The
Voting Rights
Act

The
Voting Rights
Act

CONSEQUENCES AND IMPLICATIONS

Edited by Lorn S. Foster

PRAEGER SPECIAL STUDIES • PRAEGER SCIENTIFIC

New York • Philadelphia • Eastbourne, UK
Toronto • Hong Kong • Tokyo • Sydney

Library of Congress Cataloging in Publication Data
Main entry under title:

The Voting Rights Act.

Includes index.
1. Afro-Americans—Suffrage. 2. Voters,
Registration of—United States. I. Foster, Lorn S.
KF4893.V68   1985   342.73'072 85-6600
ISBN 0-03-070684-X (alk. paper)   347.30272

To Rosalyn Louise, Hope springs eternal

Published in 1985 by Praeger Publishers
CBS Educational and Professional Publishing, a Division of CBS Inc.
521 Fifth Avenue, New York, NY 10175 USA

© 1985 by Praeger Publishers

56789 052 987654321

Printed in the United States of America on acid-free paper

INTERNATIONAL OFFICES

Orders from outside the United States should be sent to the appropriate address listed below. Orders from areas not listed below should be placed through CBS International Publishing, 383 Madison Ave., New York, NY 10175 USA

Australia, New Zealand
Holt Saunders, Pty, Ltd., 9 Waltham St., Artarmon, N.S.W. 2064, Sydney, Australia

Canada
Holt, Rinehart & Winston of Canada, 55 Horner Ave., Toronto, Ontario, Canada M8Z 4X6

Europe, the Middle East, & Africa
Holt Saunders, Ltd., 1 St. Anne's Road, Eastbourne, East Sussex, England BN21 3UN

Japan
Holt Saunders, Ltd., Ichibancho Central Building, 22-1 Ichibancho, 3rd Floor, Chiyodaku, Tokyo, Japan

Hong Kong, Southeast Asia
Holt Saunders Asia, Ltd., 10 Fl, Intercontinental Plaza, 94 Granville Road, Tsim Sha Tsui East, Kowloon, Hong Kong

Manuscript submissions should be sent to the Editorial Director, Praeger Publishers, 521 Fifth Avenue, New York, NY 10175 USA

Acknowledgments

This volume results from the collective efforts of several people and from a two-day conference held in February 1983 by the Intercollegiate Department of Black Studies of the Claremont Colleges and the Department of Government of Pomona College. Professors John Higginson, Jeffrey Stewart, Leo Flynn, and Fred Krinsky helped in the preparation of the conference, and many thanks are due to Penny Arn and Donna Whitsitt for all of their assistance. My wife Gloria, who was helpful in more ways than I can name, also provided invaluable encouragement.

Preface

The adage, "The more things change, the more they remain the same," describes the state of minority voting rights in the United States. For example, in 1968 there were 29 black elected officials in Mississippi; in 1984 the Joint Center for Political Studies reported that there were 430 black elected officials in the magnolia state. On the basis of these facts one would assume there had been a considerable change in black voting rights in Mississippi. Yet, when William Bradford Reynolds, the assistant attorney-general for civil rights and the nation's chief enforcement officer for voting rights, visited Mississippi in June of 1983 with the Rev. Jesse Jackson, he was appalled by the discriminatory practices he observed. During their visit, Reynolds and Jackson saw that would-be black voters are still disenfranchised and discriminated against 18 years after the initial passage of the Voting Rights Act and a year after its renewal.

Reynolds no doubt learned that in Mississippi a person must register at the circuit clerk's office, which is usually in the county courthouse. Registration normally takes place during business hours, nine-to-five, with no weekend or evening registration available. State law does not permit the use of deputy registrars who can go out and register voters in places where they might congregate—such as churches, shopping centers, and schools—and until last year had a system of dual registration that required voters to sign up in one place for city elections and in the county seat for county, state, and federal elections.

It is significant that these barriers to voting exist so long after the enactment of the Voting Rights Act, but what is more significant is that the chief enforcement officer for voting rights claimed ignorance of these violations. All Reynolds had to do before his visit to Mississippi was read the testimony given to both the House and Senate Judiciary Committees, testimony that confirmed the existence of barriers to voting in Mississippi and in many other covered jurisdictions. Moreover, the staff of the Justice Department's voting section knew of the problems with minority voting rights and could have briefed the assistant attorney-general before his trip.

There is no doubt that passage of the Voting Rights Act in 1965 brought some change to the South, where there are now nearly 5 million registered black voters. Overcoming disenfranchisement, however, has been a rather easy process compared to overcoming vote dilution, a variety of practices—usually involving electoral changes—that diminish the impact of the minority vote.

Section 5 of the Voting Rights Act requires all jurisdictions covered by the act to preclear any electoral changes with either the U.S. District Court for the District of Columbia or with the Department of Justice. Most jurisdictions have opted to preclear their changes with the Department of Justice. The types of electoral changes processed most often are: redistricting, annexations, changes in polling places, precinct changes, re-registration procedures, incorporations, filing fees, and at-large elections. If Section 5 did not exist, minority voters would have to file lawsuits challenging each of these changes. Such lawsuits would be very time-consuming and expensive, and in a number of cases minority plaintiffs would lack sufficient resources to contest voting suits.

The essays in this volume assess the changes that have been created as a result of the Voting Rights Act and the implications of these changes. They deal also with the impact of the "new" Section 2, the minority language requirement, and the legislative history of the Voting Rights Act. Together these essays should make clear where, in the case of minority voting rights, things have changed and where they have stayed the same.

Contents

PART I
Overview

1
The Voting Rights Act of 1965, As Amended

Don Edwards

When the long and bloody Civil War was drawing to a close, Congress overwhelmingly believed it must ratify President Lincoln's freeing of the slaves. This was done by the enactment of the Thirteenth Amendment, which became a part of the Constitution in 1865.

The next step, Congress thought, was to guarantee all the rights, privileges, and responsibilities of citizenship, of which voting is the most fundamental. So in 1869 the Fifteenth Amendment was proposed, which guaranteed to black Americans the right to vote.

Out in the states the idea of former slaves voting and getting elected to, what had been up to then, white folks' political offices was not particularly popular. Then, as now, racial prejudice stood in the path of social progress and our democratic ideals.

Kentucky, Maryland, and Tennessee rejected the amendment. New York "withdrew" its approval. Ohio and New Jersey first rejected it, then rather reluctantly changed their minds and voted to approve. This amendment was ultimately ratified by the states in 1870.

Despite this discernable lack of enthusiasm for the Fifteenth Amendment, our congressmen of a hundred years ago went ahead and enacted legislation designed to enforce the Fifteenth Amendment, laws to guarantee the right of all Americans to vote. And for a few years after the end of the Civil War, black Americans freely voted in the "old Confederacy" and were elected to public office in substantial numbers.

Beginning in the early 1870s, however, whites in many parts of the South were in virtual rebellion against the new power and influence of black Americans. They joined secret organizations like the Ku Klux Klan. They terrorized whites who supported blacks, and they abused blacks who refused to resume their hat-in-hand subservience to whites.

For a short time the federal government tried to enforce the civil rights laws. Congress passed laws making Klan-like violence a federal crime. President Grant even sent federal troops to the South to stop the violence.

Sadly, the concern of the federal government did not last. Northern congressmen tired of the constant disorder. They decided it was futile to resist the commitment of southern whites to white supremacy.

White dominance returned to the South. Black agricultural workers were reduced to peonage. The courts operated only for whites. Outright assaults on blacks by whites went unpunished. Finally, between 1890 and 1910, the ruling Democratic legislatures effectively disfranchised nearly all blacks in the deep South with voting requirements such as literacy tests. Black Americans in the South had lost the right to vote. In the 1890s there were 154 lynchings per year, all were in the South, and all of the victims were blacks.

This dismal picture of discrimination, of disfranchisement, and indeed of semislavery continued, decade after decade. It wasn't until after World War II that white Americans started to realize that this terrible situation must be addressed.

The right to vote was strengthened in three Civil Rights Acts enacted by Congress in 1957, 1960, and 1964, but none of these was totally successful. It was still dangerous business for blacks to attempt to vote. Voter registration drives were welcomed with snarling police dogs, fire hoses, clubs, jail, and even murder.

White northerners who went to the South to help in voter registration drives found a brutal world. James Reeb, a Palo Alto Unitarian minister, was murdered. Three students—James Chaney, Michael Schwerner, and Andrew Goodman—were lynched.

I, too, had a taste of the violence and hatred. In the summer of 1964 I was driving through Mississippi to visit and encourage my son and the other young people who were conducting the voter registration campaigns. My son and I spent one night at the registration campaign headquarters in McComb, Mississippi. Next morning, an hour after we had departed, a bomb went off, seriously injuring several of the young people.

I should point out that the country was in a new era, the age of television. The violence against black Americans seeking only the right to vote was there on television screens in the living rooms of most American families. The crude, brutal behavior of Sheriff Bull Conner of Selma, Alabama, and of other white police was compelling evidence that federal intervention was essential. The ordinary American finally understood the issue and demanded action.

Early in 1965, a really strong voting rights bill was drafted and referred to the House Judiciary Committee, of which I was then and am now a member. But even the persuasive skills of President Lyndon

Johnson were not enough to obtain enactment. Resistance from southern members of Congress and conservative northerners was immense. Voting by millions of blacks could tip the balance of political power in many fiefdoms controlled for a hundred years by whites.

The resistance melted with the national outrage caused by the murder of Viola Liuzzo, a white middle-class mother from Michigan, who was working on voter registration in Alabama and was shot from a passing car by a Ku Klux Klan member. On August 6, 1965 the Voting Rights Act was signed into law.

The 1965 Voting Rights Act had teeth. It suspended the use of literacy tests and other devices historically used to prevent blacks from voting. In addition, Congress wanted to provide an expeditious and effective review process that would assure that outlawed devices would not be replaced with new discriminatory voting practices. Thus, southern jurisdictions were required by Section 5 to submit for preclearance any and all proposed changes to their existing voting laws or practices to the U.S. attorney-general or the U.S. Court of Appeals for the District of Columbia. These changes could not be put into operation until the attorney-general or the district court reviewed the proposal to assure that it would not discriminate against minority voters.

Section 2 was the other key provision of the 1965 act. It applied nationwide, and it outlawed existing voting procedures that denied or abridged the right to vote. Preexisting racial gerrymandering could be reached through lawsuits based on Section 2.

To describe the impact of the 1965 Voting Rights Act as anything less than sensational would be an understatement. For example, from 1964 to 1976 Mississippi black voter registration increased from 29,000 to 286,000, an 886.2 percent increase.

Despite this progress, however, widespread discrimination in voting continued. Thus, the Voting Rights Act was extended for five years in 1970. Then, in 1975, we held extensive hearings and found that while there continued to be improvement in voter participation among blacks, there still existed significant disparities between the percentage of black and white registered voters in the areas covered by Section 5 preclearance. Moreover, we learned that enforcement of Section 5 by the Department of Justice was only beginning in earnest following initial judicial interpretations of the scope of Section 5. Since Section 5 was viewed by Congress as one of the strongest provisions in the act, we extended it again to August 6, 1982.

In this extension we added an important provision to reduce voting discrimination against minority Americans whose primary language was other than English. We provided that, in jurisdictions impacted by minority language voters, oral and/or written bilingual assistance, including bilingual ballots, must be provided throughout the election process.

The basis for this new provision was an extensive record before the Congress, including a number of federal court decisions, which showed that barriers to registration and voting effectively disfranchised language-minority citizens. Both Congress and the courts found that such citizens had been denied equal educational opportunities by state and local governments, resulting in severe disabilities and continuing illiteracy in the English language. Thus, we required that these citizens be given the assistance necessary to exercise effectively their vote.

In addition, in limited jurisdictions such as Texas, where voting discrimination against Mexican-Americans was found to be as egregious as that outlined against southern blacks in 1965, we applied the Section 5 preclearance requirement.

When the Voting Rights Act was first enacted in 1965, we knew there were hundreds of counties, cities, towns, and school districts in the South that for decades had had voting laws designed with care to make certain that white people were in charge. Since the Section 5 preclearance provision only applied to changes made after November 1, 1964, Congress also included, in Section 2, a provision that would allow people to go to court and prove that these preexisting local laws discriminated against minority voters.

On April 22, 1980 the U.S. Supreme Court rendered a decision that gravely damaged Section 2 in a case styled City of Mobile v. Bolden. The plurality decision in Mobile held that to attack successfully the offending laws, an intent to discriminate on the part of the city council or other enacting body had to be shown. In most cases this would be an impossible requirement. We were in real trouble.

Such was the situation in early 1981. Depressing, yes. We had a new president who was publicly hostile to the extension of the Voting Rights Act unless devastating amendments were added. We had a Republican Senate with Strom Thurmond of South Carolina as chairman of the Judiciary Committee. We had as the U.S. attorney-general the president's personal attorney, William French Smith. We faced the difficult situation not only of having to extend the law, but in addition having to reverse the Mobile decision.

As we prepared for the hearings there was little optimism. It seemed that almost everyone, newspaper writers included, believed that voting discrimination was a part of this country's past—that we did not need an extension of the Voting Rights Act.

So began the public hearings in early May of 1981, continuing on into mid-July, in Washington, D.C., in Alabama, and in Texas. One hundred twenty-two witnesses testified—national, state, and local civil rights leaders, religious, union, and civic leaders, two former assistant attorneys-general of the Department of Justice, and ordinary local citizens.

What we learned in those 18 days of hearings was shocking—and sad. All seven members of the subcommittee, Republicans and Democrats alike, were dismayed.

Yes, all of the witnesses reported major gains had been made and acknowledged that many blacks and Hispanics had been elected to important posts, such as mayors of Birmingham and San Antonio, as well as the mayor of Los Angeles. But they also presented compelling evidence that discrimination against racial and language minorities still persisted and was widespread:

- In one Alabama town the voter registration book was kept under the local judge's desk, so that blacks were afraid to register.
- In Pickens County, Alabama, there was no such thing as a secret ballot. Black voters had to fill out their ballots at a table with white poll watchers looking on.
- A black woman running for mayor in one southern town was told two weeks before the election that she had three days to pay up the bank loan on her home. The bank officer giving the notice was the current mayor.
- Texas witnesses testified to widespread voting discrimination against Hispanics—falsification of election returns, voter harassment, and the refusal of state officials to prosecute violators.

These were typical examples of discrimination in voting procedures testified to by many witnesses. In addition, we were told how structural devices—such as at-large election schemes, majority vote runoffs, and the existence of racial bloc voting—together with racial gerrymandering, continued to dilute the voting power of minorities.

When the hearings ended in mid–July 1981, a majority of the subcommittee was convinced that extension was essential, and an amendment reversing the Mobile decision was critical.

In addition, subcommittee members agreed that by amending the limited bailout provision already in the act, we might finally encourage states, counties, and other jurisdictions covered by Section 5 to provide equal and permanent access to their political process for minority citizens. Thus, the bailout provision adopted during the Ninety-seventh Congress provides a specific formula for release from coverage of the Section 5 preclearance requirements.

A state or county is entitled to bailout from Section 5 coverage if the D.C. District Court finds that in the preceding ten years the state or county has complied with all federal and state laws designed to protect the voting rights of minorities. In addition, the jurisdiction must show that it has taken positive steps to eliminate discrimination throughout its electoral system. For example, it can show that it has eliminated discriminatory voting practices—such as unreasonable registration hours and locations—and discriminatory methods of election—such as numbered posts, majority runoffs, at-large elections, and racially gerrymandered districts.

This last requirement is an important element in the act because, as the Supreme Court has recognized, the right to vote can be affected by diluting or weakening the voting power of minorities as well as by an absolute prohibition on the casting of a ballot. It is a tough but workable bailout and its elements are grounded in the record before the subcommittee. The incentive to the covered jurisdictions exists because their ability to bail out rests on their own action.

But one problem remained. The president of the United States refused to lend his support to the bill. He was silent. We asked his attorney-general to testify. He refused. We asked him again. He refused.

We wanted very badly the testimony of the Reagan administration. The president of the United States is elected by all the people as their spokesperson. Both Democrats and Republicans on the subcommittee wanted his advice. He was silent.

We knew we were running out of time. The act expired on August 5, 1982 and the Senate subcommittee, chaired by Orrin Hatch, had not even scheduled hearings. We took the bill to the House floor on October 5, 1981, where it was approved overwhelmingly by a vote of 389 to 24. All harmful amendments were defeated by enormous margins. So compelling was the record in the House regarding the need to extend Section 5 preclearance and the language-minority provisions that the focus of the Senate deliberations shifted almost exclusively to the critical Section 2 amendment.

We held our collective breaths while the maneuvering went on in the Senate. For weeks the prospects were dim. At one time we heard the president was willing to accept the complete House bill, but the attorney-general rushed to the White House and urged a negative decision on the Section 2 amendment. Again, action on the bill was stalled.

But as the weeks wore on it became clear that the American people wanted the Voting Rights Act. An effective, well-organized, and sophisticated lobbying effort by civil rights, labor, religious, and civic organizations went into high gear. Every senator was visited by constituents, at home and in Washington. Mail poured in, all in support of the strong House bill.

Finally, Republican Senator Robert Dole, a most distinguished legislator, decided it was time to move ahead. He crafted the Dole Compromise to the Section 2 amendment, which essentially retained the integrity and intent of the House bill.

On June 17, 1982, the full Senate approved the bill. The House accepted the Dole Compromise, and President Reagan invited us all to the East Room at the White House for the bill–signing celebration on June 29.

The 1965 Voting Rights Act not only had been extended; it had been made stronger. And in the process of strengthening it, we had done much to revitalize the civil rights movement and to serve notice to the administration that the American public will not accept silence from its leadership on questions of civil rights and social justice.

P A R T II
Judicial Impact

2
Racial Vote Dilution: The Concept and The Court

Richard L. Engstrom

Since passage of the Voting Rights Act in 1965, the formal barriers to black people registering to vote and actually casting ballots have been largely removed throughout the United States. Black voter registration and electoral participation, as a consequence, have increased significantly. Although the overall levels of conventional political participation by blacks are still usually below the levels for whites, social science research now regularly documents the fact that within social class or status groups, blacks usually participate at rates equal to (sometimes greater than) those for whites, suggesting that the remaining barriers to equal participation are primarily socioeconomic and not structural.[1]

Despite these obvious advances, however, the issue of racial discrimination within the electoral process continues to be a serious political—and legal—issue within this country. A significant disillusionment with the franchise is said to be evident among many blacks today.[2] This disillusionment is at least partly a function of perceptions that their participation in the electoral process is too often meaningless. Electoral systems, blacks complain, are frequently arranged in such a fashion that, given the racial polarization commonly found within the electorate, their participation is of little significance.

Race unfortunately remains a fundamental source of political division in the United States today; indeed, "no other social cleavage approaches it in importance."[3] Whites and blacks are often on different sides of the political fence, and racially based bloc voting is extremely common.[4] When voting patterns are polarized along racial lines, the manner in which electoral competition is structured can have an enormous impact on the black minority's ability to compete politically. Whether elections will be decided by majority or plurality vote, how large electoral districts will be, and where the district boundaries will be located are just some examples of the various dimensions of electoral systems that can seriously affect black people's ability to convert their voting strength into the election of public officials who feel politically accountable to them.

The issue of racial discrimination within the electoral process, therefore, has not been eliminated from the U.S. political scene simply because racially discriminatory barriers to voting itself have been removed. Rather, a "second generation" of racially discriminatory election laws—those that organize electoral competition in ways that are believed to dilute the impact of the minority's vote—are under increasing scrutiny by blacks across the nation. The presence of these dilutive arrangements is certainly a major factor contributing to blacks' perceptions that "genuine political power" has continued to elude them, despite impressive gains in voter registration.[5] The voting rights issue, therefore, continues to be an important issue in U S. politics, although the problem on which it is focused has changed significantly—the previous concentration on denial of the vote has now shifted to a more contemporary concern, dilution of the vote.

DILUTION AS A LITIGATION ISSUE

Dilution of the vote refers to the practice of limiting the ability of blacks to convert their voting strength into the control of, or at least influence with, elected public officials. The racial gerrymandering of electoral district boundaries and the use of at-large (citywide or countywide) elections to select representatives are the two electoral arrangements most frequently cited by blacks as having dilutive consequences. These arrangements have often, as a consequence, been the subject of litigation, as blacks have sought relief from these electoral situations through the federal judiciary.

Racial gerrymandering, of course, refers to the delineation of representational district boundaries in such a fashion that a substantial portion of the black vote is "wasted," that is, politically inconsequential. This can be accomplished by dispersing black voting strength across districts so that blacks constitute ineffective minorities of voters within those districts, or by concentrating black voting strength into districts in which blacks comprise extraordinary majorities of voters. The cumulative effect is to waste a substantial proportion of the group's vote—either in support of losing candidates or through excessive support of winning candidates. This practice has become especially threatening to blacks since computers have become widely utilized in the districting process, as computer-assisted gerrymandering is much more sophisticated than what occurred in the past.[6]

At-large elections are used extensively in this country to select the members of local governing boards; entire county delegations to state legislative bodies are sometimes elected at-large (countywide). Blacks have long complained that this format is discriminatory toward racial minorities. When voting patterns are racially polarized, a black minority has enormous difficulty electing the candidate of its choice, especially black candidates. The white majority, it is argued, effectively controls access to all of the at-large seats, an especially serious matter when an entire council or board is elected in that manner. White legislators electorally accountable to a white majority, they complain, are not likely to be responsive to the needs of the black minority. If the county or city is divided into districts, however, the black minority can often take advantage of being residentially concentrated and control the selection of one or more representatives, who will be more directly accountable to and presumably responsive toward the black electorate. That blacks are much less likely to be elected to governing bodies when at-large rather than district elections are employed is one of the most thoroughly verified generalizations in political science today. [7]

The perception among blacks that these electoral arrangements have invidiously diluted their voting strength, reducing significantly the political impact of their votes, has stimulated numerous efforts to have such arrangements declared invalid by the judiciary. Black plaintiffs have initiated litigation asserting that such schemes violate their right to vote on an equal basis with that of the white majority. These cases—which have usually revolved around the equal protection clause of the Fourteenth Amendment—present the U.S. judiciary with an exceedingly serious, and apparently difficult, adjudication issue.

The dilution question has had a rather strange career as a litigation issue. The Supreme Court has yet to confront the concept of dilution directly. When presented with evidence strongly supportive of an inference that an electoral arrangement has a dilutive effect, the Court has responded by demanding additional data addressing other, largely extraneous, questions of discrimination. When evidence concerning these other matters was forthcoming, the Court responded by elevating even further the evidentiary burden plaintiffs must face, this time demanding proof of a discriminatory intent behind the use of a particular election scheme. A review of the case history in this area could easily lead one to conclude that the behavior of the justices on this issue (at least a majority of the justices) is far more consistent with a hypothesis that they have sought to evade, rather than decide, the issue. The following examines the Supreme Court's response to allegations of unconstitutional racial vote dilution, and suggests an approach to the issue which, if followed, would permit the Court to be more directly responsive to dilution claims, especially those raised under the recently revised section 2 of the Voting Rights Act.

DELINEATIONAL GERRYMANDERING

Until 1980 the evidentiary standards applicable to delineational gerrymandering cases and those applicable to at-large election cases appeared to be different. The Supreme Court has directly confronted an allegation of unconstitutional racial gerrymandering only once: a 1964 case, Wright v. Rockefeller. [8] At issue in Wright was the manner in which four congressional districts in Manhattan had been drawn. The districting plan passed by the state legislature had concentrated much of the minority voting strength (black and Puerto Rican) in that area into one district, resulting in the population of that district being 86.3 percent black and Puerto Rican. In the three adjoining districts, blacks and Puerto Ricans comprised only 28.5 percent, 27.5 percent, and 8.5 percent of the district populations. This arrangement, which was based on "zigzag tortuous lines,"[9] had the purpose and effect of concentrating the minority voting strength, plaintiffs complained, so that minority voters would have a serious impact on the election of only a single representative. This violated their rights under both the due process and equal protection clause of the Fourteenth Amendment, the plaintiffs maintained, as well as abridged their right to vote in violation of the Fifteenth Amendment.

The Court's response to this allegation focused exclusively on the question of the line drawers' intentions, and did not address the effect of the districting scheme. The plaintiffs were rejected—not because a significant dilution in minority voting strength would not in fact result from the plan, but because it had not been demonstrated that the plan was the product of discriminatory motives. According to a majority of the Court, the plaintiffs had "failed to prove that the New York legislature was either motivated by racial considerations or in fact drew the districts on racial lines," and had "not shown that the challenged part of the New York Act was the product of a state contrivance to segregate on the basis of race or place of origin."[10]

Wright is the only case in which the Court has dealt directly with an allegation of unconstitutional racial gerrymandering, [11] and it has placed an exceedingly demanding evidentiary burden on plaintiffs in these cases. Proof of a discriminatory intent, independent of an inference based on the effects of a districting scheme, will rarely be available. As Robert Dixon has noted, "If those who district in discriminatory fashion 'cover their tracks' by having an anonymous staff attend to political details, evidence of intent may be unavailable, and gerrymandering would be immune to effective judicial review."[12] Indeed, racial gerrymandering has been largely immune to judicial invalidation on constitutional grounds. Satisfactory proof of purpose has been "well-nigh impossible" to produce, and judgments in favor of plaintiffs have been extremely rare. [13]

Gerrymandering is undoubtedly a difficult adjudication issue. It has been described, quite accurately, as "the thorniest nettle in the political thicket"[14] because there are no widely agreed upon, objective standards through which the practice can be identified. Indeed, it is not uncommon to hear that gerrymandering is analogous to pornography: "You know it when you see it, but it's awfully hard to define."[15] Given the absence of easily manageable inferential standards, it would not be surprising to discover that the judiciary is less than eager to confront the issue; the adoption of an intent requirement may well relate to such a hesitation. The Court in Wright offered no jurisprudential treatise for its adoption of the intent standard in that case, but a legal commentator may have identified the Court's own motive when he correctly noted:

> Because a racially discriminatory motive is often far
> more burdensome to prove than is a racially discrim-
> inatory effect, emphasizing the former helps to assure
> a minimum of judicial involvement.[16]

THE SUBMERGENCE ISSUE: PHASE I

The decision in Wright v. Rockefeller was announced on the same day the Supreme Court handed down the first of its "one person, one vote" decisions, Wesberry v. Sanders.[17] Wesberry, and especially the soon to follow Reynolds v. Sims,[18] made it clear that the right to vote, at least on an individual basis, can be violated by reducing the competitive value of a vote, as well as by the denial of the franchise itself. As expressed in Reynolds:

> the right of suffrage can be denied by a debasement or
> dilution of the weight of a citizen's vote just as effec-
> tively as by wholly prohibiting the free exercise of the
> franchise.[19]

Plaintiffs alleging that a malapportioned electoral arrangement unconstitutionally prohibited them from participating equally in the political process were not required to provide proof of anyone's motives.[20]

Not surprisingly, subsequent allegations of unconstitutional racial vote dilution that reached the Supreme Court—involving the submergence of minority voting strength within at-large or multi-member districts—relied heavily on the malapportionment cases for their rationale.[21] Wright, and the intent standard expressed therein, had virtually no impact on this litigation. The two types of dilution issues were treated as distinct problems by the Court, and at least until 1980, Wright was all but ignored in the Court's subsequent decisions concerning racially based dilution.

The Court's first response to the submergence issue came only one year after the Wright decision. In Fortson v. Dorsey[22] the issue was raised as part of a challenge to a 1962 redistricting plan for the Georgia state senate. At-large (countywide) elections had been adopted as the means for selecting state senators within each of the state's populous, urban counties, and plaintiffs claimed this was done to dilute the significance of the racial minority's votes within those counties. According to the Court, however, this issue was "never seriously pressed" by the plaintiffs, and no proof had been presented to support this "bald assertion."[23] The allegation was rejected. The Court did suggest in Fortson, however, that it would not limit itself to the question of intent when it reviewed allegations of institutional gerrymandering, but would consider the possible dilutive effects of such schemes as well. The Court stated:

> It might well be that, designedly or otherwise, a multi-member constituency apportionment scheme, under the circumstances of a particular case, would operate to minimize or cancel out the voting strength of racial or political elements of the voting population. When this is demonstrated it will be time enough to consider whether the system still passes constitutional muster.[24]

The expression designedly or otherwise clearly conflicted with the Wright decision of the previous term, and no effort was made to reconcile the difference. In fact, the Wright case was cited only once in the majority opinion in Fortson, in a context that did not address the question of evidentiary standards.[25]

The submergence issue was again raised in a 1966 case, Burns v. Richardson.[26] This time the Court clearly held that the dilutive effects of an electoral arrangement would be relevant to the judiciary's assessment of the constitutionality of that arrangement. Burns involved the presence of multimember districts in a 1965 redistricting plan for the Hawaii state senate. A three-judge federal district court, maintaining that "truly representative government" was not possible unless an election system "provides potentially equal representation to the divergent factors incorporated within the body politic,"[27] rejected the proposed districts because the multimember districts, in its opinion, interfered with the realization of that goal. The court focused on the overlapping of multimember districts between the proposed senatorial plan and the plan used to select members of the other chamber of the state legislature, the House of Representatives. One senatorial district that would elect three senators, for example, also served as a district from which four state representatives were to be elected. Another six-member representative district comprised three-fourths of a proposed four-member senatorial district. The district court concluded that this overlapping unjustifiably concentrated political power in the hands of the majority group in these districts, "negat[ing] any notion of equality of representation for the minorities entrapped therein."[28]

The Supreme Court reversed the district court, however, stating that the dilutive consequences of the multimember districts had not been demonstrated, as required by Fortson. The Court criticized the lower court for "relying on conjecture as to the effects of multimember districting rather than demonstrated fact" and stated that "Speculations do not supply evidence that the multimember districting was designed to have or had the invidious effect necessary to a judgment of the unconstitutionality of the districting."[29] The Court again made it clear that proof of intent was not a necessary condition for a finding of unconstitutionality when it rephrased the language in Fortson, stating that an electoral scheme was subject to constitutional challenge if it "was designed to or would operate to minimize or cancel out the voting strength of racial or political elements of the voting population."[30] The Court also expanded on its Fortson decision, stating:

> It may be that this invidious effect [of multimember districts] can more easily be shown if, in contrast to the facts in Fortson, districts are large in relation to the total number of legislators, if districts are not appropriately subdistricted to assure distribution of legislators that are resident over the entire district, or if such districts characterize both houses of a bicameral legislature rather than one. But the demonstration that a particular multimember scheme effects an invidious result must appear from evidence in the record.[31]

Once again, no effort was made to reconcile this broader evidentiary standard (purpose or effect) with the Wright decision, which was not referenced at all by the Court in Burns.

Following the Fortson and Burns decisions, it appeared that "the door remained ajar for any future appeals which relied on proof rather than on hypothetical speculation."[32] The Court's next—and more extensive—confrontation with the institutional gerrymandering issue, Whitcomb v. Chavis,[33] produced a significant deviation from the Fortson-Burns approach. It elevated significantly the evidentiary burden facing plaintiffs attacking racially dilutive electoral arrangements.

THE SUBMERGENCE ISSUE: PHASE II

Whitcomb v. Chavis was the Burger Court's first confrontation
with the racial vote dilution issue. It concerned the election at-large
of 15 state representatives and eight state senators from Marion
County, Indiana, in which the city of Indianapolis is located. The
plaintiffs in Whitcomb did not allege that a discriminatory purpose
underlie the at-large arrangement, which had been used for many
years in Marion County, but only that the effect of the arrangement
was to dilute the voting strength of the county's black residents, thereby denying them adequate representation. A federal district court
agreed and invalidated the election system, demonstrating in a very
systematic fashion how the arrangement satisfied the standard developed by the Warren Court in Fortson and Burns. [34]

After carefully defining the term ghetto, the district court identified within Indianapolis a heavily poor and black area designated as
the "Center Township Ghetto." To meet the first requirement of
Fortson and Burns—that "an identifiable racial or political element
within the multimember district" be shown to exist—the court cited
data concerning the housing conditions (absentee landlords or owners,
crowded, dilapidated, and deteriorated units), social characteristics
(old-age assistance, education, juvenile delinquency, unemployment),
and economic characteristics (median family income, automobile
ownership) of the area. The court stated these data demonstrated that

> These Negro residents have interests in areas of substan-
> tive law such as housing regulations, sanitation, welfare
> programs (aid to families with dependent children, medi-
> cal care, etc.), garnishment statutes, and unemployment
> compensation, among others, which diverge significantly
> from the interests of nonresidents of the Ghetto. [35]

The second Fortson-Burns requirement—that the voting strength
of the group be shown to be "severely minimized" by the electoral
arrangement—was also satisfied. The court's examination of the
residences of Marion County legislators selected in the five most
recent elections (between 1960 and 1968) showed that very few residents of the ghetto area had been elected under the at-large system.
The inequality was quite extreme, as demonstrated by a comparison
with a socially and economically more advantaged area:

> Washington Township, the upper middle-class and wealthy
> suburban area having 14.64% of the population of Marion
> County, was the residence of 52.27% of the senators and
> 41.79% of the representatives. Center Township [within

which the "ghetto" area was located] having 41.14% of the
population (approximately three times as large), was the
residence of 9.51% of the senators (less than one-fifth of
Washington Township) and 17.91% of the representatives
(approximately three-sevenths of Washington Township). [36]

The court, in holding that the second Fortson-Burns requirement had
been satisfied, did not rely only on the fact that disproportionately few
ghetto residents were chosen, however. It further concluded that the
resulting Marion County legislative delegation had not been adequately
representing the ghetto residents. The members of the delegation
tended to adopt "a common, undifferentiated position" on issues before the legislature, which in the court's view was "largely the result
of election at-large from a common constituency, and obviates representation of a substantial, though minority, interest group within that
common constituency."[37] Reinforcing this cohesive behavior, the
court noted, was the strong control over nominations exercised by
the political parties within Marion County. Legislators who consistently deviated from the delegation's positions on issues were subject
to being denied renomination by their party. [38]

The district court also noted that the additional factors identified in Burns as contributing to a showing of invidious effect were all
present in this case. The at-large district was sizable, electing 15
representatives (15 percent of the total House membership) and eight
senators (16 percent of the Senate membership), and it was not sub-
districted for residency purposes. [39]

The Whitcomb case appeared to provide the hard evidence the
Warren Court had found missing in Fortson and Burns. The lower
court opinion, based on those two earlier decisions, was meticulously
prepared, and the evidence impressively documented. As one commentator stated, the Whitcomb case "went to the Supreme Court with
a record equal to any the plaintiffs will generally be able to establish
in a gerrymandering [by submergence] case."[40] The Burger Court,
however, approached the issue in a different manner, and concluded
that the evidence was not sufficient to prove invidious discrimination.

Although the Court's opinion, authored by Mr. Justice White,
referenced Fortson and Burns, those cases were virtually ignored in
the Court's actual response to the dilution issue. [41] The Court, for
example, did note that Fortson had held that multimember districts
were subject to challenge if they "minimize or cancel out" the voting
strength of a black minority, and that the dilutive impact of such electoral arrangements may be especially egregious when the systemic
conditions identified in Burns are present. [42] But the Court proceeded
to ignore the evidentiary standard that had been expressed through
those cases, and demanded instead that evidence be presented showing

that black people were not being permitted to participate generally in the electoral process on the same basis as whites. The fact that disproportionately few ghetto residents had been elected was not itself significant, according to the Court, unless the plaintiffs could demonstrate that "ghetto residents had less opportunity than did other Marion County residents to participate in the political process and to elect legislators of their choice."[43] This was not the situation in Marion County. Responding as if the case concerned a "white primary" rather than a countywide multimember district, the Court noted that no evidence had been presented showing that "poor Negroes were not allowed to register to vote, to choose the political party they desired to support, to participate in its affairs or to be equally represented on those occasions when legislative candidates were chosen."[44]

The "underrepresentation" of ghetto residents within the Marion County delegation was not, in the Court's view, attributable to racial discrimination, but rather to partisan competition in Marion County. Residents of the Center Township ghetto had been voting heavily Democratic, and the Court therefore assumed that the party must have been slating candidates satisfactory to those voters. Republican candidates, however, had swept all of the legislative seats in four of the previous five countywide elections. Thus, the relative absence of ghetto residents in the delegation was dismissed simply as "a function of losing elections."[45] As expressed by the Court, "The voting power of ghetto residents may have been 'cancelled out' as the District Court held, but this seems a mere euphemism for political defeat at the polls."[46] Being "outvoted," the Court held, did not result in a constitutional violation unless there was also evidence that the group had been "denied access to the political system" generally.[47]

The Supreme Court was also unimpressed with the lower court's conclusion that the legislative delegation had not been responsive to the legislative concerns of the ghetto residents. On this dimension, the Court stated:

> We see nothing in the findings of the District Court indicating recurring poor performance by Marion County's delegation with respect to Center Township ghetto, nothing to show what the ghetto's interests were in particular legislative situations and nothing to indicate that the outcome would have been any different if the 23 assemblymen had been chosen from single-member districts.[48]

The Whitcomb decision was a significant step back from the Fortson and Burns decisions. The plaintiffs had claimed vote dilution because, in their view, the countywide electoral arrangement resulted in their voting strength being submerged within the large, majority

white electorate, and they could not, as a consequence, elect legislators of their choice. The Court responded by stating that they were
only losing elections. That this constituted a rather evasive reply has
not escaped attention. As one commentator has noted:

> plaintiffs had complained that the electoral deck was
> stacked against them. The Court answered that there
> was no valid complaint because plaintiffs had been let
> into the game. The answer hardly seems responsive.[49]

Requiring plaintiffs to demonstrate a "denial of access" appears to be
little more than a way to avoid the dilution issue itself, and the motivation for avoiding that issue may be readily inferred from the Court's
expressed concern that an affirmance of the district court's decision
"would spawn endless litigation" initiated by other groups feeling submerged within multimember districts.[50]

Wright v. Rockefeller was still effectively contained in the Whitcomb opinion. Justice White referenced Wright only once, in a footnote
in which he stated that whether it was better for a minority to have its
voting strength spread or concentrated was a matter of dispute, even
among minority voters themselves.[51] Wright's intent standard was
clearly not treated as controlling in this decision. But Whitcomb did
significantly alter the burden confronting plaintiffs in submergence
cases. The participation standard enunciated within Whitcomb was a
much more demanding evidentiary hurdle than the more straightforward effects test expressed in Fortson and Burns, and would clearly
reduce the probability of judicial involvement with this issue.

The more formidable nature of the new standard was stressed
by the Court's most liberal members, who complained that "It is ask-
ing the impossible . . . to demand that the blacks first show that the
effect of the scheme was to discourage or prevent poor blacks from
voting or joining such party as they choose."[52] Indeed, Whitcomb
placed upon plaintiffs a surprising responsibility: to be freed from
an electoral arrangement they believed minimized the impact of their
vote, they would have to prove discrimination at other points within
the electoral process (such as when registering to vote, when participating in the nomination process, or when attempting to cast a ballot).
This would be an especially difficult problem for plaintiffs in states
such as Indiana, which do not have a long history of overt, state-
supported efforts at minority disfranchisement and vote dilution.[53]
To expect a demonstration that legislative outcomes would have been
different had single-member districts been employed is especially
unreasonable. As one commentator has stated, "Proof as to how a
hypothetical representative would have affected previous legislative
results is a preposterous demand to be made of any litigant."[54]

The Whitcomb standard, however, did not turn out to be impossible to satisfy. In 1973, in White v. Regester,[55] the Supreme Court affirmed a district court ruling invalidating countywide multimember state legislative districts in the Texas counties of Dallas and Bexar. The Court in White unanimously accepted the lower court's conclusion that past and present discrimination against black people in Dallas and Chicanos in San Antonio (located in Bexar County) had resulted in those groups being denied equal access to the political processes within those districts. The district court distinguished the situation in Texas from that present in the Whitcomb litigation by noting that Texas, unlike Indiana, utilized a place system with a majority vote requirement within its at-large arrangement, and had, in addition, "a rather colorful history of racial segregation."[56] While the court expressed the belief that, given this racial history and the continued use of antisingle-shot voting devices, all of the multimember legislative districts in Texas might be unconstitutional, it did not base its decision on these grounds. Rather, it limited its ruling to Dallas and Bexar Counties, and held that, as a factual matter, the Whitcomb burden had been met by the black litigants from Dallas and Chicano litigants from San Antonio.

Democratic Party nominations in one-party Dallas County, which were tantamount to election, were found to be controlled by the Dallas Committee for Responsible Government, an organization that endorsed a list of favored candidates for legislative seats. This organization, according to the district court, did not take the interests of blacks into account when constructing its slate of candidates, and had even used racist campaign tactics in support of its tickets. The court therefore concluded:

> In essence, we find that the plaintiffs have shown that
> Negroes in Dallas County are permitted to enter the
> political process in any meaningful manner only through
> the benevolence of the dominant white majority. If par-
> ticipation is to be labeled "effective" then it certainly
> must be a matter of right, and not a function of grace.[57]

No comparable slating organization controlled the Democratic Party nominations in one-party Bexar County. But election returns did show that the local electorate was polarized between Chicanos and Anglos, and that this division was "still an important issue" in Bexar County politics.[58] The court focused on the cultural and language differences between the Chicano minority and Anglo majority, and on the effects of a long and continuous history of pervasive discrimination toward Chicanos, and concluded that Chicanos were also being denied effective access to the political system. The Supreme Court's affirmance, which did not contain a single reference to <u>Wright</u> v. <u>Rockefeller</u>, did little more than repeat the lower court's findings and agree that the evidentiary standard expressed in <u>Whitcomb</u> had been satisfied.[59]

<u>White</u> v. <u>Regester</u> was the first case in which the Supreme Court responded favorably to a plaintiff's allegation of dilution through submergence, and as such did demonstrate that "multimember districts can be unconstitutional in fact, not just in theory."[60] The constitutional vulnerability of these arrangements under <u>Whitcomb</u> and <u>White</u>, however, was largely limited to the South. Following <u>White</u>, black plaintiffs were able to win numerous cases challenging at-large, multimember electoral arrangements within the South, where the "hangover" effects of past discrimination[61] and the racially polarized nature of recent elections were often easily documented.[62] One example of this occurred in Mobile, Alabama, where a federal district judge on October 22, 1976, concluded that the black plaintiffs challenging the at-large elections used to select the entire Mobile city commission had satisfactorily demonstrated that their access to the political process in Mobile was not equal to that of the white majority. The judge therefore held that, under the <u>Whitcomb</u> and <u>White</u> precedents, the election system was constitutionally infirm.[63]

THE SUBMERGENCE ISSUE: PHASE III

Mobile, a city with almost 200,000 residents in 1970, was governed through a three-member city commission, an arrangement in which both legislative and executive responsibilities are centralized within one small elected body. Commissioners within this system each serve as the head of one of the major departments of the municipal government, and collectively serve as the legislative body for the municipality. Because each commissioner has citywide administrative responsibilities, each is usually elected at-large.

Despite the fact that blacks, by 1970, constituted approximately 35 percent of Mobile's population, no black had ever been elected to the city commission. Prior to the passage of the 1965 Voting Rights Act, this exclusion was readily explicable—most blacks in Mobile, as in Alabama generally, were disfranchised.[64] Following that act, however, blacks were permitted to register and vote in Mobile "without hindrance,"[65] but still no black person was elected to the commission. The plaintiffs contended that this continued exclusion, even after blacks had been granted access to the ballot, was also easily explained—it was a consequence of the severe racial polarization within the Mobile electorate. Commissioners were elected at-large through a place system, with a majority vote required to be elected to each place. Blacks, being a minority, were politically impotent under these electoral rules.

As one observer of the situation remarked, "It soon became apparent to local Blacks that even if every eligible Black in Mobile was registered, and even if every registered Black voted for Black candidates, Blacks would still lose because of deep-seated racial division and at-large voting."[66]

The polarized electoral environment in Mobile, plaintiffs further argued, also prohibited the development of effective electoral coalitions through which blacks could help to elect sympathetic whites to the commission. Black support for a candidate produced a white "backlash," whether that candidate was black or white. This election system, they maintained, virtually guaranteed the election of an all-white commission, none of the members of which would feel politically accountable to blacks. The problem in Mobile, according to the plaintiffs, was that

> In form blacks are able to mark and cast ballots, but in
> substance they are disenfranchised. They cannot elect
> any black to the city commission. They cannot elect to
> the commission any white known to support fair treatment
> for the black community. And they cannot protect them-
> selves against a pervasive policy of discrimination which
> runs rampant through the operations of the city govern-
> ment.[67]

Blacks in Mobile therefore challenged the city's election system. Relying heavily on the Supreme Court's recent White v. Regester decision, they argued that they were being denied equal access to the local political system as a consequence of this electoral situation, and requested that single-member districts be adopted in its place.

The federal district court in Mobile, in Bolden v. City of Mobile,[68] granted the plaintiffs the relief they sought. That no black had ever been elected to the commission was, in the district judge's opinion, an indication that the local political process was "not equally open."[69] Referencing statistical analyses documenting the racial polarization in local elections, recent instances in which qualified black candidates had been defeated in Mobile elections because they had received virtually no white support, and the opinions of candidates expressed during testimony, the judge concluded that "There is no reasonable expectation that a black candidate could be elected in a city-wide election race because of racial polarization."[70] This virtual certainty of electoral defeat, along with the history of discrimination in Mobile's electoral process, repressed black participation, resulting in a denial of equal access. In the judge's view:

> the at-large election of city commissioners combined
> with strong racial polarization of Mobile's electorate

continues to effectively discourage qualified black citizens from seeking office or being elected <u>thereby denying blacks equal access</u> to the slating or candidate selection process.[71]

A further indication that the political process was not equally open, in the judge's opinion, was that the white officials who had been elected at-large had not been responsive to the needs and concerns of Mobile's black community. The judge cited public employment figures showing blacks to be significantly underrepresented in the city's work force, especially in positions of responsibility, and noted the relative (and sometimes total) absence of blacks on important city boards and committees. In addition, the provision of public services such as drainage facilities, street maintenance, and park programs demonstrated, in the court's words, a more "sluggish," "slow," and "timid" response to the needs within the city's black residential areas.[72] This, the judge concluded, reflected the political impotence of blacks in the polarized at-large context.[73] Within the Mobile city commission, responsiveness to the needs of black citizens was inhibited by a "fear of a white backlash vote," and these needs, therefore, were given "low priority."[74]

The district court held explicitly that the Mobile plaintiffs had satisfied the burden of proof established by the Supreme Court in <u>Whitcomb</u> and <u>White</u>. Black people in Mobile did not have equal access to the local political process under the commission government at-large election arrangement, and the judge ordered that the structure of government be changed to the mayor/council form, with the council members elected from nine single-member districts. Because residential patterns in Mobile have been among the most segregated in the United States, with black people largely concentrated in the central and northern portions of the city and white residents in the southern and western sections,[75] the change to single-member districts was expected to result in some districts that would contain sufficient proportions of black voters so as to give blacks "a realistic opportunity" to elect candidates of their choice.[76]

This district court decision, however, did not survive Supreme Court review. A few years after the <u>White</u> decision, the Burger Court embarked on a revisionary course that would result in a significant change in the jurisprudence concerning the Fourteenth Amendment's equal protection clause. This would in turn produce another alteration in the Court's approach to the submergence issue, elevating even higher the burden of proof faced by plaintiffs in these actions.

The watershed case in the Supreme Court's revisionary journey was <u>Washington</u> v. <u>Davis</u>,[77] decided in 1976, three years after <u>White</u> v. <u>Regester</u>. The case concerned the use of a written examination as a screening device for selecting among applicants seeking to become police officers in the District of Columbia Metropolitan Police Department. The exam, which was administered generally throughout the federal civil service, was designed to measure the verbal skills of prospective employees. One effect of the exam, however, was to filter black applicants out of the competition for these positions at a much higher rate than white applicants, the percentage of blacks failing the exam being approximately four times that of whites. The complainants, two black men whose applications had been rejected after failing the examination, claimed that the use of the exam violated their rights under the due process clause contained in the Fifth Amendment.[78] They did not allege that the exam was being used for the purpose of excluding blacks, but only that the exam was not related to performing the job of a police officer and that it had an invidiously discriminatory impact.

The Court rejected the black applicants' complaint, holding that racially discriminatory treatment alone does not establish a sufficient presumption of unconstitutionality to require that such treatment be scrutinized strictly by the judiciary. Acting as if the precedents were far clearer than they are in fact, the Court stated that "the basic equal protection principle" had always been "the invidious quality of a law claimed to be racially discriminatory must ultimately be traced to a racially discriminatory purpose."[79] A disproportionate impact, under this standard, can be cited as evidence supporting an inference of a discriminatory intent, but that alone is not a sufficient condition for such an inference.[80]

Among the cases cited by the Supreme Court as demonstrating the previous application of this "basic principle" was Wright v. Rockefeller, the delineational gerrymandering case. Conspicuously absent from the Court's opinion, however, was any reference to the more recent submergence decisions, Whitcomb v. Chavis and White v. Regester, in which findings concerning racial motivations were never expressed. The precedential value of Washington v. Davis for subsequent submergence cases was therefore questionable. The Davis decision, for example, was handed down a few months before the district court announced its decision in the Mobile case. The defendants in the Bolden litigation had argued that Davis required the plaintiffs to show a racially discriminatory purpose behind the at-large electoral arrangement. The district judge rejected this argument, however, and refused to treat Davis as controlling. Noting that the submergence cases had not been referenced in that decision, the district judge concluded that Davis had not changed the adjudication standards governing this issue. In the district judge's opinion, "Had the Supreme Court intended the Washington case to have the far reaching consequences contended by defendants, it seems to this court reasonable to conclude that they would have made such an expression."[81]

This intent issue was raised again on appeal, of course, where
it was dealt with somewhat differently. The Fifth Circuit Court of
Appeals had, following Whitcomb and White, established guidelines
for the review of dilution allegations within that (southern) circuit.
These guidelines, which were expressed in Zimmer v. McKeithen,
held that

> where a minority can demonstrate a lack of access to the
> process of slating candidates, the unresponsiveness of
> legislators to their particularized interests, a tenuous
> state policy underlying the preference for multimember
> or at-large districting, or that the existence of past dis-
> crimination in general precludes their effective partici-
> pation in the election system, a strong case [of vote
> dilution] is made.[82]

If "an aggregate of these factors" was found to be present, then a
ruling that the Whitcomb-White standard was satisfied was justified.[83]
The district court's decision in Bolden had been based explicitly on
these Zimmer criteria.

On appeal, the circuit court held that Washington v. Davis did
require that proof of intent be shown in dilution by submergence litigation. But the circuit court still upheld the judgment of the district
court, ruling concurrently that if the factors expressed in Zimmer
were present, an inference of intentional discrimination was justified.[84] Zimmer was said to have implicitly recognized the intent requirement because the factors it focused on were "categories of circumstantial evidence of intentional discrimination."[85] In short, the
law governing vote dilution in the Fifth Circuit was changed in theory,
but not in fact; "intent" was now explicitly required, but Zimmer was
still controlling. The district court's judgment in Bolden was therefore upheld. Its findings concerning the Zimmer criteria were viewed
by the circuit court as supporting an inference that the at-large election system "has been maintained with the purpose of diluting black
votes."[86]

The district and circuit court decisions in Bolden suggested that,
at least in the South, at-large electoral arrangements might continue
to be vulnerable to constitutional litigation after Washington v. Davis.
The Supreme Court's review of Bolden, however, raised serious questions about the future utility of such litigation.

The Supreme Court was badly divided in the Bolden case. The
judgment in favor of the city government was announced in a plurality
rather than majority opinion. That opinion, authored by Mr. Justice
Stewart and joined by Chief Justice Burger and Justices Powell and
Rehnquist, held explicitly that the intent standard, as expressed in

Washington v. Davis and its progeny, [87] was applicable to the vote
dilution issue. Noting that Wright v. Rockefeller had been cited in
Davis as one of the major precedents in which the Court had previously
focused on the intentions of governmental decision-makers, Justice
Stewart concluded that the intent requirement clearly "applied to claims
of racial discrimination affecting voting just as it does to other claims
of racial discrimination."[88] The fact that the claim of discrimination
"affected voting" did not, in the plurality's view, trigger strict scrutiny under the "fundamental interest" proviso (as had been argued by
the plaintiffs),[89] because the issue concerned the weight of a group's
vote, not that of an individual:

> It is true . . . that the Equal Protection Clause confers a
> substantive right to participate in elections on an equal
> basis with other qualified voters. . . . But this right to
> equal participation in the electoral process does not pro-
> tect any "political group," however defined, from elec-
> toral defeat. [90]

Rather than overrule the Court's previous submergence decisions, the plurality, through an opinion bordering on intellectual dis-
honesty, attempted to reconcile these earlier decisions with its holding in Bolden. The language in Fortson and Burns concerning vote
dilution occurring by design "or otherwise" was simply dismissed as
dicta, [91] and Whitcomb and White were treated as if the Court's primary concern in those cases had also been the question of intent. The
plurality referenced Whitcomb as if that decision had held that proof
of intent was necessary in order for the plaintiffs to prevail. Quoting
from Whitcomb, it stated that "A plaintiff must prove that the disputed
plan was 'conceived or operated as [a] purposeful devic[e] to further
racial . . . discrimination.'"[92] This quotation, which appears again
on page 70 of the opinion, was grossly out of context. In Whitcomb,
the Court had actually stated that

> there is no suggestion here that Marion County's multi-
> member district, or similar districts throughout the
> State, were conceived or operated as purposeful devices
> to further racial or economic discrimination. As plain-
> tiffs conceded, "there was no basis for asserting that
> the legislative districts in Indiana were designed to dilute
> the vote of minorities." Brief of Appellees (Plaintiffs) 28-
> 29. [93]

Indeed, the plaintiffs in Whitcomb had explicitly stated that they did
not allege a discriminatory motivation behind the use of the county-

wide at-large elections, and based their case solely on the discriminatory impact of that electoral arrangement. The Court in Whitcomb,
after noting that intent was not an issue, still continued to review the
plaintiffs' evidence concerning the effect of the scheme. If Whitcomb
had in fact treated intent as a necessary condition, no further inquiry
would have been required.

The plurality also attempted to reconcile the White decision with
its holding in Bolden. Although there were absolutely no findings concerning the purpose of the countywide at-large elections at issue in
White, the plurality argued that the White decision was "consistent"
with the intent requirement. [94] The Court in White had stated that "we
have entertained claims that multimember districts are being used
invidiously to cancel out or minimize the voting strength of racial
groups," and cited Fortson, Burns, and Whitcomb in that context.[95]
The plurality in Bolden seized upon that passage, highlighting the
"being used invidiously" expression to argue that the Court in White
was "strongly indicating that only a purposeful dilution of the plaintiffs' vote would offend the Equal Protection Clause."[96] This interpretation was bolstered, in the plurality's view, by the Court's subsequent review of the evidence concerning the lack of equitable access
to the political process for the blacks and Hispanics in the two Texas
counties. This evidence, the plurality maintained, was relevant only
because it related to the question of purpose. [97]

Although the evidence presented in White concerning the relative
access to the political process available to the minority groups in
Texas supposedly addressed the issue of intent, evidence of "precisely
the [same] type" was found inadequate in Bolden. [98] The plurality flatly
rejected the circuit court's interpretation that the presence of the conditions identified in the Zimmer guidelines provided an adequate basis
for inferring a discriminatory purpose. These guidelines had been
adopted by the Fifth Circuit following the White decision and were
based explicitly on the type of evidence referenced by the Supreme
Court in that case. [99] Yet, in Bolden the plurality held that the Zimmer
criteria were "most assuredly insufficient" to prove intent. [100]

That no black person had ever been elected to the Mobile city
commission did not demonstrate, in the plurality's view, that "the
processes leading to nomination and election were not equally open
to Negroes."[101] The plurality focused on the district court's finding
that since the adoption of the federal Voting Rights Act, there have
not been any "official obstacles" preventing black people from registering to vote, casting ballots, or becoming candidates for office in
Mobile. [102] That the racial polarization in Mobile elections left these
black votes and candidacies largely meaningless—given the at-large
elections, place system, and majority vote requirement—apparently
was of no importance. The extensive evidence concerning the severity

of the racial polarization within the Mobile electorate was ignored, presumably because it did not constitute an "official obstacle." The alternative perspective, that in this polarized context the election system itself might be viewed as "an official obstacle," was never addressed.

The plurality also found the evidence concerning discrimination within the municipality's employment practices and provision of services to be "relevant only as the most tenuous and circumstantial evidence,"[103] and the evidence concerning the "hangover" effects of past, state-supported racial discrimination, which had been extremely important in White v. Regester, to be of only "limited help."[104] In addition, the features of the electoral system that exacerbate its dilutive potential—such as the place system and majority vote requirement—were found to contribute little to an inference of purpose, because those features "tend naturally to disadvantage any voting minority."[105]

As noted above, the Court was badly divided in Bolden. Two justices, Stevens and Blackmun, concurred in the result. Mr. Justice Stevens agreed that the city should prevail, despite his conclusion that the at-large system was being maintained in Mobile partly as a consequence of racially discriminatory motives, because there were other "legitimate" considerations supporting its retention.[106] Mr. Justice Blackmun actually concluded that the plaintiffs' evidence was sufficient to support an inference of intent, but still voted to overrule the lower court determinations because, in his view, the district court judge had gone too far in ordering a complete change in Mobile's structure of government as a remedy for the electoral discrimination.[107]

Vigorous dissents were registered by Justices White and Marshall. Mr. Justice White, who had authored the majority opinions in Whitcomb, White, and Davis, agreed with the plurality that proof of intent was necessary in order for the plaintiffs to prevail, but he (like Stevens) found the evidence adequate to support such an inference. White agreed that White v. Regester had been decided consistently with the "totality of the facts" approach to the question of intent expressed in Washington v. Davis, but found the evidence in Bolden "even more compelling" than that present in White.[108] Mr. Justice Marshall, who was joined in dissent by Mr. Justice Brennan, argued that the intent standard was not applicable in Bolden. Marshall noted that the Court's previous decisions concerning submergence had never required a showing of intent, and maintained that this situation had not been affected by Davis and its progeny because none of those cases involved a "fundamental interest," whereas the vote dilution issue does (the right to vote). Marshall and Brennan also argued that if proof of intent were required, they too would be satisfied with the evidence presented by the plaintiffs in this case.[109]

The Bolden decision has been subjected to considerable criticism.

The plurality's effort at reconciling the intent standard enunciated in Bolden with the Court's earlier decisions concerning dilution by submergence has not been very convincing. Bolden has been widely recognized as constituting a dramatic break with those precedents, and the plurality's effort to suggest the contrary has even been described as an example of "legal double think."[110] Not only is the intent standard not consistent with the earlier decisions, but the plurality's approach to the intent question, critics feared, may have effectively placed the burden of proof in these cases well beyond the reach of plaintiffs. Although the plurality explicitly adopted the "totality of circumstances" approach to inferring a discriminatory intent, it also, in the words of one voting rights attorney, "rejected circumstantial proof of the strongest possible kind."[111] Indeed, the plurality's response to the evidence in Bolden suggested that it would not be very amenable to sustaining an inference of racially discriminatory intent, prompting one observer to comment "perhaps nothing short of a patent declaration of racial animus will suffice."[112] Such declarations are now exceedingly rare, of course, and voting rights attorneys expressed the fear that the burden of proof faced by plaintiffs would be "all but impossible to meet."[113]

Predictions that Bolden had created an impossible hurdle for black plaintiffs, like the similar predictions after Whitcomb, turned out to be less than accurate. Voting rights attorneys marshalled the assistance of historians and social scientists in an effort to demonstrate the presence of discriminatory motives at the time electoral arrangements were adopted, or to justify an inference that certain arrangements had been maintained subsequently for the purpose of diluting minority voting strength.[114] These efforts have not been without success in the lower courts,[115] and a finding of discriminatory purpose was upheld in the first case to reach the Supreme Court following Bolden.

The Supreme Court's first post-Bolden submergence case was decided in 1982.[116] At issue was the use of at-large elections to select the five-member board of commissioners for Burke County, Georgia. The election system in Burke County was the same type as that in Mobile—each at-large seat was contested separately, and a candidate had to receive a majority of the vote to be elected. Despite the fact that blacks constituted a majority of the county's population (53.6 percent), they were a minority of both the voting-age population and the registered voters within the county (38 percent), and no black had been elected to the commission since the system was adopted in 1911.

The proceedings in the district court took place prior to the Bolden decision, but after the Fifth Circuit, in Nevitt v. Sides, had held that dilution claims required a showing of intent and that the Zimmer factors were sufficient to justify such an inference.[117] The

district court therefore applied the Zimmer criteria and concluded
that although the election system had not been adopted originally for
a discriminatory purpose (blacks were disfranchised at the time in
Burke County), it had subsequently been maintained for the purpose
of diluting black votes. The court ordered that five single-member
districts be employed in place of the at-large elections.[118] On appeal,
the Fifth Circuit affirmed the district court because its findings were
not "clearly erroneous"; indeed, the appellate court found the inference of discriminatory intent to be "virtually mandated by the overwhelming evidence."[119]

The Supreme Court's response to Rogers was virtually the same
as the appellate court's; it declared that none of the district court's
findings was "clearly erroneous," and therefore refused to disturb the
decision. The Court's opinion was authored by Mr. Justice White, who
had dissented in Bolden on the grounds that the Zimmer-based evidence presented in that case was sufficient to establish a finding of
intent. In Rogers, five other justices joined White's opinion, explicitly
acknowledging the Zimmer-Nevitt basis to the district court's conclusions,[120] and simply ignoring any conflict with the Bolden holding (a
conflict that was accurately explicated in the dissenting opinion of Mr.
Justice Powell).[121] The Whitcomb-White participation test, it now
appears, is once again controlling, although it is now recognized as
an "intent" rather than "effects" test.

THE NEW SECTION 2

Civil rights forces not only sought to marshall evidence of "intent" following Bolden, they also sought to have that decision in effect
overruled by Congress. While the issue of whether to extend the special provisions of the Voting Rights Act was before the Ninety-seventh
Congress (1981-82), civil rights advocates assumed the offensive and
sought to insert an effects test for vote dilution cases into section 2
of that act.[122] Section 2 was a general statutory prohibition against
any racially based interference with the right to vote:

> No voting qualification or prerequisite to voting, or stan-
> dard, practice, or procedure shall be imposed or applied
> by any State or political subdivision to deny or abridge the
> right of any citizen of the United States to vote on account
> of race or color.[123]

The plaintiffs in the Bolden litigation had argued that the Mobile election structure had violated this statutory provision as well as the Fourteenth and Fifteenth Amendments. The Court dismissed this allegation,

holding that section 2 was nothing more than a restatement of the Fifteenth Amendment, which applied only to the issue of vote denial, not dilution.[124]

With the Voting Rights Act already on the congressional agenda, voting rights advocates successfully seized the opportunity to contain the impact of Bolden by having Congress establish a statutory protection against dilution that did not require a finding of intent. Section 2 now reads:

> No voting qualification or prerequisite to voting or standard, practice, or procedure shall be imposed or applied by any State or political subdivision in a manner which results in a denial or abridgement of the right of any citizen of the United States to vote on account of race or color.[125]

The congressional intent in adopting this revision to section 2 was quite explicit—it was "to restore the legal standard that governed voting discrimination cases prior to the Supreme Court's decision in Bolden."[126] Indeed, the Whitcomb-White participation standard was codified by the following addition to section 2:

> A violation [of section 2] is established if, based on the totality of circumstances, it is shown that the political processes leading to nomination or election . . . are not equally open . . . in that [blacks] have less opportunity than other members of the electorate to participate in the political process and to elect representatives of their choice.[127]

The impact the amended section 2 will have on the next round of voting rights litigation cannot be predicted with certainty at this time, but it is expected to be profound. Frank Parker, a leading voting rights attorney, has described the revised section 2 as "the key feature" of the new act, one that "breathes new life" into the voting rights movement.[128] The subsequent judicial response to this statutory provision may well propel us into phase IV of the dilution struggle.

CONCLUSION

The Supreme Court's response to the issue of racial vote dilution has been far more evasive than confrontational. Demanding proof of discrimination at other points in the electoral or political process is hardly responsive to an allegation that the rules under which the winners of electoral contests are determined are systematically disadvantageous to a racial minority, and demanding proof of discriminatory motives seems little more than a means of minimizing judicial involvement with the dilution question. Blacks understandably have found the Court to be far less supportive during this phase of the voting rights struggle than during the earlier vote denial phase.

The reason for this evasive posture may have been articulated well by Mr. Justice Powell, who when dissenting in Rogers v. Lodge stated:

> This is inherently a political area, where the identification of a seeming violation does not necessarily suggest an enforceable judicial remedy—or at least none short of a system of quotas or group representation. [129]

Mr. Justice Frankfurter, while addressing the individual-based vote dilution issue present in Baker v. Carr, correctly noted that "one cannot speak of 'debasement' or 'dilution' of the value of the vote until there is first a standard of reference as to what a vote should be worth."[130] Undoubtedly underlying the jurisprudential detours that seem to have been thrown into the path of those alleging group-based (racial) dilution is a fear that responding directly to such claims may imply that minorities have a right to "proportional representation," something the Constitution (nor section 2 of the Voting Rights Act) certainly does not acknowledge, and something that seems to carry primarily negative connotations within our political culture. Proportional representation is neither the only, nor the proper, standard against which dilution should be measured, however.

Computer programs have been developed that, with certain specified constraints such as contiguity and minimal deviations from population equality, produce randomly generated districting plans. When such plans are drawn without regard to race, the resulting distribution of either all possible plans, or a random sample of possible plans, can serve as the standard of reference against which a given set of districts can be evaluated. The standard in this case is not proportional representation, but simply racially neutral treatment. This standard is established by applying a quantitative measure of minority voting strength to each of the computer-produced plans. The frequency distribution of these scores is then treated as a probability distribution of the minority's expected electoral impact (as measured) occurring by chance, given the racially neutral districting constraints and the residential distribution of the minority. When the same measure of voting strength is applied to another set of districts (single member or at-large), the result can be compared to the probability distribution; the probability of less voting strength, or more dilution, than

that within the challenged electoral arrangement can then be estimated.[131] If that probability is low, it can be viewed as establishing
a presumption of invidious dilution, which those responsible for the
arrangement can then rebut. This approach to the assessment of dilution avoids any suggestion that a group has a right to proportional
representation, but does recognize a right to racially neutral treatment. Such an approach provides a promising pathway through which
the judiciary can address more directly, and therefore more fairly,
the concept of racial vote dilution.

NOTES

1. See Jewel A. Prestage, "The Study of Black Politics in
America: The State of the Art," paper presented at the 1982 Annual
Meeting of the American Political Science Association, September
2-5, Denver, Colorado.
2. Harrell R. Rodgers, "Civil Rights and the Myth of Popular
Sovereignty," Journal of Black Studies 12 (1981): 53-70.
3. Paul R. Abramson, John H. Aldrich, and David W. Rhode,
Change and Continuity in the 1980 Elections (rev. ed.; Washington,
D.C.: Congressional Quarterly Press, 1983), p. 96; see also Bruce
A. Campbell, The American Electorate: Attitudes and Action (New
York: Holt, Rinehart and Winston, 1979), pp. 171-173; Norman H.
Nie, Sidney Verba, and John R. Petrocik, The Changing American
Voter (enlarged ed.; Cambridge, Mass.: Harvard University Press,
1979), pp. 104-105; and J. B. McConahay, B. B. Hardee, and V.
Batts, "Has Racism Declined in America? It Depends on Who is Ask-
ing and What is Asked," Journal of Conflict Resolution 25 (1981):
563-579.
4. See, e.g., Richard Murray and Arnold Vedlitz, "Racial Voting Patterns in the South: An Analysis of Major Elections from 1960
to 1977 in Five Cities," Annals of the American Academy of Political
and Social Sciences 439 (1978): 29-39, and Katharine I. Butler, "Constitutional and Statutory Challenges to Election Structures: Dilution
and the Value of the Right to Vote," Louisiana Law Review 42 (1982):
875.
5. See Rodgers, "Civil Rights and the Myth."
6. John O'Loughlin, "Racial Gerrymandering: Its Potential Impact on Black Politics in the 1980s," in The New Black Politics: The
Search for Political Power, eds. Michael B. Preston, Lenneal J.
Henderson, Jr., and Paul Puryear (New York: Longman, 1982), pp.
241-263.
7. See, e.g., Richard L. Engstrom and Michael D. McDonald,
"The Election of Blacks to City Councils: Clarifying the Impact of

Electoral Arrangements on the Seats/Population Relationship," American Political Science Review 75 (1981): 344–354; Richard L. Engstrom and Michael D. McDonald, "The Underrepresentation of Blacks on City Councils: Comparing the Structural and Socioeconomic Explanations for South/Non-South Differences," Journal of Politics 44 (1982): 1088–1099; Chandler Davidson and George Korbel, "At-Large Elections and Minority-Group Representation: A Re-Examination of Historical and Contemporary Evidence," Journal of Politics 43 (1981): 982–1005; Albert K. Karnig and Susan Welch, "Electoral Structure and Black Representation on City Councils," Social Science Quarterly 63 (1982): 99–114; and Peggy Heilig and Robert J. Mundt, "Changes in Representational Equity: The Effect of Adopting Districts," Social Science Quarterly 64 (1983): 393–397.

    8. 376 U.S. 52.

    9. Ibid., at 59 (Douglas, J., dissenting).

    10. Ibid., at 56, 58.

    11. The Court's 1960 decision in Gomillion v. Lightfoot, 364 U.S. 339, which involved a redelineation of the municipal boundaries of Tuskegee, Alabama, is often cited as a racial gerrymandering decision. The issue in Gomillion, however, was vote denial, not dilution, as the blacks in Tuskegee had lost their right to cast ballots in municipal elections as a result of having their residencies placed outside the new municipal boundaries. The gerrymandering issue has been addressed by the Court, however, in the context of section 5 of the Voting Rights Act, which requires federal "preclearance" of changes in election systems enacted by selected (primarily southern) states and localities. For an examination of the Court's decisions concerning section 5, see Richard L. Engstrom, "Racial Vote Dilution: Supreme Court Interpretations of Section 5 of the Voting Rights Act," Southern University Law Review 4 (1978): 139–164.

    12. Robert G. Dixon, Jr., Democratic Representation (New York: Oxford University Press, 1968), p. 496.

    13. Armand Derfner, "Pro Affirmative Action in Districting," Policy Studies Journal 9 (1980–81): 852.

    14. Robert G. Dixon, Jr., "The Court, the People, and 'One Man, One Vote'," in Reapportionment in the 1970's, ed. Nelson Polsby (Berkeley: University of California Press, 1971), p. 31.

    15. See generally Richard L. Engstrom, "Post-Census Representational Districting: The Supreme Court, 'One Person, One Vote,' and the Gerrymandering Issue," Southern University Law Review 7 (1981): 207–217.

    16. Comment, "Political Representation: The Search for Judicial Standards," Brooklyn Law Review 43 (1977): 452–453.

    17. 376 U.S. 1 (1964).

    18. 377 U.S. 533 (1964).

19. Ibid., at 555.

20. See, e.g., Engstrom, "Post-Census Representational Districting," pp. 185-207.

21. See Butler, "Constitutional and Statutory Challenges," p. 876.

22. 379 U.S. 433 (1965).

23. Ibid., at 439.

24. Ibid. (emphasis added).

25. The Court in Wright had made a special note of the fact that the related issue of equipopulous districting ("one person, one vote") had not been raised in the Wright litigation, and that its decision therefore had no affect on that issue (376 U.S. 52, at 58). The Court in Fortson simply referenced this portion of the Wright decision while stating that the vote dilution allegation in Fortson had not been developed sufficiently and therefore the Court would not fully respond to it (379 U.S. 433, at 439).

26. 384 U.S. 73.

27. Holt v. Richardson, 240 F. Supp. 724, 729 (1965).

28. Ibid., at 730 (emphasis added).

29. Burns v. Richardson, 384 U.S. 73, 88-89 (emphasis added).

30. Ibid., at 89 (emphasis added).

31. Ibid., at 88 (emphasis added).

32. Gordon E. Baker, "Gerrymandering: Privileged Sanctuary or Next Judicial Target?" in Reapportionment in the 1970's, ed. Nelson Polsby (Berkeley: University of California Press, 1971), p. 125.

33. 403 U.S. 124 (1971).

34. Chavis v. Whitcomb, 305 F. Supp. 1364 (1969).

35. Ibid., at 1386 (emphasis added).

36. Ibid., at 1385.

37. Ibid.

38. Ibid., at 1386.

39. Ibid., at 1386-87.

40. Robert N. Clinton, "Further Explorations in the Political Thicket: The Gerrymander and the Constitution," Iowa Law Review 59 (1973): 19.

41. Ignoring precedents established by the Warren Court apparently was not an uncommon phenomenon during the early years of the Burger Court [see, e.g., Charles A. Johnson, "Personnel Change and Policy Change on the U.S. Supreme Court," Social Science Quarterly 62 (1981): 751-757].

42. Whitcomb v. Chavis, 403 U.S. 124, 143-44 (1971).

43. Ibid., at 149 (emphasis added).

44. Ibid.

45. Ibid., at 153. In the one election won by the Democratic

Party, which was also a partisan sweep, the party had slated one
senator and one representative from the Center Township ghetto.

46. Ibid. (emphasis added).

47. Ibid., at 155 (emphasis added).

48. Ibid. (emphasis added).

49. W. L. Carpeneti, "Legislative Apportionment: Multimember
Districts and Fair Representation," University of Pennsylvania Law
Review 120 (1972): 684.

50. Whitcomb v. Chavis, 403 U.S. 124, 157 (1971).

51. Ibid., at 156, n. 34. Adam Clayton Powell, the black incumbent congressman in the district that was 86.3 percent black and
Puerto Rican, had entered the Wright litigation as an intervening de-
fendant in support of the state legislature's proposed districting plan.

52. Ibid., at 180 (Douglas, J., dissenting) (emphasis added).
The dissent by Justice Douglas was joined by Mr. Justice Brennan
and Mr. Justice Marshall.

53. See, e.g., Armand Derfner, "Multi-Member Districts and
Black Voters," Black Law Journal 2 (1972): 120-128, and Kenneth L.
Karst, "Not One Law at Rome and Another at Athens: The Fourteenth
Amendment in Nationwide Application," Washington University Law
Review (1972): 401.

54. Note, "Supreme Court Declares New Standard of Proof for
Groups Alleging Submergence in a Multi-Member Election District,"
Seton Hall Law Review 3 (1971): 185-186 (emphasis added); see also
Carpeneti, "Legislative Apportionment," p. 684.

55. 412 U.S. 755.

56. Graves v. Barnes, 343 F. Supp. 704, 725 (1972).

57. Ibid., at 726.

58. Ibid., at 732.

59. White v. Regester, 412 U.S. 755.

60. Gerhard Casper, "Apportionment and the Right to Vote:
Standards of Judicial Scrutiny," in 1973 Supreme Court Review, ed.
Philip B. Kurland (Chicago: University of Chicago Press, 1973), p. 26.

61. "Hangover effects" refers to the contemporary socioeconomic
and political disadvantages minority groups suffer as a consequence of
earlier discriminatory treatment [see Comment, "The Voting Rights
Act of 1965 and Minority Access to the Political Process," Columbia
Human Rights Law Review 6 (1974): 133-134, 153].

62. See, e.g., Ronald Claunch and Leon C. Hallman, "Ward
Elections in the South: Electoral Change Through Federal Court
Order," GPSA Journal 6 (1978): 3-15, and Davidson and Korbel, "At-
Large Elections," p. 984.

63. Bolden v. City of Mobile, 423 F. Supp. 384.

64. Disfranchisement was accomplished in Alabama through the
use of such devices as the literacy test, "good character" test, con-

stitutional interpretation test, poll tax, and white primary. On the history of racial discrimination in Alabama's electoral process, see Brief for the United States as Amicus Curiae at 67–74, City of Mobile, Alabama v. Bolden, 446 U.S. 55 (1980).

65. Bolden v. City of Mobile, 423 F. Supp. 384, 387.

66. Laughlin McDonald, "The Bolden Decision Stonewalls Black Aspirations," Southern Changes 2 (1980): 13.

67. Brief for Appellees, City of Mobile, Alabama v. Bolden, 446 U.S. 55 (1980), at 90–91.

68. 423 F. Supp. 384 (1976).

69. Ibid., at 388–389.

70. Ibid., at 389.

71. Ibid. (emphasis added).

72. Ibid., at 391–392.

73. Ibid., at 392.

74. Ibid.

75. Ibid., at 386. See also Thomas L. Van Valey, Wade Clark Root, and Jerome E. Wilcox, "Trends in Presidential Segregation: 1960–1970," American Journal of Sociology 82 (1977): 833.

76. Ibid., at 403.

77. 426 U.S. 229.

78. The due process clause of the Fifth Amendment has been interpreted as prohibiting the federal government from invidiously discriminating against individuals or groups in the same way that the Fourteenth Amendment's equal protection clause prohibits discrimination by state and local governments [see Bolling v. Sharpe, 347 U.S. 497 (1954)]. Because the District of Columbia is under the jurisdiction of the federal government, the plaintiffs' claim in Washington v. Davis was based on the Fifth Amendment [see Washington v. Davis, 426 U.S. 229, 239 (1976)].

79. Washington v. Davis, 426 U.S 229, 240.

80. Ibid., at 242.

81. Bolden v. City of Mobile, Alabama, 423 F. Supp. 384, 395.

82. 485 F. 2d 1297, 1305 (1973) (emphasis added).

83. Ibid.

84. See the companion case to Bolden, Nevitt v. Sides, 571 F. 2d 209 (1978).

85. Nevitt v. Sides, 571 F. 2d 209, 215.

86. Bolden v. City of Mobile, Alabama, 571 F. 2d 238, 245 (1978).

87. See, e.g., Village of Arlington Heights v. Metropolitan Housing Development Corporation, 429 U.S. 252 (1977), and Personnel Administrator of Massachusetts v. Feeney, 442 U.S. 256 (1979).

88. City of Mobile, Alabama v. Bolden, 446 U.S. 55, 67 (1980).

89. See Brief for Appellees, City of Mobile, Alabama v. Bolden, 446 U.S. 55 (1980), at 53–61.

90. City of Mobile, Alabama v. Bolden, 446 U.S. 55, 77.

91. Ibid., at 67, 68 n. 13.

92. Ibid., at 66 (emphasis added).

93. Whitcomb v. Chavis, 403 U.S. 124, 149 (1971) (emphasis added).

94. City of Mobile, Alabama v. Bolden, 446 U.S. 55, 69 (1980).

95. White v. Regester, 412 U.S. 755, 765 (1973).

96. City of Mobile, Alabama v. Bolden, 446 U.S. 55, 69.

97. Ibid., at 70.

98. Armand Derfner, "Section 2 of the Voting Rights Act and City of Mobile v. Bolden," paper read at the Symposium on the Voting Rights Act, sponsored by the American Bar Association's Special Committee on Election Law and Voter Participation, April 9-10, 1981, Washington, D.C.

99. See Zimmer v. McKeithen, 485 F. 2d 1297 (1973). Mr. Justice White, the author of the Court's opinions in Whitcomb v. Chavis and White v. Regester, has stated that the conditions identified in Zimmer v. McKeithen were "the very factors deemed relevant by White v. Regester and Whitcomb v. Chavis" [City of Mobile, Alabama v. Bolden, 446 U.S. 55, 101 (1980), (White, J., dissenting) (emphasis added)].

100. City of Mobile, Alabama v. Bolden, 446 U.S. 55, 73.

101. Ibid.

102. Ibid.

103. Ibid., at 74.

104. Ibid.

105. Ibid., at 74 (emphasis added).

106. Ibid., at 92 (Stevens, J., concurring).

107. Ibid., at 80-83 (Blackmun, J., concurring).

108. Ibid., at 103 (White, J., dissenting).

109. Ibid., at 103-141 (Marshall, J., dissenting).

110. Bernard Grofman, "Alternatives to Single-Member Plurality Districts: Legal and Empirical Issues," Policy Studies Journal 9 (1980-81): 880. See also Derfner, "Section 2 and the Voting Rights Act," p. 1, and Comment, "Voting Rights: Stuck Inside of Mobile with the Voting Blues Again. Vote Dilution Claims Confined," Stetson Law Review 10 (1981): 365, 375.

111. Derfner, "Pro Affirmative Action," p. 852.

112. Comment, "Voting Rights," p. 375.

113. McDonald, "The Bolden Decision," p. 11; see also Derfner, "Pro Affirmative Action," p. 852, and Grofman, "Alternatives to Single-Member Plurality Districts," p. 880.

114. See, e.g., Peyton McCrary, "History in the Courts: The Significance of Bolden v. City of Mobile," in Ethnic Vote Dilution, ed. Chandler Davidson (Washington, D.C.: Howard University Press,

forthcoming), and Charles Cotrell, "Reflections of a Political Scientist as Expert Witness," paper read at the 1982 Annual Meeting of the American Political Science Association, September 2-5, Denver, Colorado.

115. See, e.g., McMillan v. Escambia County, Florida, 638 F. 2d 1239 (1981), and Bolden v. City of Mobile, Alabama, 542 F. Supp. 1050 (1982).

116. Rogers v. Lodge, 458 U.S. 613 (1982).

117. Nevitt v. Sides, 571 F. 2d 209 (1978).

118. Lodge v. Buxton, Civil No. 176-55 (S.D. Ga. 1978).

119. Lodge v. Buxton, 639 F. 2d 1348 (1981).

120. Rogers v. Lodge, 458 U.S. 613, at slip op. 11.

121. Ibid., at 458 (Powell, J., dissenting).

122. See, generally, Richard L. Engstrom, "The (New) Voting Rights Act: Continuity and Change in Black Politics," in Contemporary Southern Politics: Continuity and Change, ed. Jimmy Lea (Baton Rouge: Louisiana State University Press, forthcoming).

123. 79 Stat. 437, as amended, 42 U.S.C. §1973.

124. City of Mobile, Alabama v. Bolden, 446 U.S. 55, 60-61 (1980).

125. §3, 96 Stat. 131, 134 (amending 42 U.S.C. §1973) (emphasis added).

126. Senate Committee on the Judiciary, Voting Rights Act Extension, S. Rep. No. 97-417, 97th Cong., 2d Sess. 15 (1982).

127. §3, 96 Stat. at 134.

128. Frank R. Parker, "The New 'Results' Test of the Voting Rights Act: A New Sparkle for the Crown Jewel of American Liberties," in Section 2 Litigation Manual (Washington, D.C.: Lawyer's Committee for Civil Rights Under Law, 1982), p. 2.

129. Rogers v. Lodge, 458 U.S. 617 (1982) (Powell, J., dissenting).

130. 369 U.S. 186, 300 (1962), (Frankfurter, J., dissenting).

131. See, e.g., Richard L. Engstrom and John K. Wildgen, "Pruning Thorns from the Thicket: An Empirical Test of the Existence of Racial Gerrymandering," Legislative Studies Quarterly 2 (1977): 465-479; John O'Loughlin, "The Identification and Evaluation of Racial Gerrymandering," Annals, Association of American Geographers 72 (1982): 165-184; and John O'Loughlin and Anne-Marie Taylor, "Choices in Redistricting and Electoral Outcomes: The Case of Mobile, Alabama," Political Geography Quarterly 1 (1982): 317-339.

3
Denial or Abridgment of the Right to Vote: What Does It Mean?

Katharine I. Butler

> "But my dear, we never compromise virtue," quoth the
>   Queen.
> "Horrors, no," exclaimed Alice, "but what is virtue?
>   That is the question."
>
> > Lewis Carroll
> > Through the Looking Glass[1]

Few can be found who favor denying or abridging the right to vote on account of race or for any reason. But when is the right denied or abridged? That is the question, and the answer cannot be provided until the scope of the right has been defined.

As the law has developed, the Supreme Court has implicitly recognized several different "rights to vote," all having a different scope, and often afforded different levels of protection according to the source of the right. This chapter will contrast the Court's definition of the right arising under Section 5 of the Voting Rights Act with that arising under Section 2 and the Constitution.

CONSTITUTIONAL DENIAL OF THE RIGHT TO VOTE

The most basic aspect of the right to vote must be access to the ballot, or enfranchisement. Despite the Supreme Court's exaltation of the right in the 1868 case of Yick Wo v. Hopkins[2]—"the right to vote is a fundamental political right because preservative of all rights"— for nearly one hundred years before and after that pronouncement, the states were given a free hand in the restrictions they could impose upon this right. Early state constitutions imposed limitations on the franchise based upon property ownership, poll taxes, personal wealth, religion, sex, age, race, and durational residency.[3] Following the Civil War, vague restrictions for illiteracy, economic and social status, and conviction of certain crimes served as not-so-subtle means to continue to disfranchise blacks, despite the Fifteenth Amendment.[4]

Sex was effectively outlawed as a basis for disfranchisement by passage of the Nineteenth Amendment, but early Supreme Court interpretations of the Civil War amendments rendered them impotent to effect a similar enfranchisement of blacks.[5] Gradually, however, the more blatant discriminatory devices—grandfather clauses, all-white primaries, and discriminatory use of literacy tests—were outlawed.[6]

Even the certainty that a particular disfranchising device would ultimately be judicially outlawed proved an insufficient barrier to state and local officials intent upon discrimination. No sooner would one device be declared unconstitutional than another would be enacted in its place. Under pressure from civil rights groups, Congress responded to the widespread disfranchisement of blacks in the South with passage of the 1965 Voting Rights Act. The act's plethora of administrative remedies had an overwhelming impact on the registration of blacks.[7] If the right to vote includes only unrestricted access to the ballot, we could today for the most part declare securing of this right for black voters a "fait accompli."[8]

Shortly after the Supreme Court demonstrated a willingness to give some clout to the Fifteenth Amendment, nonminority voters began to utilize the Fourteenth Amendment to elevate the right to vote in nonracial areas to the status attributed to it by Yick Wo. Oddly, the highest elevation was achieved in the apportionment cases, where no claim of denied franchise could be made.[9] In Baker v. Carr[10] the Supreme Court held that the equal protection clause of the Fourteenth Amendment mandates an equally weighted vote for all voters. This rule was eventually extended to require election districts at every level of state and federal government to comply with one person–one vote standards.[11]

The equal protection rationale was quickly adopted to scrutinize outright restrictions on the franchise as well. Property ownership as a prerequisite to voting in a school board election was struck down in Kramer v. Union Free School District,[12] and the poll tax was outlawed in Harper v. Virginia Board of Electors.[13] In Carrington v. Rush,[14] the Supreme Court struck down a Texas statute prohibiting military personnel from voting in state elections. A Maryland statute denying the ballot to residents of a federal enclave was outlawed in Evans v. Cornman.[15] Even durational residency requirements must be necessary to promote a compelling state interest in order to survive constitutional challenge. See Dunn v. Blumstein.[16]

The underlying rationale of these cases was that voting is a "fundamental right." Any state action that denies or abridges this right must be closely scrutinized and carefully confined. See Harper v. Virginia Board of Electors. [17] In the franchise limitation cases, the right was clearly denied, and in the absence of a compelling state interest, the offending legislation could not stand. Likewise, in the malapportionment cases, unequal election districts resulted in some voters' ballots counting for less than those of others. According to these cases, once the "right" is involved, strict scrutiny is to be applied, which generally means the infringing legislation cannot stand.

DILUTION OF MINORITY VOTING STRENGTH

Despite general elimination of barriers to registration and balloting following implementation of the Voting Rights Act, minorities quickly recognized that their political fortunes often were not thereby improved. Frustration over the constant defeat of black and other candidates sympathetic to black interests led to the development of the so-called dilution suits. The dilution cases have been adequately discussed in earlier papers. [18] In essence, minority plaintiffs in these cases argued that the election structure (generally at-large elections or multimember districts) in combination with racial-bloc voting prevented their ballots from counting in the election contest. Black candidates could not be elected without white support, which was not forthcoming. White candidates did not need black votes to be elected, and once in office were free to ignore the interests of the group without fear of future political defeat. Blacks were therefore effectively fenced out of the political process. For years the courts applied the fundamental rights analysis, developed in apportionment cases, to cases involving dilution of minority voting strength. If dilution were established (and the problems of proof were considerable), the right to vote was deemed to have been denied to members of the minority group, even though no claims of disfranchisement or malapportionment were raised. [19]

Until the Supreme Court's decision in Washington v. Davis[20] and the advent of the "intent" requirement in equal protection cases, the primary issue in dilution cases was not whether dilution denied or abridged the right to vote, but rather whether dilution had in fact been established by the evidence in the case. Although there was significant case authority to the contrary, some courts and most commentators were of the opinion that the fundamental rights analysis removed dilution from the general intent requirement applicable in other disproportionate impact cases, such as those involving employment and housing. [21] This belief was shattered by the Supreme Court's decision in Mobile v. Bolden, [22] where a majority of the Court held that demonstration of a racially discriminatory purpose behind the dilution-causing legislation is an essential element of the plaintiffs' case.

Although there was no majority opinion as to how this discriminatory purpose was to be established, a majority of the Court did agree that its establishment is essential. The upshot of the Mobile decision is that the Court does not see dilution as an infringement upon the right to vote, at least not the right that is "fundamental." The Court cited with approval the franchise and malapportionment cases where strict scrutiny is applied, and where there is no requirement that a discriminatory motive be established. The constitutional right involved in a dilution case is therefore not the right to vote, but rather the right not to have legislative decisions based on an impermissible basis, for the purpose of depriving minorities of the opportunity to elect candidates of their choice.

The plaintiffs' unsuccessful claim in Mobile was based on the Fifteenth Amendment as well as the Fourteenth. The Court has interpreted the Fourteenth Amendment to reach all denials of equal protection, including both infringements of fundamental rights and state action based on race. The Fifteenth Amendment, however, is more limited in that it deals only with denials or abridgments of the right to vote on account of race. With one exception, all Fifteenth Amendment cases decided by the Supreme Court involved actual denials of access to the ballot. [23] The exception is Wright v. Rockefeller, [24] which involved a claim of racial gerrymandering of Manhattan's four congressional districts. All qualified voters in Manhattan were permitted to vote for some congressman, so no question of access to the ballot was raised. The plaintiffs lost, but not because the Court believed the right to vote was incapable of being infringed by a districting scheme. They lost because they failed to demonstrate that the authors of the scheme were motivated by racial concerns.

The Mobile plurality cited Wright for the proposition that the Fifteenth Amendment requires a discriminatory purpose, implying that if a discriminatory purpose had been established the amendment would have been violated. Thus, even though districting does not involve the "fundamental" right to vote (Mobile), discriminatory districting will violate the Fifteenth Amendment (Wright), which by its very language applies only to denials or abridgments of the right to vote. The Fifteenth Amendment's right to vote must therefore be broader in scope than the "fundamental" right to vote, since it includes a prohibition against dilution, but it is narrower in the protection afforded. Only intentional, racially motivated schemes are actionable.

On the same day the Court decided in Mobile that dilution does not involve a violation of the right to vote of the fundamental variety, it also decided a dilution case, City of Rome v. United States, [25] under

Section 5 of the Voting Rights Act. Like the Fifteenth Amendment, Section 5 protects only the right to vote, but the answer the Court gave in Rome for when the right has been denied or abridged was very different from the answer given in Mobile. In essence, the Court in Rome held that the right to vote protected by Section 5 includes the "right" of minorities not to have their ability to elect candidates of their choice diminished by changes in election laws. The development of this expansive definition of the right to vote will be considered below.

DENIAL OF THE RIGHT TO VOTE UNDER SECTION 5

Section 5 of the Voting Rights Act of 1965 was the congressional response to the practice of many political subdivisions in the South of adopting new discriminatory devices to prevent the political participation of blacks as soon as old devices were outlawed. Section 5 provides that all election law changes enacted in covered jurisdictions after the effective date of the act must obtain federal preclearance before implementation.[26] The political subdivision enacting the change must obtain from either the attorney-general of the United States or the District of Columbia District Court a declaration that the new law will not have the purpose or effect of denying or abridging the right to vote on account of race.

Every change that affects voting in even the slightest way must obtain preclearance. The burden of proof on the issues of purpose and effect is on the submitting political subdivision. The standard for judging when a change is free from discriminatory effect and thus entitled to preclearance was set out by the Supreme Court in Beer v. United States.[27] If a change is not retrogressive, it does not violate Section 5 unless "the [newly adopted law] itself so discriminates on the basis of race or color as to violate the Constitution."[28] The Court saw Congress' interest in enacting Section 5 as insuring that changes in voting procedures would not lead to retrogression in the position of racial minorities in their exercise of the electoral franchise so recently guaranteed by other parts of the act.

The plan in Beer was submitted by the city of New Orleans, which at the time had a 45 percent black population. The submitted councilmanic districting plan was drawn so that the election of a black to one of the seven council seats was probable. Because under the displaced plan the election of a black was unlikely, the Supreme Court found the new plan to be ameliorative rather than retrogressive: it enhanced blacks' opportunity to elect a candidate of their choice vis-à-vis the plan it replaced. The Court also noted that the plan did not even approach a violation of previously enunciated constitutional standards set out in dilution cases brought under the Fourteenth Amendment, and thus the Court reversed the lower court's denial of preclearance.

In Beer there were extensive findings of fact by the trial court establishing that black citizens were not effective participants in the political processes of the city because of the presence of the factors associated with dilution cases. The trial court reasoned that any plan that failed to correct this exclusion by providing a reasonable opportunity for blacks to achieve proportional representation produced a discriminatory effect and should be denied preclearance.

The Supreme Court's rejection of the absolute test of discriminatory effect adopted by the lower court in favor of a relative test was seriously criticized by the Beer dissenters and by commentators.[29] One consequence of the retrogression standard is that jurisdictions that had more repressive election systems on the effective date of the act may be rewarded with easier preclearance because any slight improvement will be sufficient to qualify as ameliorative. Strangely, however, this result may be entirely consistent with the original congressional intent to "freeze" election laws in covered jurisdictions as of the effective date of the act in order to prevent further retrogressive tactics. Furthermore, the effect of a Section 5 objection is to prevent the implementation of the new law. No further remedy is provided; therefore, if an ameliorative change were to be denied preclearance, the more repressive system would be resurrected.

Several factors prevent the retrogression standard from impairing the effectiveness of Section 5. First, the primary benefit of Section 5, regardless of the standard applied, is that legislators know their actions will be scrutinized. Section 5 forces legislators, who would otherwise intentionally or inadvertently ignore the impact of election laws on minorities, to give serious attention to minority interests. Second, most submissions are made to the attorney-general, whose decisions are seldom challenged. In actual practice the attorney-general denies preclearance on bases other than retrogression.[30] Finally, recent Supreme Court interpretations of Section 5 adopt a definition of "retrogression" that implicitly extends the right to vote far beyond the scope of the "right," even as defined by the pre-Mobile dilution cases.

"Retrogression" Clarified

In City of Rome v. United States,[31] the city of Rome, Georgia, sought district court preclearance of a number of election changes implemented since 1966, but inadvertently not submitted until 1975. There were a number of changes in the methods of electing both the city commission and the school board, the net result of which was to increase the number of votes needed for candidates to be elected. The Supreme Court agreed with the district court's conclusion that when those changes were combined with racial bloc voting, the effect was dilution of the voting strength of the city's 23 percent black population. Under the old system blacks had a slightly better chance to elect a candidate of their choice than under the new system. Thus, concluded the Court, the change "would lead to a retrogression in the position of racial minorities with respect to their effective exercise of the electoral [process]."[32]

Both the old and the new election system called for at-large elections, which as a practical matter meant that the city's registered black voters, who were less than 20 percent of the total, could not elect a black candidate under either system without substantial white support. Furthermore, the evidence reported by the lower court established that despite the absence of black elected officials, Rome's black citizens were effective participants in the political life of the city. They frequently provided the margin of victory for winning candidates, and elected officials were correspondingly responsive to the needs of the black community. In short, dilution, even under the pre-Mobile effects test, was not established.

In light of these findings (which were not disturbed on appeal), it can be assumed that any change that produces even a theoretical decrease in the minority group's ability to elect a candidate of its choice—regardless of how effectively the group is participating politically—will be equated with "retrogression in the exercise of the electoral process" and will be denied preclearance. It is obvious then that the standard for when the right to vote has been abridged is different when the right protected by Section 5 is involved.

Even if Congress has the authority to ordain such a result in the name of affirmatively providing greater protection for a previously excluded minority, one may question its desirability. Although in the case of Rome blacks were elected to both bodies under the "revised" plan (notably with considerable white support),[33] whether the black community will receive greater value from their vote remains to be seen. The Court may have negotiated for them a trade of political clout for a token representative.

The Supreme Court's inclination to evaluate the impact of election law changes on minorities' exercise of the right to vote solely in terms of the group's ability to elect a candidate of their choice was taken a disturbing step further in Port Arthur v. United States.[34] Port Arthur, decided in early 1983, involved the submission of an annexation of outlying areas to the city, and a consolidation with several smaller surrounding municipalities. A strict application of the Beer retrogression standard would preclude all annexations in covered ju-

risdictions unless the added area mirrored the racial composition of
the existing city. Annexations, and therefore the submission in Port
Arthur, are evaluated under a slightly different standard. The annexation preclearance standard was developed in Richmond v. United
States.[35]

Richmond involved an annexation to the city of Richmond, Virginia. Before annexation blacks were a majority of the city's population, but afterward they were in the minority. City elections were held
at-large, and racial bloc voting was common. Thus the effect of the
annexation was to deprive blacks of their majority status in the city
and thereby of potential control of the government. Furthermore, in
light of the prevalent racial bloc voting, a situation was created where
blacks were not likely to have much impact on election outcomes. The
District Court denied preclearance because the proportion of blacks
in the new city was less than in the old, thereby diluting their voting
power. The Court continued to refuse preclearance even after the city
agreed to adopt single-member districts that would provide blacks
with proportional representation within the new city. The Supreme
Court reversed, holding that "As long as the ward system fairly reflects the strength of the Negro community as it exists after annexation we cannot hold . . . that such an annexation is nevertheless barred
by §5."[36]

In Port Arthur blacks constituted 45.21 percent of the preannex-
ation population of the city. By virtue of the annexation-consolidation,
that percentage was decreased to 40.56 percent. Prior to the enlarge-
ment, city elections were conducted at-large with candidates required
to run from residency wards, and a majority vote was required for
election. This system was retained after the annexations, thereby
increasing slightly the number of white votes a black candidate would
need to be elected.

The city initially attempted to obtain preclearance of the annexation-consolidation without modifying the city's election structure.
Subsequently, however, after the attorney-general refused preclearance and the city had filed for a declaratory judgment in the District
Court, the city and the attorney-general agreed to a plan, which they
jointly submitted to the District Court. The plan called for the election
of eight council members plus a mayor. Six council members were to
be elected by districts, and two at-large, but from residency districts.
A majority vote was required for election to all seats. Population distribution within the wards was such that blacks were virtually assured
control of three seats, or one-third of the council counting the mayor
as a part of the council (and a greater percentage if the mayor was
not considered). The District Court refused preclearance because the
city would not agree to drop the majority vote requirement for the
two at-large seats. The Supreme Court affirmed.

The Supreme Court's decision was based on three factors. First, the Court concluded that adequate reflection of black political strength in the enlarged city was a question upon which reasonable minds could differ. Because the District Court was devising a remedy to cure a statutory violation, the Supreme Court "should not rush to overturn its judgment."[37]

Second, the "plan undervalued to some extent the political strength of the black community."[38] Blacks were assured of one-third of the seats, but they were 40.56 percent of the population and 34.6 percent of the voting-age population. The majority vote requirement, in combination with racial bloc voting, would preclude a black candidate from ever winning an at-large seat. Eliminating the requirement, reasoned the Court, made it possible for a black to win, but would not guarantee that result.

Finally, opined the Court, the District Court had found previous plans presented by the city to be tainted by an impermissible purpose. Although no such finding was made as to the plan under consideration, "It seems to us that in light of the prior findings of discriminatory purpose such action was a reasonable hedge against the possibility that the [proposed] scheme contained a purposefully discriminatory element."[39]

The Court's reasoning, particularly on the issue of "effect," is nothing short of baffling. Under any reasoned analysis of the effect of the change in Port Arthur, blacks were considerably better off in the enlarged city with its mixed plan than in the preexisting city. Port Arthur was not like Richmond, where blacks lost their majority status and potential control of the government by virtue of the annexation. In Port Arthur blacks went from a situation where no black could be elected, absent white support, to a situation where they were assured control of one-third of the governmental body—just slightly more than one percent less than their percentage of the voting age population. They were assured proportional representation as close as possible to what they would have received under the most ideal, race-free circumstances. Admittedly, under the rationale of City of Richmond, blacks were entitled to some compensation for their diminished influence in city elections brought about by the annexation. Why the assurance of proportional representation, coupled with the "margin of victory" vote for the at-large seats, did not provide adequate compensation is difficult to imagine.

Ironically, the Court's action has the potential for decreasing the chances that a black will be elected to one of the at-large seats. The residency ward for one of the at-large seats is 70.83 percent black, raising the distinct possibility that white candidates will be in short supply. Elimination of the majority vote requirement will increase chances of a black victory only where white candidates outnumber black ones. The opposite situation is likely to exist in the 70.83 percent black ward, and thus the plurality rule will be of no assistance for that seat. Any effort among blacks to propose a single candidate could prompt a similar move by whites, possibly turning the election into a racial confrontation. As for the other at-large seat, the ward contains so few blacks of voting age (less than 10 percent) that black candidates are unlikely.

The upshot of Rome and Port Arthur is that the right to vote under Section 5 includes the "right" for minorities not to have their chances of electing a candidate of their choice depend upon gaining more white support than that needed under the existing system (Rome). If an otherwise legitimate election law change, such as an annexation, increases the number of white votes a black candidate must obtain to be elected, blacks must be compensated for this decrease in their influence by adjustments in the election system that virtually guarantee proportional representation consistent with their numbers in the changed political subdivision. Furthermore, all doubts as to what "consistent with their numbers" means must be resolved in favor of greater representational opportunities for minorities (Port Arthur). This appears to be adequate compensation for the occasional ameliorative, but nevertheless discriminatory, system that might be precleared as a result of Beer's retrogression standard.

DENIAL OF THE RIGHT TO VOTE
AS DEFINED BY SECTION 2

Section 2 of the Voting Rights Act originally contained a general prohibition, almost identical to the Fifteenth Amendment, against denial or abridgment of the right to vote on account of race. Unlike Section 5, Section 2 has nationwide application. So long as vote dilution cases could be maintained under the Fourteenth Amendment's "fundamental rights" analysis, Section 2 was of no particular importance. With the advent of the intent requirement, however, plaintiffs began to argue that, regardless of the constitutional standard, dilution suits could be maintained under Section 2 without a showing of discriminatory purpose. A plurality of the Supreme Court rejected this argument in Mobile, but in 1982 Congress amended Section 2 to clarify that discriminatory results are also prohibited. As amended, Section 2 now reads in pertinent part:

> (a) No voting . . . practice . . . shall be imposed by
> any . . . political subdivision in a manner which results
> in a denial or abridgement of the right of any citizen . . .
> to vote on account of race or color, or [membership in
> language minority groups protected by the Act].

(b) A violation of subsection (a) is established if, based
on the totality of circumstances, it is shown that the
political processes leading to nomination or election in
the State or political subdivision are not equally open to
participation by members of a class of citizens protected
by subsection (a) in that its members have less opportunity than other members of the electorate to participate
in the political process and to elect representatives of
their choice. The extent to which members of a protected
class have been elected to office in the State or political
subdivision is one circumstance which may be considered:
Provided, That nothing in this section establishes a right
to have members of a protected class elected in numbers
equal to their proportion in the population. [40]

From the legislative history of the amendment, it is clear that
Congress intended to restore the pre–Mobile standard developed in
White v. Regester[41] and Zimmer v. McKeethen. [42] The language of
Section 2(b) is from the Supreme Court's opinion in White, the only
Supreme Court case in which plaintiffs prevailed on a dilution theory.
Zimmer, an early, influential dilution case decided by the Fifth Circuit Court of Appeals, provided a list of primary and enhancing factors,
some aggregate of which would establish dilution.
    One can agree with the spirit of the amendment to Section 2 and
yet disagree with the decision to resurrect the Zimmer standard. Many
commentators thought that Mobile was wrongly decided. [43] If dilution
results in an abridgment of the right to vote, a remedy should be provided for those affected, regardless of the purposes behind the adoption
or maintenance of the election structure. The cases following White
and Zimmer, however, did little to tie the Zimmer factors to a theoretically sound definition of dilution. The justification was not apparent
for why one "aggregate of factors" equalled dilution while another aggregate did not. Absent also was an explanation of why dilution resulted
in an abridgment of the right to vote. If blacks were allowed to register
and vote freely, how could they be seen as having less opportunity to
participate in the political process than others whose candidates also
lost? The "totality of the circumstances" or "aggregate of factors"
test from Zimmer produced inconsistent results, not clearly justified
by factual differences in the cases. [44]
    Neither the practical problem of defining dilution nor the theo-
retical problem of why dilution abridges the right to vote is solved by
redefining the claim as arising under Section 2 rather than the Constitution. Even under Section 2, a claim for relief is stated only if the
right to vote is denied or abridged. Perhaps with a little fine tuning
the "totality of the circumstances" test could have been reorganized

to produce a workable and theoretically sound definition of dilution. But the legislative history of the 1982 amendment suggests that Congress was opposed to a more concrete formulation, and chose instead to continue what might more appropriately be called the "Chinese menu" approach to dilution. According to the Senate Judiciary Committee, a violation can be established by a variety of factors, but "there is no requirement that any particular number of factors be proved, or a majority of these points one way or the other." The net result of this open-ended standard, coupled with a recent Supreme Court decision defining "discriminatory results" as a factual finding seldom to be reversed on appeal, [45] is sure to be that cases will be decided by the trial judge's nose.

IMPLICATIONS AND CONCLUSIONS

In the final analysis, there is no unified definition of what is included within the scope of the right to vote—aside from perhaps unrestricted access to the ballot. The fundamental right to vote, protected by the Fourteenth Amendment, includes only enfranchisement and an equally weighted vote. Clearly, this definition is too narrow. Recognition must be given to the fact that in certain circumstances this is not enough to assure some classes of voters that the right will serve its function of "protecting all other rights."

While the Supreme Court's interpretation of the Fifteenth Amendment suggests a broader right to vote—one that encompasses the right to have one's ballot matter in election contests—this expanded "right" is protected only from intentional infringement.

Section 5's right to vote is broader in that it includes the right to effective exercise of the political process, and can be violated without regard to the intent of the violators. While recognizing that there is more to the "right" than just casting a ballot is a step in the right direction, the definition the Court has selected for "effective exercise" is, unfortunately, not particularly well related to the underlying values to be protected. Section 5's retrogression standard is both underprotective and overprotective of minority rights. The problems caused by underprotection are somewhat mitigated by the availability of Section 2. In the long term, the greater danger may come from the overprotective interpretation.

In Rome and Port Arthur the Supreme Court equated effective political participation with "ability to elect a candidate of one's choice" and, it is implied, without white support. While in some circumstances the only opportunity for any political voice may be through the assurance of electing a candidate, this will by no means always be the case. To insist upon a guaranteed seat is an acceptable remedy for exclusion

from the political process. To make that assurance absent evidence
of exclusion is quite something else.

If blacks and other minorities are able to form political alliances,
to have their interests considered by elected officials through threat of
political action, and are generally able to secure through their ballots
the benefits of citizenship, they are effectively participating in the
political process. They are receiving from the right to vote the same
value as others. To guarantee more may disrupt the functioning of the
pluralist bazaar, the long-term consequence of which cannot be fully
predicted. Conceivably, one result may be the perpetuation of racial
distinctions long beyond the point where they may otherwise have dis-
sipated.

The Section 2 "right to vote" has the potential for striking an
acceptable medium between the extremes of Mobile and Rome. The
language of the section reflects an awareness that political effectiveness cannot be assumed from mere access to the ballot. At the same
time, it rejects the notion that absence of black elected officials alone
is proof that the election system causes a discriminating result.
Whether courts deciding cases under Section 2 will be able to strike
an appropriate balance remains to be seen.

The existence of different "rights," regardless of how defined,
means that challenges to election laws can be determined more by the
source of the challenge than by the actual impact of the law on the ability of minorities to participate in the political process. The situation
in Port Arthur provides a good backdrop to demonstrate the general
irrationality of the law as it has developed in voting cases.

Had Port Arthur been in a noncovered jurisdiction, such as
Florida, it could have retained the at-large election system, absent
proof by challengers that the retention was for the purpose of preventing the election of blacks (Fourteenth and Fifteenth Amendments), or
that the system deprived blacks of an equal opportunity to participate
in the electoral process (Section 2). If the pre-Mobile dilution cases
are followed for this latter determination, much more is required for
plaintiffs to prevail than just the inability of blacks to elect a candidate
without white support. Perhaps plaintiffs could have prevailed in an
attack on the original at-large system, but clearly the mixed plan
finally proposed by the city would have easily withstood a Section 2
challenge.

Even under Section 5, the outcome of the preclearance issue
could have been entirely different, depending upon the prechange condition in Port Arthur, even though the postchange impact could be precisely the same. If, for example, instead of an annexation, the city
had changed from an at-large system of election to a district system
with even a single district potentially controlled by blacks, the change
would have been nonretrogressive, and, absent evidence of discrimi-

nating purpose, entitled to preclearance. Likewise, had the annexation and consolidation increased the number of black voters in the city by even a fraction of a percentage point, preclearance would have been compelled by Beer. Yet, in none of these situations would black voters be in as advantageous a position as they were in Port Arthur under the mixed plan, which assured them three seats on the council.

This irrational result is not necessary. The right to vote should have a single meaning—one that recognizes the values the right protects and the function it serves in a democratic society. That value comes not from proportional representation, nor is it always assured by the right to cast a ballot. Rather, it comes from the ability to join together with others to make one's numbers felt in the political process and, therefore, in societal decision-making. It comes from being able to form alliances to further common goals. In short, it comes from being able to participate in the pluralist bazaar of politics.

The 1982 extension of the Voting Rights Act is history, and the continuation of the shield of Section 5 is assured for another 25 years. We can all now safely drop the rhetoric that characterized the extension debates and put our efforts into the development of a workable, theoretically sound definition of the right to vote.

NOTES

1. St. Martin's Press (New York: 1977).
2. 118 U.S. 356 (1886).
3. F. LeClercq, The Emerging Federally Secured Right of Political Participation, 8 IND. L. REV. 607, 610 (1975).
4. Id. at 619.
5. See, e.g., Civil Rights Cases, 109 U.S. 3 (1883); Slaughter-House Cases, 83 U.S. 394 (1883).
6. See generally, Derfner, Racial Discrimination and the Right to Vote, 26 VAND. L. REV. 523 (1973).
7. See Butler, Constitutional and Statutory Challenges to Election Structures: Dilution and the Value of the Right to Vote, 42 LA. LAW REV. 851, 858-62 (1982) [hereinafter cited as Butler].
8. Black registration rates still lag somewhat behind rates for whites in most states. The difference is so slight as to negate any inference that this is the product of discriminatory registration practices. Registration rates by states compiled by the Bureau of Census, November 1980, are reprinted in Report No. 97-417, Report of the Committee on the Judiciary, United States Senate on S. 1992, 167.
9. The irony of the Civil War amendments (passed for the protection of blacks) being used to expand the political rights of whites is ably discussed in Blacksher and Menefee, From Reynolds v. Sims

to City of Mobile v. Bolden: Have the White Suburbs Commandeered the Fifteenth Amendment, 34 HAST. L. J. 1 (1982).

    10. 369 U.S. 186 (1962).

    11. Avery v. Midland County, 390 U.S. 474 (1968).

    12. 395 U.S. 621 (1969).

    13. 383 U.S. 663 (1966).

    14. 380 U.S. 89 (1965).

    15. 398 U.S. 419 (1970).

    16. 405 U.S. 330 (1972).

    17. 383 U.S. 663 (1966).

    18. See also, Butler, supra, note 7.

    19. These cases are discussed in J. Dantzler, Election Law, 1978 Annual Survey of American Law 91 (1979); Note, Discriminatory Effect of Elections At-Large: The "Totality of the Circumstances" Doctrine, 41 ALB. L. REV. 363 (1977); and Bonapfel, Minority Challenges to At-Large Elections: The Dilution Problem, 10 GA. L. REV. 353 (1976).

    20. 426 U.S. 229 (1976). In this case black plaintiffs challenged an aptitude test developed by the Civil Service Commission and administered by the District of Columbia Police Department for the purpose of screening applicants to be police officers. Evidence indicated that a disproportionately higher number of minority applicants failed the test. The Supreme Court held that disproportionate impact was not sufficient to establish a denial of equal protection. In order to prevail plaintiffs must demonstrate that the device was conceived for the purpose of furthering racial discrimination. This reasoning was extended to decisions having a disproportionate impact on minorities securing housing in Arlington Heights v. Metropolitan Housing Development Corp., 429 U.S. 252 (1977). See also Personnel Administrator of Massachusetts v. Feeney, 442 U.S. 256 (1979).

    21. See generally, Note, Racial Vote Dilution in Multi-Member Districts: The Constitutional Standard after Washington v. Davis, 76 MICH. L. REV. 694 (1978).

    22. 446 U.S. 55 (1980).

    23. The Supreme Court has utilized the Fifteenth Amendment as the basis for invalidating state action only eight times in a century. See Derfner, Racial Discrimination and the Right to Vote, 26 VAND. L. REV. 523, at 561 (1973). Gomillion v. Lightfoot, 364 U.S. 339 (1960), the most famous Fifteenth Amendment case, involved a redrawing of the city limits of Tuskegee, Alabama, in such a way as to exclude all black voters from the city. The other cases were Louisiana v. United States, 380 U.S. 145 (1965) and Terry v. Adams, 345 U.S. 461 (1953), which outlawed an all-white, supposedly private, preprimary procedure; Schnell v. Davis, 336 U.S. 933 (1949), involving the discriminatory use of literacy tests; Smith v. Allwright, 321 U.S. 649

(1944), outlawing an all-white political party primary; <u>Lane</u> v. <u>Wilson</u>, 307 U.S. 268 (1939), outlawing "grandfather clauses"; <u>Guinn</u> v. <u>United States</u>, 238 U.S. 347 (1915); and <u>Myers</u> v. <u>Anderson</u>, 238 U.S. 368 (1915).

24. 376 U.S. 52 (1964).

25. 446 U.S. 156 (1980).

26. The covered jurisdictions were initially Alabama, Georgia, Louisiana, Mississippi, South Carolina, Virginia, 40 counties in North Carolina, and a smattering of counties in nonsouthern areas. For those jurisdictions the effective date for the act was November 1, 1964. Amendments in 1975 added Texas, parts of Arizona, and New Mexico, as well as counties from a number of other states. The 1975 amendments extended the act's protection to other language minorities, most notably Mexican Americans and American Indians.

27. 425 U.S. 130 (1976).

28. Id. at 141.

29. See, i.e., Engstrom, <u>The Supreme Court and Equipopulous Gerrymandering: A Remaining Obstacle in the Quest for Fair and Effective Representation</u>, 1976 ARIZ. ST. L. J. 275, 333.

30. See generally, H. Motomura, <u>Preclearance Under Section Five of the Voting Rights Act</u>, 61 N.C. L. REV. 189 (1983).

31. 446 U.S. 156 (1980).

32. Id. at 185.

33. See D. Mathis & L. Mathis, <u>The Voting Rights Act and Rome (Georgia) City Elections</u>, 11-12 (1981).

34. 103 S. Ct. 530 (1982).

35. 422 U.S. 358 (1975). These standards actually had their origin in an earlier annexation case, <u>City of Petersburg, Va.</u> v. <u>United States</u>, 410 U.S. 962 (1973). The Supreme Court merely affirmed without opinion the lower court's decision in that case. Thus, Richmond, where the Supreme Court elaborated upon the standard, is the case more typically cited.

36. 422 U.S. at 371.

37. 103 S. Ct. at 535.

38. Id.

39. Id. at 536.

40. 42 U.S.C. §1973 (Supp. 1982).

41. 412 U.S. 755 (1973).

42. 485 F.2d 1297 (5th Cir. 1973) (en banc), <u>aff'd sub nom</u>, East Carroll Parish School Bd. v. <u>Marshall</u>, 424 U.S. 636 (1976).

43. Butler, supra note 7; Note, <u>The Supreme Court, 1979 Term</u>, 94 HARV. L. REV. 75, 138 (1980); Comment, <u>City of Mobile v. Bolden: A Setback in the Fight Against Discrimination</u>, 47 BROOKLYN L. REV. 169 (1980).

44. See Butler, supra, note 7, at 886-88.

45. <u>Rogers</u> v. <u>Lodge</u>, 102 S. Ct. 3272 (1982).

PART III
Legislative Enactment

4
The Voting Rights Act As an Intervention Strategy For Social Change: Symbolism or Substance?

Mack   H.   Jones

> Political analysis must . . . proceed on two levels
> simultaneously. It must examine how political actions
> get some groups the tangible things they want from gov-
> ernment and at the same time it must explore what these
> same actions mean to the mass public.[1]

> One alternative to the obvious inadequacies of an orthodox
> behaviorist perspective, is to focus on the relative power
> and status of different groups in the society and to proceed
> from the assumption that dominant groups are in conflict
> with subordinate groups and will seek to maintain their
> dominant position, particularly in matters of importance
> to them. . . . While this perspective on politics is prom-
> ising, it is somewhat sterile unless one begins to explicate
> the mechanisms by which elites maintain advantage over
> nonelites. It is not enough to say that some groups have
> power, others do not, and that these relationships are
> fairly stable. For this view to be persuasive, it is nec-
> essary to demonstrate that this stability, this structuring
> of power, is itself dynamic, that this stability is not sim-
> ply a social fact but a social process.[2]

INTRODUCTION

Murray Edelman, one of the most perceptive scholars of our
generation, has challenged political scientists to go beyond the conventional pluralist interpretations of U.S. political life—an interpre-

63

tation that implies that the outcomes of the political process are determined by open competition in the political marketplace—and address the more fundamental question of how do dominant elements maintain their position of dominance through political forms or structures that appear to be democratic or even egalitarian, but perpetuate an inegalitarian social reality.

Edelman's contribution, however, is not limited to his challenge; he has done considerable work toward developing a theory, albeit a controversial one, which attempts to explain how dominant forces maintain their position of dominance, while at the same time commanding the respect and loyalty of those being dominated. Problems associated with the black struggle for full political participation in the United States would seem to be an ideal vehicle for an elaboration of Edelman's thesis. In this chapter I identify some of the major elements of the Edelman thesis and use them to analyze the implementation of the 1965 Voting Rights Act (VRA).

Edelman argues, among other things, that acts of the state are both instrumental and expressive. They are instrumental to the extent that they convey tangible rewards to some and reciprocal deprivations to other competing interests, and they are expressive to the extent that they become emotion–laden symbols that may be used to arouse some, while placating others.

In general, the theory goes, well–organized groups that petition government for specific tangible payoffs or for the allocation of substantive power are more likely to receive benefits commensurate with their demands than are large social groups, which are less likely to be organized and more inclined to make demands in broad symbolic terms such as freedom, civil rights, and justice. The large social groups, according to Edelman, are more likely to become satiated through expressive or symbolic state action and withdraw from the fray, while governing authorities and organized groups collaborate on implementing public policies in a fashion especially deferential toward the latter. Indeed, the success of organized groups in obtaining material payoffs or substantive power is facilitated by the tendency of unorganized groups to settle for symbolic reassurance and become quiescent even when their objective conditions remain unchanged or are worsened by state intervention.

The Edelman thesis argues, or at least intimates, that when a public policy issue involves a confrontation between dominant and subordinate elements, or elites and nonelites, the official action taken by the state will often appear to be deferential toward the subordinate element or the nonelites, but the actual implementation of the policy may favor the elite. The language and provisions of the intervention statute and the public discussion surrounding enactment of the measure may induce quiescence among the advocates of change, but subsequent interpretation and implementation of the statute by the bureaucracy will defer to the interests of the dominant elite.

Edelman's thesis also calls our attention to the fact that although dominant forces maintain their advantageous position over time, and as such, the unequal relationship between them and the subordinate group is static, the process of maintaining such an unequal relationship is a dynamic one. The dynamism, however, is in the process through which certain patterns of social relations are maintained, rather than in the patterns of social relations themselves. Unless analysis goes beyond appearances, the dynamism of the process may easily be mistaken for dynamism in the relationship itself. Thus, passage of statutes ostensibly designed to alter patterns of social relationships do not constitute prima facie evidence of such alterations. Rather, it represents only another point of engagement in the ongoing struggle among contending forces.

The idea for this chapter grew out of an earlier work in which I attempted to assess the significance of post-VRA black officeholding in the rural South. [3] In that work, I discovered that while the changes that had transpired in the South had been both highly visible and significant, they had been far less than some had hoped. On the positive side, I found that the political culture of the region had changed noticeably and that more respectful patterns of social relations had replaced some of the more repressive ones of the past. Black deference to the caste mores of the old Black Belt South had been fatally undermined. But on the other hand, in many respects the material quality of black life in the rural South remained unchanged. I also discovered that in many jurisdictions in which blacks had a majority, systemic forces prevented them from gaining political control. In other jurisdictions where blacks had achieved formal political authority, the substantive outcomes of the political process were not unlike those of predecessor governments. These factors and others convinced me that the real meaning and significance of VRA could be understood only when the act was viewed as part of a broader social process, a process in which dominant white elements attempt to maintain certain patterns of social relationships that insure their superordinate position.

This chapter attempts to develop such an understanding by: first, placing the passage of VRA in the appropriate historical and theoretical context by conceptualizing it as an intervention strategy perceived by blacks as a device designed to begin a transformation of then-existing patterns of repressive social relationships into more emancipatory ones; second, using Edelman's thesis as an orienting device to describe and analyze the response of southern officials to VRA, and to assess the Department of Justice's (DOJ) enforcement of the act; and third, discussing the symbolic and substantive impact of VRA on the black condition in the South.

HISTORIC BACKGROUND

The repressive apartheid system that the white ruling class successfully imposed on the old South following Reconstruction remained virtually undisturbed for more than half a century. The principle that blacks had no rights that whites were bound to respect, as enunciated in the Dred Scott decision of 1857, remained the central theme of interracial social relationships.

In spite of decades of agitation by blacks for political and social rights, until 1965 whites successfully used a judicious mixture of legal stratagems and physical and psychological coercion to maintain their hegemonic position. The apartheid system they fashioned was able to absorb or adapt to a series of interventions undertaken by the national government in response to black protest without altering in a fundamental way those patterns of relationships. These interventions included the 1915 invalidation of the grandfather clause to maintain white-only elections; outlawing the white primary in 1944; overturning the separate-but-equal doctrine in 1954; establishing the Civil Rights Commission and mandating federal protection against denial of the franchise in 1957; and insuring equal access to public accommodations, employment opportunities, and educational institutions in 1964. It was in this context of continued white resistance that the civil rights campaigns that led to passage of the 1965 VRA were launched.

As white intransigence intensified in the early 1960s, blacks mounted an assault to destroy once and for all the repressive social system of the Old South. Groups such as the Student Nonviolent Coordinating Committee and the Congress on Racial Equality developed programs that encouraged blacks to challenge and defy apartheid relationships in their day-to-day encounters with whites. Reverend Martin Luther King, Jr. and others embarked upon highly visible campaigns to dramatize the repressive character of existing relationships and to create sufficient tension to convince national authorities that more forceful intervention was in the public interest. The march from Selma to Montgomery, Alabama, to highlight continued white opposition to black voting rights captured international attention and persuaded the president and Congress to act.[4]

On its face, VRA as passed in 1965 and amended in 1970, 1975, and 1982 is the most comprehensive voting rights legislation passed since Reconstruction. Some provisions of the act are permanent and general while others are temporary, discretionary, and apply only to specific jurisdictions. If all of the provisions were implemented fully, the act could bring about full political participation in the southern region. On the other hand, limited use of the discretionary prerogatives would diminish considerably the potential for instrumental payoffs and the development of substantive political power. Initially, VRA was drafted expressly to apply to those southern states that had been most flagrant in denying blacks the right to vote: Alabama, Mississippi, Louisiana, Georgia, South Carolina, Virginia, and 40 counties in North Carolina. This was accomplished through a triggering formula, which made the act applicable to those states or counties that used some form of literacy test, good moral character test, or related devices as a prerequisite for voting, and in which less than 50 percent of the voting age population was registered by November 1, 1964 or less than 50 percent actually voted in the 1964 presidential election.

The key provisions of the act are Section 4, which suspended the use of these tests or devices, first for five years and later extended to 2002 by subsequent amendment; Section 5, which sought to prevent state and local governments from changing electoral procedures to discriminate against black citizens by requiring that all proposed electoral changes be submitted to either the District Court of Washington, D.C., or the U.S. attorney-general for preclearance—if either determined that the proposed change was racially discriminatory, it could not be implemented; Sections 3 and 6, which authorized the assignment of federal examiners to list (in actuality register) voters in jurisdictions whenever the attorney-general institutes a proceeding under any statute to enforce the guarantees of the Fifteenth Amendment; Section 8, which authorized the attorney-general to have observers sent to counties to see whether persons are being permitted to vote and whether their votes are being tabulated properly; Section 12, which provided for fines of not more than $5,000 or imprisonment for no more than five years or both for depriving or conspiring to deprive any persons of rights secured by VRA. Section 12 also gave the attorney-general authority to seek preventive relief when there are reasonable grounds to believe that any person has or is about to engage in acts prohibited by VRA.

In summary, the law forbade the use of current discriminatory devices, provided a mechanism to prevent implementation of new ones, allowed the national government to register voters, and dispatch observers to note and report on compliance with the law; it also provided penalties for those violating the act.

As suggested earlier, VRA should be conceptualized as an intervention strategy. Generically speaking, intervention strategies are designed to transform existing patterns of relationships in the direction of some desired future. Proponents of intervention begin with a definition of existing reality and a preconceived notion of a desired future state of affairs. They then develop an intervention strategy that would transform the present in the direction of that desired future. The constituent elements of the intervention strategy, to the extent practicable, are then reduced to statutory provisions. Thus, an intervention statute mandates certain patterns of human

conduct which, if followed, would bring about the desired change or
at least set in motion a process that would lead to such change.

The ultimate effectiveness of such intervention strategy depends
primarily upon two things: the logical consistency among the definition
of the problem, the intervention strategy, and the desired future;
and the faithfulness with which the provisions of the act are implemented. If the definition of the problem does not reflect the empirical
reality, an intervention strategy based upon such a definition will fail;
of course, failure to implement the intervention strategy would lead
to a similar outcome.

This chapter will not address the question of logical consistency,
which is to say the appropriateness of VRA as an intervention strategy.
Our concern will be limited to the interpretation and implementation
of VRA and the reaction of the relevant publics.

Ideologues of the civil rights movement defined the black condition in the South as one of total political, social, and economic subordination. Politics and political power were not only the cement that
held the repressive caste system together, but also the most auspicious
mechanism for transforming the social order. Given the relatively advantageous numerical position of blacks in the region, it was felt that
if blacks were guaranteed unfettered access to the political process
they would be able to elect members from their own group in black
majority jurisdictions and have a salutary influence on the election of
officials in the others. This enhanced political power of blacks would
eventually lead to a more equitable socioeconomic order.

Having described VRA as an intervention strategy, we now attempt to determine the extent to which the interpretation and implementation of the act by DOJ, along with the response of the relevant
publics, is explained by Edelman's thesis.

Passage and implementation of VRA did not involve the classic
case of an organized interest pitted against an unorganized one. Neither
the black nor white community could be said to have been organized.
However, within both communities there were organized forces that
phrased their demands with considerable specificity and were therefore less likely than their mass counterparts to be reassured through
symbolic political acts. The organized black interest demanded unfettered access to the franchise as a device to facilitate the realloca-
tion of substantive political power, while the organized white faction
sought to preserve the status quo. Thus, in this situation there are
two mass publics, unorganized and distant from the policy-formulation
process and hence susceptible to symbolic manipulation; and there are
also two organized intermediate factions, making specific demands
and expecting instrumental payoffs.

Under such conditions, what behaviors would the Edelman thesis
lead us to expect? Before attempting to answer that question, further

elaboration of the contending forces may be helpful. The dominant white elites on both the state and local levels constitute the forces with direct material stakes in minimizing the substantive changes that could be induced by implementing of VRA. Control of local government, particularly county governments in the rural South, translates into considerable economic power. It allows for influence on land use and development decisions, the allocation of local functions, the dispensing of public sector jobs, tax assessments and collections, and other important economic decisions. Quite often the economic and political elite are one. Since historically these functions had been carried out in a manner prejudicial to black interests, unfettered black participation constituted a clear and present threat. The interests of the local elite were often articulated at the state level through such devices as "local courtesy." The local elite generally preferred the most conservative interpretation of the act because it tended to preserve their interest.

Inasmuch as the federal government, which was responsible for implementing the act, was widely perceived by both the mass black and white publics to be an ally of sorts of the organized black faction that pushed for passage of the act, we might expect the latter to defer, at least initially, to DOJ's interpretation and implementation of VRA. Having been aroused by the setting, a sharp increase in voter-registration activity by both groups would be expected.

As for the pivotal actor, the federal government, Edelman's theory would lead us to expect that DOJ would attempt to placate both the dominant white elite and white mass public by giving a conservative interpretation of the act and minimizing the federal presence in the South.

USE OF EXAMINERS

What does an empirical analysis reveal? At the outset, the key provision of VRA as an intervention strategy was Section 6, which gave federal officials discretionary authority to list or, for all intent and purposes, to register black voters. Prior to passage of VRA, only 29.3 percent of eligible blacks were registered in the covered jurisdiction, with percentages ranging from a low of 6.7 in Mississippi to a high of 46.8 in North Carolina. The gap between the percentages of eligible whites and blacks registered ranged from 63.2 in Mississippi to 22.8 in Virginia. [5]

To facilitate black registration, the attorney-general was authorized to send examiners to counties from which he received 20 meritorious complaints from residents alleging discrimination. He could also send examiners to counties which, in his judgment, the appointment of examiners was necessary to enforce the guarantees of the Fifteenth Amendment.

The attorney-general developed a most conservative interpretation of the role of DOJ in registering black voters. In a memorandum of procedure shortly after passage of the act, DOJ announced that the fact that 20 meritorious complaints of racial discrimination had been filed by citizens would not compel the appointment of examiners. Rather, the complaints would constitute only one factor on a scale used to determine whether compliance existed.[6] Thus, with a stroke of the pen, the power of local blacks to determine when there was a need for federal examiners was eliminated, and the issue was reduced to a two-way relationship involving only DOJ and local whites. Furthermore, there is no evidence that local blacks were given any additional information on the other items that comprised the scale used by DOJ to measure compliance.

Attorney-general Katzenbach, in a letter to registrars in covered jurisdictions in January 1966, did list the criteria that would influence his decision. They were:

> Whether the percentage of Negroes and whites over 21 in the county was disproportionate to the percentage of each which was registered and, if so, whether this was attributable to violations of the 15th amendment; whether the registrar had adopted application procedures to insure that all persons eligible under the Act had an opportunity to become registered; whether officials were taking affirmative steps to overcome the effects of past discrimination.[7]

To operationalize the above criteria, a staff large enough to conduct field examinations throughout the counties of the various states would have been necessary. The Civil Rights Division never had such a staff. Furthermore, there is no evidence that DOJ ever attempted a comprehensive investigation using criteria found in Katzenbach's letter.

DOJ also took pains to insure that it did not appear to be an ally of black citizens. No effort was made to advertise the presence or schedule of examiners, and no special appeals were made to potential black registrants. The assistant attorney-general took the position that the federal government had no business encouraging voter-registration drives. Moreover, he argued that an aggressive position by the federal government would lead the public to believe that federal examiners were substitutes for local organizations. This, he asserted, would be counterproductive.[8] Before a county could be designated for examiners, he further argued, there should be potential for registering at least a thousand black voters.[9]

DOJ's strategy resulted in examiners being sent to only a small fraction of covered jurisdictions, and significant examining activity occurring only in Mississippi and Alabama, and only during the first two years after passage of the act.

There were some 533 counties covered by the act as passed in 1965. Black registration was less than 50 percent in 243 of them. Only 63 counties were ever to receive examiners to register or list voters. During the crucial first year, no examiners were sent to North Carolina, Virginia, or Georgia. Only two South Carolina counties and five Louisiana parishes received examiners in 1965. Seventeen Mississippi and 11 Alabama counties received examiners in 1966.

As Table 4.1 shows, no significant examining activity ever occurred in Georgia and South Carolina, although both had counties that were infamous for their discriminatory practices.

As early as 1967, DOJ was severely criticized for its sparing use of examiners. Both the Washington Research Project[10] and the U.S. Commission on Civil Rights[11] published thoroughly documented reports of continued disfranchisement in covered jurisdictions and called for more comprehensive and vigorous application of the act.

The former report charged that:

The inadequate enforcement of Voting Rights Act of 1965 by the Department of Justice has frustrated achievement of equal political rights by black Southerners.

In recent years, the Department has practically

TABLE 4.1: Number of Counties in Which Federal Examiners Listed Voters by States

State	Total	Years Examining Took Place				
		1965	1966	1967	1971	1974
Alabama	12	11	1	—	—	—
Georgia	3	—	—	3	—	—
Louisiana	9	5	1	3	—	—
Mississippi*	34	17	6	9	1	1
North Carolina	0	—	—	—	—	—
South Carolina	3	—	—	3	—	—
Virginia	0	—	—	—	—	—

*Between 1975-1980 examiners were sent to two Mississippi counties initially designated in 1965, Madison and Humphreys.
Source: Unfulfilled Goals, pp. 103-104.

abandoned the federal examiner program as a major tool
authorized by the Voting Rights Act to insure registration
of voters in the South. [12]

DOJ defended its implementation strategy by citing the fact that
within two years after passage of VRA, more than 150,000 blacks had
been listed by federal examiners, an additional 416,000 had been registered by local registers, and that more than 50 percent of the black
voting age population was registered in every southern state. By 1971
a million new black voters had been registered in the seven covered
states.

At first appearance, DOJ's explanation and defense of its strategy may seem convincing. But as is often the case, appearance may
be misleading, for subsequent research demonstrated that black political mobilization was much more likely to occur in jurisdictions in
which examiners were present. Terchek found that nongovernmental
political inputs were greater in examiner than in nonexaminer counties,
and that twice as many counties with examiners had black candidates
for public office in the late 1960s than did nonexaminer counties. This
is especially significant when it is recalled that DOJ sent examiners
to the most recalcitrant counties. [13] Thus, rather than reinforcing
dependency, the presence of examiners, it can be reasonably inferred,
stimulated black political activity, a development diametrically counter
to the argument advanced by DOJ.

As the data in Table 4.2 attest, it is true that the voter-registration rate among blacks increased substantially during the first two
years after passage of the act, and has increased modestly yet steadily
since then. However, the gap between the percent of eligible blacks
and eligible whites remains substantial in four of the seven states:
14.9 percent in North Carolina and Louisiana, 16.9 in Georgia, and
17.3 in Alabama.

Moreover, statewide voter-registration figures mask as much
as they reveal. Wide disparities in the level of black and white voter
registration still exist in many counties, particularly rural counties
in which blacks comprise a high percentage of the population. This
can be seen by examining figures from the three states that make
voter-registration figures by race available. In 1974[14] in Louisiana,
the gap between the percentage of eligible blacks and whites registered
was more than 15 percent in 36 of 64 parishes; in 25 parishes it was
in excess of 20 percent; in eight parishes the gap was more than 30
and more than 40 percent in two. Twenty of the 40 North Carolina
counties covered by the act had gaps greater than 15 percent, while
six South Carolina counties had gaps in excess of 20 percent.

A 1982 study of black voter registration in Georgia[15] revealed
similar disparities with one county, a majority black county, having

TABLE 4.2: Registration by Race and State in Southern States Covered by the Voting Rights Act (percent)

	Pre-Act Estimate			Post-Act Estimate			1971-72 Estimate			1976 Estimate		
	White	Black	Gap	White	Black	Gap	White	Black	Gap	White	Black	Gap
Alabama	69.2	19.3	49.9	89.6	51.6	38.0	80.7	57.1	23.6	75.5	58.1	17.3
Georgia	62.6	27.4	35.2	80.3	52.6	27.7	70.6	67.8	2.8	73.2	56.3	16.9
Louisiana	80.5	31.6	48.9	93.1	58.9	34.2	80.0	59.1	20.9	78.8	63.9	14.9
Mississippi	69.9	6.7	63.2	91.5	59.8	31.7	71.6	62.2	9.4	77.7	67.4	10.3
North Carolina	96.8	46.8	50.0	83.0	51.3	31.7	62.2	46.3	15.9	63.1	48.2	14.9
South Carolina	75.5	37.3	38.4	80.7	51.2	30.5	51.2	48.0	3.2	64.1	60.6	3.5
Virginia	61.1	38.3	22.8	63.4	55.6	7.8	61.2	54.0	7.2	67.0	60.7	6.3

Sources: Pre-act, Post-act and 1971-72 estimates adapted from U.S. Commission on Civil Rights, The Voting Rights Act: Ten Years After. The 1976 estimates taken from U.S. Commission on Civil Rights, The Votings Rights Act:Unfulfilled Goals, 1981.

a gap of 54 percent and 16 counties with gaps in excess of 20 percent. The gaps were greatest in heavily black rural counties "where the black voting strength poses the greatest threat to altering existing political structures."[16]

Such black-white voter registration differentials explain to a great extent the failure to elect significant numbers of black county officials in the vast majority of Black Belt counties, including the preponderance of those with black majorities. Aggressive federal examining activity in the period immediately following passage of the act might have produced different results.

SECTION 5 PRECLEARANCE

If Section 6 authorizing the use of federal examiners to list voters was the key to setting in motion the process of social change envisaged by proponents of VRA, the preclearance provisions of Section 5 were the heart of the act because they were crafted to insure continuity of the process. Southern states had proven to be especially ingenious in developing "legal" means to circumvent earlier intervention strategies designed to give blacks the vote. For example, the Guinn decision of 1915, which invalidated the grandfather clause, was replaced with white primary legislation that survived as a "legal" device until 1944 and which, in turn, was replaced with literacy and character tests. The latter endured until 1965. Thus, in spite of several court decisions to the contrary, blacks were legally excluded from the electorate for more than 50 years. Section 5 was designed to end such legal subterfuge once and for all.

As noted above, Section 5 required all covered jurisdictions to submit any proposed changes in their voting practices or procedures to either the U.S. attorney-general or the U.S. District Court of the District of Columbia. If the proposed change is submitted to the attorney-general, DOJ determines within 60 days whether it would have a racially discriminatory effect. The change cannot be implemented if DOJ concludes that such is the case. Thus, the ultimate effectiveness of VRA hinges on Section 5 enforcement.[17]

DOJ enforcement of Section 5 has been consistent with the assumption of Edelman's thesis. Throughout the life of the act, DOJ, regardless of the ideology or political party of the administration or the assistant attorney-general in charge, has followed a policy of minimal federal involvement. It has never developed a system that would allow it to monitor covered jurisdictions, nor has it developed procedures to insure compliance, even after noncompliance has been identified. Moreover, office procedures within the voting rights section of DOJ are such that DOJ cannot make a systematic assessment of its own Section 5 activities.

Further, in the face of extensive violations of Section 5 by both state and local jurisdictions, DOJ has never sought to use the criminal sanctions included in the act. As a result, local officials have knowingly and in some instances contemptuously violated the act, rendering it in many jurisdictions more symbolic than substantive.

The denuding of Section 5 began in the beginning. During the Johnson administration no guidelines or procedures for enforcing Section 5 were developed. During that period, only the South Carolina state government made a reasonable effort to comply. Of 325 submissions during this period, North Carolina submitted no changes, Alabama only two, Louisiana three, Virginia ten, and Mississippi eighteen.[18]

When the act came up for extension in 1970, the Nixon administration proposed the elimination of Section 5. Attorney-general John Mitchell advanced the dubious argument that the law should be scrapped because "when local officials have passed discriminatory laws they have usually not submitted them to the Attorney-General for approval."[19]

Guidelines were established in 1971, but only after the special provisions of the act had been extended and the Nixon administration had been challenged in court for its conservative interpretation of its responsibilities under Section 5. The guidelines required submission of all proposed changes, including redistricting and annexations, although the attorney-general had wanted to exclude the latter two categories. Mitchell also wanted the burden of proof of discriminatory impact to rest with federal authorities rather than with submitting jurisdictions, but was forced to relent in the face of intense objections from civil rights groups.

The failure of the Johnson administration to develop Section 5 guidelines and the publicly demonstrated opposition of the Nixon administration certainly did not encourage compliance. Once guidelines were established, office procedures developed by the voting rights section did not enhance efforts to either identify instances of nonsubmission or insure that proposed changes objected to by DOJ were not implemented anyway.

DOJ compiles and circulates weekly a roster of proposed changes submitted by covered jurisdictions. Individuals who feel that proposed changes are discriminatory are invited to register objections with DOJ. Although DOJ claims that it checks every submission to assess its potential discriminatory effect, it has never had a staff of sufficient size to make its claim credible. In 1974 the Voting Rights Section had a staff of 19 attorneys and eight research associates.[20] A total of 988 submissions, including 299 that involved redistricting and annexation, were filed that year.[21]

The voting rights section staff was expanded and reorganized in

1976, following the 1975 extension that broadened coverage of the act to include discrimination against language minorities. After 1975 the act covered 927 jurisdictions in 23 states, including nine states covered entirely. [22] Under the new arrangement, the section is divided into two units: submissions and litigative. [23] The submissions unit, which was responsible for preclearance activities in 1977, was comprised of a senior attorney advisor, a paraprofessional director, and 11 paraprofessionals. Some 4,007 proposed changes were submitted that year.

The paraprofessionals are responsible for initial screening of submissions and flagging those that might have discriminatory effects. DOJ had developed a roster of contact persons—primarily minority citizens scattered throughout covered jurisdictions—who are consulted regarding the discriminatory potential of submissions from their jurisdiction. The paraprofessional makes a recommendation that is reviewed by the paraprofessional director and submitted to the senior attorney for a decision. If the decision is to interpose an objection, the matter goes to the head of the division. Thus, the burden for insuring that discriminatory changes are not approved falls upon a small group of nonspecialists who have no training nor experience to qualify them for their tasks.

These staffing deficiencies are reinforced by inadequate and inefficient office procedures. The GAO criticized DOJ for: having no systematic procedures for identifying nonsubmissions; when nonsubmissions are detected, having no mechanism to insure submission; having no mechanism to insure that changes objected to by DOJ are not implemented anyway; not requiring sufficient data to make reliable assessment of proposed changes. For example, GAO charged that in cases involving redistricting and annexation, DOJ did not consistently require information about boundaries and racial distribution of existing and proposed units.

Extensive evidence of nonsubmissions has been documented by DOJ and by other public and private agencies. For example, a 1972 DOJ review of state laws passed in Louisiana between 1965 and 1972 resulted in 149 previously unsubmitted changes being submitted. [24] A similar review of 1971 Alabama session laws identified 161 unsubmitted changes, while a 1975 review of session laws of six southern states revealed 305 nonsubmissions. [25]

Noncompliance is commonplace, as is open defiance. As a prelude to the 1975 hearings on extension of VRA, a DOJ review identified local jurisdictions that had never made a submission. The FBI identified specific unsubmitted changes in Alabama, Georgia, Louisiana, Mississippi, North Carolina, and South Carolina. Letters were sent to jurisdictions requesting submission within 30 days. If the changes were not submitted within the alloted time, an FBI investigation could be requested. However, according to the GAO report:

Department of Justice officials stated that no formal reports were prepared summarizing the results of their
various compliance efforts. However, the Department's
records showed that responses to submission requests
were often not received within 30 days and, in fact, some
requests have been pending for at least 2 years. We found,
for example, that the Federal Bureau of Investigation identified 102 unsubmitted changes, of which 60 were still unsubmitted in 1976. [26]

Such defiance remains a problem. In 1980 124 letters were sent
to covered jurisdictions where it was believed that unsubmitted changes
were made. Seventy-nine jurisdictions responded by submitting 78
changes that had been made, but as of January 27, 1981 no response
had been received from 45 jurisdictions. [27]

In the face of such noncompliance, DOJ has steadfastly adhered
to its conservative enforcement strategy; it has never even threatened
to invoke criminal penalties authorized by Section 12.

LITIGATIVE ACTIVITY

VRA gave the attorney-general litigative authority to enforce
preclearance provisions and also to protect voting rights in jurisdictions not covered by the special provisions of the act. This gives DOJ
authority to file suit to have dismantled discriminatory provisions both
in noncovered jurisdictions and in covered jurisdictions where such
provisions may have been adopted prior to 1965. Many jurisdictions
in Mississippi and Georgia adopted such provisions in anticipation of
passage of the act. Other states, such as Virginia, which already had
relatively high levels of black voter registration, adopted racially
discriminatory provisions to dilute black political strength prior to
1965. [28]

The GAO study reported that DOJ had been unable to litigate
adequately matters related to special provisions; that it had no system for identifying needed litigation; and that it had failed to pursue
litigation connected with citizen complaints.

VRA provides that citizens may submit complaints of voting
rights violations to DOJ, and if found to be meritorious, could lead
to DOJ litigation. DOJ assigned the lowest priority to such action.
According to GAO:

Our review of these files [citizens' complaints] showed
432 complaints had not been officially closed. In 157 of
these the last update was made approximately 3-1/2

years before our review. We also found 217 complaints
which were assigned to attorneys no longer employed by
the voting section.[29]

In summary, DOJ's enforcement strategy has been consistent
with the Edelman thesis. Provisions relating to the use of examiners,
preclearance, and litigation have been interpreted and implemented
in ways that minimize federal involvement and encourage evasion of
VRA by covered jurisdictions.

The behavior of officials in covered jurisdictions too has been
consistent with Edelman's argument. Beginning with the months when
Congress was debating VRA and continuing to the present, jurisdictions have passed acts designed to minimize black voting strength.
Reports of the Commission on Civil Rights of 1968, 1975, and 1981
cited above, along with other documents, present compelling evidence
of racially discriminatory activity.

The 1968 report Political Participation, under the heading
"Obstacles to Negro Participation in the Electoral and Political Process," included the following chapters:

- Diluting the Negro Vote
- Preventing Negroes from Becoming Candidates or Obtaining Office
- Discrimination Against Negro Registrants
- Exclusion of and Interference with Negro Poll Watchers
- Vote Fraud
- Discriminatory Selection of Election Officials
- Intimidation and Economic Dependence

The 1975 report The Voting Rights Act Ten Years After included
chapters on:

- Barriers to Registration
- Barriers to Voting
- Barriers to Candidacy
- Physical and Economic Subordination

Chapter headings in the 1981 report, Voting and Registration,
are less descriptive than those of the previous reports, but the con-
tents are not. They are replete with discussions of the use of conventional illegal contrivances to minimize black political participation.[30]

Indeed, testimony at the 1981 hearings on extension of the act
suggest that white intransigence, especially in Alabama, may be increasing. In several rural, majority-black counties in southwest Alabama, after sustained efforts, blacks have succeeded in electing candidates to countywide offices. In 1978 in Wilcox, a black sheriff was

elected. The white-controlled board of registrars responded by purging the voter-registration list in 1980 without notifying those whose names had been purged. Black voters were successful in enjoining the board of registrars from proceeding with the illegal purge.[31]

In 1981, however, the Alabama state legislature passed a "re-identification" bill applying to three majority black counties, Wilcox, Sumter, and Perry.* The bill requires that all registered voters appear at the courthouse or the beat in which they live to reidentify themselves. The registrar will visit each beat only one weekday between 9 a.m. and 4 p.m. Voters who do not reidentify themselves are dropped from the voter-registration list. A similar reidentification bill was enacted previously for Choctaw, a neighboring county, and resulted in black registration declining from 5,269 to less than 3,000, while white registration dropped from 6,679 to 5,200. Blacks as a percent of total registered voters declined from 44 to 33 percent. DOJ did not object to the Choctaw statute. Thus, it is clear that the behavior of white officials, like that of DOJ, was consistent with the assumptions of the Edelman thesis.

Two issues remain to be investigated: the effectiveness of VRA as an intervention strategy and the behavior of the organized black interest. A thorough analysis of the effectiveness of VRA would require a much greater allocation of time and other resources than that presently at hand. For present purposes, an analysis of black success in winning elective positions, particularly countywide elective positions, will be used as a crude measure of effectiveness.

As Table 4.3 conveys, no state has a level of black officeholding that is remotely proportionate to the percentage of the population that is black. Moreover, even in those counties where blacks constitute population majorities as can be gleaned from Tables 4.4 and 4.5, black officeholding remains anemic. Only in Alabama have blacks been successful in gaining majority control of county governments. As of 1982, blacks controlled the county legislative body in six of ten black majority counties; in Mississippi, they controlled only two of 11; only one of 19 in Georgia; and two of five in Virginia. Blacks control no county governments in the Carolinas and Louisiana.

Black officeholding, of course, is only an intermediate objective of VRA as an intervention strategy. The end objective is the enhancement of the quality of black life in the region. Such enhancement would be reflected in a narrowing of the gap between black and white south-

---

*The bill was introduced by the white state representative as local legislation. Under the local courtesy rules, such legislation is more or less passed automatically if it is supported by the local delegation.

TABLE 4.3: Blacks as Percentage of Population and Elected
Officials in Southern States Covered under the Preclearance
Provisions of the Voting Rights Act, July 1980

State	Population		Black Officials	
	Percent Black, 1980	Total Officials	Number	Percent of Total
Alabama	25.6	4,151	238	5.7
Georgia	26.8	6,660	249	3.7
Louisiana	29.4	4,710	363	7.7
Mississippi	35.2	5,271	387	7.3
North Carolina*	22.4	5,295	247	4.7
South Carolina	30.4	3,225	238	7.4
Virginia	18.9	3,041	124	4.1

*Statewide data, including the 40 counties subject to preclearance.

Sources: Joint Center for Political Studies, National Roster of Black Elected Officials, vol. 10 (1981). Data on Virginia supplied by Virginia State Conference NAACP.

Taken from The Voting Rights Act: Unfulfilled Goals, p. 15.

erners, and between southern blacks and national norms on accepted indicators of socioeconomic well-being.*

Finally, has the behavior of black actors been consistent with the Edelman thesis? The Edelman model assumes a highly organized group seeking instrumental payoffs on one side, and a large unorganized force on the other; but in our case there were highly organized factions on both sides. While the organized black faction did not settle for symbolic reassurance, it did not challenge DOJ with the intensity that the evidence would seem to justify. Groups such as the Lawyers Committee for Civil Rights and Alabama Legal Services along with countless other local groups took initiatives to insure implementation of VRA.

However, no black group, particularly no national black organization, has mounted a direct attack on DOJ for its conservative enforcement policies. When the act came up for extension in 1970, 1975, and 1982, practically all national black civil rights organizations sent

---

*I am in the process of examining these data.

TABLE 4.4: Black Elected Officials as Percentage of All Elected Officials in Southern States Covered under the Preclearance Provision of the Voting Rights Act, July 1980

State	U.S. Congress		State Legislature		County Governing Body	Local School Board	Municipal Governing Board	Population Percent Black, 1980
	Senate	House	Senate	House				
Alabama	0.0	0.0	5.7	12.4	6.6	7.1	5.3	25.6
Georgia	0.0	0.0	3.6	11.7	3.4	5.9	5.2	26.8
Louisiana	0.0	0.0	5.1	9.5	13.2	13.4	9.4	29.4
Mississippi	0.0	0.0	3.8	12.3	6.6	10.3	10.4	35.2
North Carolina*	0.0	0.0	2.0	3.3	3.7	7.4	6.0	22.4
South Carolina	0.0	0.0	0.0	11.3	11.7	11.6	6.7	30.4
Virginia	0.0	0.0	2.5	4.0	6.8	†	5.2	18.9

*Statewide data, including the 40 counties subject to preclearance.
†Not an elective position.

Sources: U.S., Department of Commerce, Bureau of the Census, Popularly Elected Officials, vol. 1, no. 2 (1979), GC 77 (1)-2; and Joint Center for Political Studies, National Roster of Black Elected Officials, vol. 10 (1981). Data on Virginia supplied by Virginia State Conference NAACP.

Taken from The Voting Rights Act: Unfulfilled Goals, p. 15.

TABLE 4.5: Black Representation on County Governing Body of
Majority Black Counties, 1982

	Majority Counties	Membership	Black Members
Alabama	10	6	3
Georgia	20	1	12
Louisiana	6*	0	0
Mississippi	22	2	8
North Carolina	6	0	3
South Carolina	12	0	0
Virginia	6	2	0

*Includes Orleans Parish, which has same political boundaries
as City of New Orleans.
Source: Voter Education Project, Atlanta, Ga.

representatives to testify to the need to extend the act because of continuing discriminatory practices. However, none of the representatives
made an issue of DOJ's halting enforcement efforts. For example, no
group has mounted a campaign to have DOJ invoke the Section 12 criminal penalties against local officials who knowingly violate the act.

Indeed, after hearing testimony of continued violations and conservative enforcement by DOJ, one congressman wondered aloud,
"Have they [civil rights groups] written to the Department of Justice
and made formal demands that they enforce these criminal sanctions
against clerks and election officials who are depriving minorities of
the right to vote?"[32]

CONCLUSION

Data presented in this chapter are consistent with the assumption
that implementation of VRA would favor the organized white faction
seeking to preserve the status quo. However, there is little evidence
that passage of the act induced quiescence among its supporters or
that subsequent inertia among supporters contributed to white success
in limiting instrumental payoffs. DOJ officials—beginning with the
Johnson administration and continuing through Nixon, Ford, Carter,
and Reagan administrations—emphasized the symbolic importance of
the act, but the organized black faction continuously pushed for substantive power. During the first years, the Voter Education Project,
the Washington Research Project, and the Commission on Civil Rights

all called attention to DOJ's ineffective implementation. Local citizens throughout the South lodged official complaints about the survival of racial discrimination in voting in their communities. During the hearings of 1969, 1974, and 1981 prior to extension of VRA, much evidence to this effect was placed in public record. Nevertheless, at no time was DOJ admonished to change its style or procedures. All five administrations took the position that VRA did not authorize the federal government to undertake affirmative action programs to encourage black voting, officeholding, and subsequent exercise of political power.

DOJ has taken great care to interpret and implement VRA in a fashion that removed arbitrary impediments to black political participation and made possible the integration of the new participants into the ongoing political process, while minimizing changes in the allocation and exercise of political power in the region. Thus, to the extent that changes in the level of black political participation were intended to be an instrumental step toward substantive political changes, the impact of VRA has been more expressive or symbolic than it has been instrumental.

NOTES

1. Murray Edelman, The Symbolic Uses of Politics (Chicago: University of Illinois Press, 1964), p. 12.

2. Michael Lipksy, "Introduction" to Murray Edelman, Political Language: Words that Succeed and Policies that Fail (New York: Academic Press, 1977), pp. xix-xx (emphasis added).

3. Mack H. Jones, "Black Officeholding and Political Development in the Rural South," Review of Black Political Economy 7 (Summer, 1976): 375-407.

4. For a good discussion of the relationship between the Selma-Montgomery March and passage of VRA, see David L. Garrow, Protest At Selma, Martin Luther King, Jr. and the Voting Rights Act of 1965 (New Haven: Yale University Press, 1978).

5. Memorandum on Procedures for the Continuous Evaluation of Counties Covered by 4(b) of the Voting Rights Act, Aug. 24, 1965, quoted in U.S. Commission on Civil Rights, Political Participation (Washington, D.C.: Government Printing Office, 1968), p. 12.

6. Ibid., p. 154, letter from Attorney-General Nicolas De B. Katzenbach to local registrars in Alabama, Georgia, Louisiana, Mississippi, North Carolina, South Carolina, and Virginia, Jan. 8, 1966, cited in text.

7. Ibid., p. 156.

8. Ibid.

9. The Shameful Blight (Washington, D.C.: Washington Research Project, 1972).

10. U.S. Commission on Civil Rights, Political Participation.

11. The Shameful Blight, p. 18.

12. See Ronald Terchek, "Changing Patterns of Southern Political Participation," in Richard Claude and James Strause, eds., Making Government Work (Washington, D.C.: University Press of America, 1981), p. 26.

13. Jones, "Black Officeholding."

14. Raymond Brown, "The State of Voting Rights in Georgia, 1982" (Atlanta: Southern Regional Council, 1982).

15. Ibid., p. 17.

16. U.S. Commission on Civil Rights, The Voting Rights Act: Ten Years After (Washington, D.C.: Government Printing Office, 1975), p 25.

17. Shameful Blight, p. 139.

18. John Mitchell, testimony before Senate Extension Hearings, July 11, 1969, quoted in Shameful Blight, p. 138.

19. Gerald Jones, Chief Voting Rights Section, November 7, 1974.

20. Howard Ball, Dale Krane, and Thomas P. Lauth, "Judicial Enforcement of Voting Rights Policy by Attorneys in the Department of Justice," paper delivered at the 1977 meeting of the Southern Political Science Association, Nov. 3-5.

21. U.S. Comptroller-General, General Accounting Office, Voting Rights Act–Enforcement Needs Strengthening (Washington, D.C.: Government Printing Office, 1978), p. 11.

22. This discussion draws on Chapter 3, "Program Improvement Needed to Strengthen Enforcement," in GAO Report.

23. Ibid., p. 13.

24. Ibid.

25. Ibid., pp. 11-12.

26. U.S. Commission on Civil Rights, The Voting Rights Act: Unfulfilled Goals (Washington, D.C.: Government Printing Office, 1981), p. 72.

27. See testimony of Michael Brown, Virginia State Conference, NAACP, Hearings on Extension of Voting Rights Act Before Subcommittee on Civil and Constitutional Rights of the Committee Session, 1981 (hereinafter cited as House Extension Hearings), pp. 321-378.

28. GAO Report, p. 26.

29. U.S. Commission on Civil Rights, Unfulfilled Goals, see especially pp. 22-37.

30. Testimony of Abigail Turner, House Extension Hearings, p. 753.

31. Testimony of Judge Eddie Hardaway, Jr., House Extension Hearings, p. 753.

32. Representative Henry Hyde, House Extension Hearings, p. 2091.

5
Political Symbols and the Enactment of the 1982 Voting Rights Act

Lorn S. Foster

INTRODUCTION

In 1965 the debate over enactment of voting rights legislation
focused upon a set of clearly defined political symbols. In 1982, however, the political symbols were not clearly defined. The forum for
the debate over voting rights legislation shifted dramatically between
1965 and 1982. In 1965 the streets of Selma, Alabama, were the forum
in which the debate over voting rights took place; in 1982 the debate
shifted to the halls of Congress. The change in settings also meant
there was a change in the actors. In 1965 the debate over voting rights
took place between black civil rights demonstrators in the streets of
Selma and bigoted white police. In the 1982 debate each side argued
that it was fighting to preserve basic constitutional principles. The
thesis of this chapter is that political symbols were very important
in shaping the debate over the 1982 renewal of the Voting Rights Act.

In 1965 the positions of both the opponents and proponents of the
Voting Rights Act were clearly stated. In 1982 the same clarity did
not exist, but both sides nonetheless used political symbols to buttress
their arguments. Proponents of an extended Voting Rights Act argued
that extension of Section 5 of the act, a "new" Section 2, a minority-
language requirement, and a strong antibailout provision were crucial
for protecting minority voting rights. Opponents of a strong Voting
Rights Act did not argue against minority voting rights; instead, they
argued that the proposed changes went too far in extending minority
voting rights by granting benefits to a group and not to individuals.
The debate over group or individual rights was at the center of the
debate over the new Section 2 of the Voting Rights Act, which established a results test to prove discrimination against minorities in

voting. The legislative history of the 1982 Voting Rights Act is quite explicit in stating that the new Section 2 is not an attempt to create proportional representation along racial lines. Nevertheless, opponents of the 1982 Voting Rights Act consistently argued that the new Section 2 conferred special privileges, group based, to minority voters. In the spring of 1979 Abigail Thernstrom stated very clearly what the Reagan administration's position was to be regarding the special provision of the 1982 Voting Rights Act:

> Today, the test of disenfranchisement is not whether one person's vote is worth more than another's, but whether the group to which that person belongs is "underrepresented" in the system. Group power, not individual worth, is made the measure of political equity.[1]

It was over the issue of whether the federal government should take affirmative steps or be passive in its enforcement of voting rights that the debate over the 1982 renewal began. Proponents believed that the Voting Rights Act and its subsequent renewals had not gone far enough to protect minority voting rights. Opponents argued that additional measures were not necessary because millions of minority voters had been enfranchised, and it was not the obligation of the law to insure that minorities won in the electoral process, but only to insure that they have access to it. This was a strawman as proponents never argued for any guarantee for minority participation.

ANALYSIS

The Setting

Mack Jones correctly assessed the impact of the Voting Rights Act as an intervention strategy that has had both a substantive and a symbolic impact upon blacks in the South.[2] The primary motive of the Voting Rights Act was to enfranchise as many blacks as possible. The evidence indicates that the Voting Rights Act was successful in achieving that goal.[3] In the years following the passage of the act in 1965, the focus of the voting rights debate shifted from the disenfranchisement of black voters to vote dilution.[4] As a consequence of this shift in focus, the principal tool of voting rights enforcement moved from the use of Section 4, which had been employed to register new black voters in the South, to Section 5.

Section 5 freezes the electoral laws and procedures as of November 1, 1964, and prohibits enforcement of any change in them until certification by the attorney-general or District Court for the District of Columbia that the changes are not discriminatory in purpose or effect.[5] After 1970 Section 5 became the primary tool used by the Department of Justice and the District Court in the area of voting rights enforcement.

The Supreme Court's decision in Allen v. State Board of Elections 393 U.S. 544 (1969) established a legal precedent and clarified the act. The act was strengthened administratively and politically by the following events:

- Reorganization of the Civil Rights Division during 1969, the first year of the Nixon administration;
- The passage of the 1970 amendments to the Voting Rights Act and defeat of the Nixon proposals for eliminating Section 5;
- The growing strength of civil rights groups in the South;
- The pressure for submission guidelines from conservative white leaders in the South; and
- Legislative oversight committee criticism.[6]

The Voting Rights Act was renewed again in 1975. This was significant because a minority-language requirement was included to protect U.S. citizens who were fluent in a language other than English. In addition, more support was given to the voting section so that it would become more vigorous in its enforcement of Section 5. Prior to the 1975 renewal, most of the attorneys in the voting section were responsible for reviewing all Section 5 preclearance submissions with the help of a small number of paralegals. The 1975 act provided additional paralegal support, which resulted in Section 5 submissions being processed by paralegals and then approved by staff attorneys. This greatly simplified the process for both covered jurisdictions and for the Department of Justice.

The evolution of the voting rights debate from vote denial to vote dilution helped set the stage for the 1982 renewal. In the years immediately following the passage of the Voting Rights Act in 1965, the actors and their positions were easy to define; through the years the debate became more complex and subtle, and as a result the issue of voting rights became more clouded, though not less important. The actors were less visible and the symbols were not clearly defined. The stage for the 1982 renewal was set in 1980 with the Supreme Court's decision in City of Mobile v. Bolden 446 U.S. 55 (1980).

The black plaintiffs in Mobile argued that the city's three-person city commission, elected at-large, diluted black voting strength. The city of Mobile had adopted the commission system in 1911 as a political reform measure. A U.S. District Court, along with U.S. Fifth Circuit Court of Appeals, had ruled in favor of the plaintiffs that the at-large commission system diluted minority voting strength. The lower courts reasoned that the commission system was unconstitutional under both the Fourteenth and Fifteenth Amendments and Section 2 of the Voting Rights Act, which was basically a restatement of the Fifteenth Amendment. A plurality of the Supreme Court ruled that plaintiffs must prove "intent" and not just "effect" in documenting vote dilution. The Supreme Court's ruling in Bolden created a political symbol that defined the roles of the actors in the 1982 debate: the proponents, the resisters, and the compromisers.

As stated previously, the issue of "intent" versus "effect" was not less important than vote denial. The major difference between the 1965 and 1982 debates was that the issue was not as clear to the general public as it had been 17 years earlier. The debate over the 1982 renewal would take place not in the streets but in the halls of Congress, where the scope of the issue was very clear to all involved. The issue of Section 2 and the "intent" test as opposed to an "effects" test were central to the larger debate that occurred regarding the individual or the group as the atom of political existence.

In addition to the Mobile decision, Ronald Reagan was elected president in the fall of 1980 by an overwhelming majority. The election of 1980 set most of the actors in the voting rights debate in their places.

Actors

Who were the proponents of a strong voting rights bill in 1982? Laura Minor Murphy, a former legislative lobbyist for the ACLU, described a series of meetings held in Washington in the fall of 1980 to discuss efforts for the passage of a strong Voting Rights Act in 1982. Present at those early meetings were Minor; William Taylor of the Center for National Policy Review and a former staff director for the U.S. Civil Rights Commission; John Shattuck of the ACLU; Laughlin McDonald of the ACLU; Armand Derfner of the Joint Center for Political Studies–Voting Rights Project; and Althea Simmons of NAACP, among others. These early meetings were held to determine what the climate would be for the 1982 extension. The consensus was that the climate would not be good for the renewal of a strong voting rights act. Those present were attempting to develop a best case-worst case scenario for the upcoming debate.[7]

Those people and groups who were initially involved in developing the agenda for the proponents of the Voting Rights Act were very knowledgeable and committed. Nevertheless, they recognized that they did not represent the appropriate constituency necessary to get a strong Voting Rights Act passed. They were Washingtonians, and therefore were going to be suspect to some of the proponents and opponents of the 1982 act. Besides being Washingtonians, the group was overwhelmingly white and male; in general, they were not the ideal group to represent the collective interests of blacks and Hispanics. The steering committee that began work over renewal set as one of its primary tasks the creation of a more diffuse grassroots constituency to lobby for the Voting Rights Act. [8]

Pinderhughes presents data suggesting that the Washington-centered coalition that came to be known as the Voting Rights Act Steering Committee (see Table 5.1) became more diffuse and inclusive at both the group and the individual level. [9] As the debate over the extension of the Voting Rights Act became more focused, the coalition supporting the Voting Rights Act became more expansive, even though the leadership pushing for the extension was largely Washington based. The membership organizations were important in marshalling support for the Voting Rights Act in the home districts of many members of Congress who otherwise would not have taken an active interest.

The coalition of groups that took an active role in lobbying was not limited to racial/ethnic organizations, but also included labor, legal, religious, and women's organizations. The ACLU is a good example of a national membership organization that had a great deal invested in the 1982 renewal. Over the years the ACLU had filed numerous briefs in both vote dilution and reapportionment cases, and therefore felt its constituency would support it in its effort to get the 1982 renewal through Congress.

Most of the traditional noncivil rights groups had a commitment to civil rights, as exhibited by their membership in the Leadership Conference for Civil Rights (LCCR). The LCCR is not a membership organization; it is a loose coalition of 160 membership organizations who have a basic commitment to civil rights. The LCCR depends upon its member organizations for funding and organizational support. The LCCR was founded in 1949 as an umbrella organization to lobby for a continuation of the Fair Employment Practices Commission. Over the years it has been the organizational focal point for civil rights legislative lobbying. It was responsible for most of the organization and lobbying at the national level, while its member organizations were able to mobilize support at the grassroots level throughout the country. In March 1981 the LCCR hired Ralph Neas, a former staff aide to Senator Edward Brooke (R-Mass.), as executive director. One major reason for hiring Neas was to help lead the fight during the forthcoming voting rights debate.

A number of factors forced the civil rights community to close ranks on the 1982 Voting Rights Act: the recent Supreme Court decision in Mobile v. Bolden; the defeat of a fair housing bill in Congress; and the election of Ronald Reagan as president. Besides the external factors, there were a number of internal issues that had to be ad-

TABLE 5.1: The Voting Rights Act Steering Committee

American Federation of State, County and Municipal Employees[a]
Leadership Conference on Civil Rights
National Association for the Advancement of Colored People[b]
Joint Center for Political Studies
Center for National Policy Review[b]
U.S. Catholic Conference[a]
League of Women Voters[b]
Common Cause
Mexican American Legal Defense and Educational Fund[b]
National Association for the Advancement of Colored People: Legal
    Defense Fund[b]
Lawyers Committee for Civil Rights Under Law[a]
American Civil Liberties Union[b]
American Federation of Labor-Congress of Industrial Organizations[b]
National Urban League[b]
Anti-Defamation League of B'Nai B'Rith[b]
National Alliance of Postal and Federal Employees[a]
National Education Association[a]
The Lutheran Council
National Women's Political Caucus[b]
Leadership Conference on Civil Rights
Congress of American Indians[a]
United Church of Christ[a]

Black Leadership Forum

Congressional Black Caucus
Urban Coalition
Joint Center for Political Studies
Operation PUSH
Southern Christian Leadership Conference[a]
National Association for the Advancement of Colored People[b]
Urban League[b]
National Business League[a]

[a]Organizations affiliated with the Leadership Conference on
Civil Rights.
[b]Organizations members of the Leadership Conference's
Executive Committee.
Source: Taken from Pinderhughes, "Interest Groups and the
Passage of the Voting Rights Act in 1982," presented at the Annual
Meeting of the National Conference of Black Political Scientists,
Houston, Texas, April 27-30, 1983.

90

dressed. What should be the stand of the civil rights community on a revised Section 2 after Bolden? What should be the stand of the civil rights community on extension of the bilingual provision of the Voting Rights Act? How strong a bailout provision should be included in the new legislation? A decision was made during an ad hoc meeting in December 1980 to push forward on all three issues. Beginning in winter 1981 the previous ad hoc meetings were institutionalized and met each Friday throughout the year. The meetings were held in the offices of Representative Don Edwards (D-Cal.), chair of the House Judiciary Subcommittee on Constitutional and Civil Rights. These meetings sometimes lasted for 15 to 16 hours. Task forces were created to deal with lobbying, grassroots organizations, and the drafting of legislation. The role of congressional staff in this process cannot be understated. As one participant in these meetings said:

> We had an accountability system, because we knew we
> had to stay one step ahead of our opponents. In order to
> do so we had to make everyone feel comfortable and cre-
> ate the best possible bipartisan bill that we could. It was
> important to stick to a strict timetable, and get at least
> 60 firm votes on the Senate side to stop a possible fili-
> buster. [10]

Beginning with the introduction of HR3112 on April 7, 1981, a great deal of the focus of the voting rights debate for the proponents centered around Edwards and his staff. Edwards has served in the House and on the Subcommittee for Constitutional and Civil Rights since 1962. In reflecting upon his service on the House Judiciary Committee, he recalled that in 1964, during the debate over the Civil Rights Bill, junior members of the committee went three or four days without being allowed to ask a question or to present opposing viewpoints. Therefore, Edwards made an effort to allow all viewpoints to be heard during the hearings on HR3112. Edwards is of the opinion that "a member is totally dependent upon staff, because other responsibilities consume a great deal of his time. Helen [Gonzalez] and Ivy Davis set up the hearings."[11] On the Senate side, with other supporters of the Voting Rights Act, Burt Wides in Senator Kennedy's office and Mike Clipper worked very hard to get cosponsors in the Senate.[12]

On May 5, 1981, the House Judiciary Subcommittee on Constitutional and Civil Rights began 18 days of hearings, spread out over three months. The hearings were held not just in Washington but also in Alabama and Texas. The House hearings were the primary responsibility of the committee staff (Davis, Gonzalez, and Katherine Leroy), working in conjunction with the civil rights lobby. As one participant in the process has stated, "the House staff did well. The House hearings were the most comprehensive hearings that I've heard. Don Edwards and his staff made the case very well."[13] Even though the House staff played a very instrumental role in the hearing process, "it was made clear that the staff would accommodate opposing viewpoints."[14]

Unlike 1965, when the president was a major proponent of the Voting Rights Act, in 1982 the president and the attorney-general supported an extension of the Voting Rights Act in only a nominal way. In 1982 most executive branch support for the Voting Rights Act came from the U.S. Civil Rights Commission and staff attorneys working in the voting section of the Department of Justice. In September 1981 the U.S. Civil Rights Commission issued a report, The Voting Rights Act: Unfulfilled Goals. The commission made eight recommendations:

1. Prior to August 6, 1982, Congress should extend for an additional 10 years the special provisions of the Voting Rights Act.
2. Prior to August 6, 1982, Congress should extend for an additional 7 years the minority language provisions of the Voting Rights Act.
3. Congress should amend section 2 of the Voting Rights Act to prohibit all states or political subdivisions from maintaining or establishing voting practices or procedures that have this "effect" of discriminating on the basis of race, color, or inclusion in a minority language group.
4. Congress should hold hearings to determine whether a nationwide Federal elections law that provides minimum standards for registering and voting in Federal elections should be implemented.
5. Congress should amend the Voting Rights Act to provide for civil penalties or damages against state and local officials who fail to comply with the preclearance provisions of the Voting Rights Act.
6. Congress should amend the Voting Rights Act by adding a section which places an affirmative responsibility on the Attorney General to enforce more vigorously compliance with the preclearance provision of Section 5.
7. The Department of Justice should amend its guidelines on implementation of the minority language provisions to include specific criteria for determining effective minority language assistance.
8. The Attorney General should provide for effective enforcement of the minority language provisions in jurisdictions subject to Section 203 of the Voting Rights Act

by requiring U.S. Attorneys to monitor regularly compliance with the provisions in every Section 203 jurisdiction in their districts. [15]

The role of the U.S. Civil Rights Commission is much more symbolic
than substantive. The commission has no enforcement policies and
simply submits reports and findings to the president and Congress.
Unfulfilled Goals was the third major voting rights study done by the
commission since the passage of the Voting Rights Act in 1965. One
factor emphasized in each of the commission's studies is that there
are still barriers to voting in most jurisdictions covered by the Voting
Rights Act. The two most important functions performed by the commission have been serving as an information source and as the con-
science of the country.

All of the staff attorneys and equal opportunity specialists in the
voting section of the Department of Justice are civil service employees
and are therefore immune to external political pressure. However,
the policymakers in the Justice Department are political appointees.
Before the Civil Rights Division of the Department of Justice was reorganized in 1969, many of the staff attorneys were thought to be ex-
tensions of the civil rights community. They spent a considerable
amount of time in the field and so became emotionally involved in
blacks' quest for full voting rights. Currently, the staff attorneys
and equal opportunity specialists are less emotionally involved.

> The Voting Section was able to help in some informal
> ways. Political appointees made statements before the
> Hatch and Edwards committees; people in the Voting
> Section were able to filter information to the various
> lobbying groups that was very helpful. [16]

During the debate over renewal, the evidence was quite clear
that both an iron triangle and an issue network existed with regard to
voting rights. An iron triangle can be described as the relationship
that exists between lobbying and special interest groups at the apex
and the executive branch and Congress and congressional staff at the
base (see Table 5.2). Issues networks have been defined as

> compris[ing] a large number of participants with quite
> variable degrees of mutual commitment or of dependence
> on others in their environment, in fact it is almost im-
> possible to say where a network leaves off and its envi-
> ronment begins. . . . Participants move in and out of
> the networks constantly. Rather than groups united in
> dominance over a program, no one, as far as one can
> tell, is in control of the policies and issues. [17]

TABLE 5.2: The Voting Rights Iron Triangle

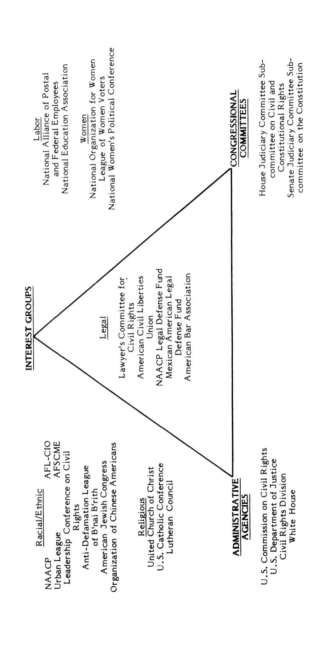

INTEREST GROUPS

Labor
National Alliance of Postal
and Federal Employees
National Education Association

Women
National Organization for Women
League of Women Voters
National Women's Political Conference

Legal
Lawyer's Committee for
Civil Rights
American Civil Liberties
Union
NAACP Legal Defense Fund
Mexican American Legal
Defense Fund
American Bar Association

Racial/Ethnic
NAACP   AFL-CIO
Urban League   AFSCME
Leadership Conference on Civil
Rights
Anti-Defamation League
of B'nai B'rith
American Jewish Congress
Organization of Chinese Americans

Religious
United Church of Christ
U.S. Catholic Conference
Lutheran Council

CONGRESSIONAL COMMITTEES

House Judiciary Committee Subcommittee on Civil and
Constitutional Rights
Senate Judiciary Committee Subcommittee on the Constitution

ADMINISTRATIVE AGENCIES

U.S. Commission on Civil Rights
U.S. Department of Justice
Civil Rights Division
White House

Source: Dianne M. Pinderhughes, "Interest Groups and the Passage of the Voting Rights Act in 1982," presented at the National Conference of Black Political Scientists Convention, Houston, 1983.

The coalition of groups and individuals that came together was very forceful and effective in marshalling support for the 1982 renewal. That both an iron triangle and an issue network were able to operate in 1981-82 is a direct result of the passage of the Voting Rights Act in 1965. Blacks and minorities over the years have been able to exert a great deal of pressure on the electoral process and to have a much greater influence over the legislative process. It is significant that when the arena for the Voting Rights Act shifted from city streets to the halls of Congress that civil rights groups were able to accommodate themselves to that shift.

Who were the resisters to the passage of strong voting rights legislation in 1982?

> neither a formal coalition of opponents nor a consistent legislative alternative ever appeared over the course of the 18-month-long debate. What ties together this loose knit group of conservatives in Congress with conservative members of the press and the Reagan Administration was a skepticism that stringent provisions of the Act were necessary in their present form. [18]

Unlike 1965, there was no organized opposition to the Voting Rights Act renewal. Most of the opposition was on an ad hoc basis. This is not to suggest that opposition in 1982 was not powerful. When the act was originally passed, southern members of Congress were able to use their powers in both houses along with their expert parliamentary skills to hinder its passage. In the years after 1965, most southern members of Congress accommodated themselves to the reality of black voting. Nevertheless, there were members who were opposed to the passage of a strong Voting Rights Act in 1982. The appeal to race was no longer a major factor in the 1982 debate; instead, the debate focused on a series of abstract symbols that centered on the issue of "fairness," that is, proportional representation and quotas. There was also another argument that felt government intervention was illegitimate. The major argument against the passage of a strong renewal was that the Voting Rights Act had accomplished what it had set out to do. Hasn't the federal government gone far enough in lessening voter discrimination? Why should it continue?

In fall 1980 there was a great deal of skepticism on the part of the civil rights community that a strong voting rights act could be enacted. Ronald Reagan was elected president by an overwhelming majority. His previous record and the electoral coalition he had put together indicated that he would not be very supportive of a stringent voting rights act. In addition, the Senate was controlled by a Republican majority for the first time since the 1950s. With a Republican majority, Strom Thurmond (R–SC) was the new chairman of the Judiciary Committee and Orrin Hatch (R–Utah) chaired the subcommittee on the Constitution. Proponents of a strong Voting Rights Act were able to win House passage of the bill they wanted, but the possibility of getting an equally strong bill through the Senate and signed by the president did not appear to be very good. No one was against voting rights per se; people were opposed to how voting rights policy had been implemented.

Armand Derfner very effectively summarized why the proponents wanted a strong Voting Rights Act renewed:

> There is a corollary which is implicit in the element of
> taking race into account, but which some think should be
> explicitly included in the definition: the idea that dis-
> crimination against the people in the particular group
> is so historic or so likely that it must be overcome by
> something more than merely neutral or colorblind action.
> This feature is generally thought to distinguish affirma-
> tive action from simple nondiscrimination and generally
> comes in only after less stringent measures have been
> unsuccessful. [19]

Proponents of a strong renewal felt that full voting rights could be assured for black and Hispanic citizens only by having a new Section 2, a continuation of bilingual ballots, and a strong bailout provision. If not, covered jurisdictions would revert to the practice of discriminating against minorities. Proponents of a strong renewal could document patterns of discrimination in covered jurisdictions, and these patterns could be overcome only by the use of affirmative legislation.

One of the themes of Reagan's 1980 campaign was a pervasive antigovernment sentiment. In particular, Reagan suggested that the federal government interfered too much in areas that should be administered by state or local governments or that should be left to the private sector. The Voting Rights Act was just such a piece of legislation. Reagan and his supporters believed that Section 5 and the minority-language requirements were an intrusion on the part of the federal government into the affairs of local governments. The fact that Section 5 created an administrative bottleneck that covered jurisdictions had to pass through was further evidence of federal intrusion. Attorney-general William French Smith was no doubt reflecting both his and the president's views when he stated before the Conservative Political Action Conference:

> Over the past five decades the Congress had ceded more
> and more authority to the federal agencies to, in a sense,

make laws through regulation. Many of those regulatory
statutes have been exceedingly broadly written—and, to
say the least, amorphous in the standards provided to
guide or limit executive action.[20]

Reagan was in a state of what social psychologists refer to as cognitive dissonance, being cross-pressured by two equally strong values:
federal intrusion versus fairness in voting. Eventually the president
conceded that he was in favor of a renewed Voting Rights Act with a
ten-year time limit, easier bailout provisions, and less stringent
minority-language requirements. The Reagan position called for an
extension of the act that was meaningless. One lobbyist for the Voting
Rights Act characterized the response of the president and the White
House as:

> Foot dragging all the way, no constructive offer was
> ever made by the White House. They were politically
> inept, their timing was bad and their understanding of
> the issue was poor. They [the White House] tended to
> treat this as a political issue.[21]

Another lobbyist suggested that the Department of Justice played a
major role in formulating the administration's position. In January
1982 the administration came out with both barrels; William French
Smith and Bradford Reynolds testified against both the new Section 2
and bilingualism. Smith invited senators over to lobby against the bill.
There were also a series of unauthorized rumors that predicted bad
things if the Voting Rights Act passed.[22] It is significant that the Justice Department would take a position in January 1982 after the House
had passed HR3112. As the agency with primary responsibility for the
enforcement of the act, it should have had a position formulated much
earlier.

Smith, along with the president, wanted to refocus the debate
over the Voting Rights Act. The attorney-general was of the opinion
that the House-passed bill would create quotas and provide for proportional representation. In addition, the administration felt the act
conferred political rights upon groups and not individuals:

> Despite our ringing endorsement of the Voting Rights Act,
> some have attempted to portray us as weak on voting rights
> because we do not support the particular bill passed by the
> House of Representatives. The House bill, however, would
> go beyond extension of the Act and change the already per-
> manent nationwide protection of the right to vote. The cur-
> rent law focuses on intent to discriminate, but the House

bill would focus instead on election results. The Act
would be triggered whenever election results failed to
mirror the racial and language makeup of a particular
jurisdiction. The end result could well be quotas in electoral politics. Election rules and systems would then be
restructured by the courts to mandate legislatures, city
councils, or school boards that mirror the racial compo-
sitions of the population. . . .

Under the House bill, the focus would be on the
group's right to have one of its members elected to office, not the individual's right to cast his vote free from
discrimination. The proposed amendment is based on the
abhorrent notion that blacks can only be represented by
blacks and whites only by whites. Our society has moved
well beyond that. Such a notion is the logical culmination
of viewing civil rights law as a means of ensuring that all
individuals are treated as individuals regardless of their
race.[23]

Smith's recommendations were structural changes that would have
hindered the capacity of the federal government to have fully enforced
the Voting Rights Act.

There was a cohort of resisters in both the House and Senate
who shared the views of Reagan, Smith, and Reynolds. The House-
passed bill was approved 389 to 24, and in the Senate there were only
eight negative votes. However, these figures do not give a true indication of how much resistance there was in Congress. An examination
of the votes in both the House and Senate Judiciary Committees and on
the floor of both houses to amend the bills will give a clearer picture
of the amount of resistance. Members were much more inclined to
vote to dilute sections of the Voting Rights Act than they were to vote
against it. Opponents of a strong act were disappointed with HR3112.
The House of Representatives had held 18 days of public hearings with
153 witnesses in three locations in order to get a wide array of views
on the issue. The chairman of the House subcommittee, Don Edwards,
made every effort to insure that the hearings were fair and that all
positions were heard. The ranking minority member of the subcommittee, Henry Hyde (R-Ill.), was provided every opportunity to participate actively in the hearing process. M. Caldwell Butler (R-Va.)
felt the Judiciary Subcommittee hearings and the floor debate were
not adequate:

In August the House Judiciary Committee of the 97th Congress had the opportunity to develop new and creative voting rights legislation for the 1980s and beyond. Accomplish-

ing this would have required a thorough, deliberate, and rational decision making process. Instead the Committee hurriedly and haphazardly passed legislation which is conceptually unsound and technically incompetent. Greater consideration was given to reporting out legislation before the August recess than to assuring that its language was accurate and its potential impact was understood.[24]

If opponents did not have the opportunity to raise questions in the House, they certainly had an opportunity to do so in the Senate.

The Senate Judiciary Committee was headed by Sen. Strom Thurmond (R-SC), who was an opponent of the Voting Rights Act in 1965 and not a vigorous proponent of the legislation in 1982. Thurmond's committee votes and his floor votes on key amendments give a clear indication of his views. During the floor debate, Sen. Hollings (D-SC) presented evidence from Edgefield County, Thurmond's home, which showed that voter discrimination existed there in 1980.[25] The chair of the Senate subcommittee on the Constitution, Sen. Orrin Hatch (R-Utah), allowed the subcommittee's hearing and its report to reflect the view of the opponents of the Voting Rights Act.

> Given the environment of the House consideration of HR3112, this subcommittee is not persuaded that special deference ought to be accorded the outcome of that consideration. This subcommittee has endeavored to provide a fair opportunity for all responsible views to be heard. It is the obligation of the United States Senate, the "world's most deliberate legislative body," to see that a different environment of debate occurs within its own chambers.[26]

The theme of the Senate debate was very different from the debate that had occurred in the House. Whereas the House debate documented numerous violations of the right to vote in covered jurisdictions, the Senate debate focused on the potential evils that would be created by the enactment of the House-passed bill.

Opponents in the Senate were very vigorous in their opposition to what they believed to be a racially biased piece of legislation:

> In addition to the serious questions inherent in adopting any legislation which recognizes interest groups as a primary unit of representation, it must be taken into account that the particular group immediately involved is defined solely on racial grounds. The subcommittee believes that special caution is appropriate when the enactment of any race based classification is contemplated

and vigorous analysis of potential undesirable social
consequences must be undertaken. [27]

The new Section 2 was one of the most objectionable parts of the Voting
Rights Act for the resisters. Their view was that Section 2 overturned
Bolden and created a "results" test that would create proportional
representation. A large part of the Senate Judiciary Committee's report was spent trying to refute the new Section 2. The issue of proportional representation was one of the key symbols raised by the resisters, even though proponents of the new Section 2 did not perceive it
to be a call for proportional representation.

Another important symbol raised by the resisters was that the
Voting Rights Act forced the South to remain as a conquered province
and therefore be subject to unfair federal intrusion into local affairs:

> Fundamental—indeed radical changes in the way our de-
> mocracy works will surely come about if Congress passes
> S1992. This measure would not only extend the extraordi-
> nary requirements of the Voting Rights Act of 1965, but
> would also place new, severe, and unconstitutional re-
> straints on local governments throughout the country.
> Before the Senate acts on this bill members should take
> adequate time to consider both the need to extend the Act
> and the wisdom of new changes in the Act that place un-
> paralleled power to alter the character of local and state
> governments in the hands of the Federal Government. [28]

The new bailout provisions along with Section 2 were the issues by
which the resisters felt most threatened.

Whatever questions were not given an adequate hearing during
the House debates were fully developed and presented during the Senate
debate. Both party affiliation and ideology were important in the re-
focusing of the Senate debate. In addition, the rules of the Senate provided members with greater latitude to debate issues. S1992 was essentially identical to HR3112 when it was first introduced. Proponents
had gathered close to 60 cosponsors before the Voting Rights Act was
introduced, and by the time it was passed in the Senate they had 78
cosponsors. The 60 cosponsors were important because it meant the
proponents had enough votes to vote cloture if there was a filibuster.
In the end, the proponents of the Voting Rights Act were able to get
all that they wanted. Section 2 was reworked to address "a totality of
circumstances" and not a results test, a stringent bailout was included
plus a 25-year extension of the preclearance provision and a strong
bilingual component.

CONCLUSION

Goldstein is correct in his assessment of the voting rights debate that

> While those symbols and images used by the proponents
> were the most persuasive, they failed to present effec-
> tively a reality that was also ignored by both resisters
> and compromisers. In this respect, the overall impact
> of all the symbols and images used in the voting rights
> debate is a public unaware of both the variety of continu-
> ing voting rights violations and the failure of the Depart-
> ment of Justice to enforce the Act adequately. [29]

In the context of a legislative debate, the symbols presented by the proponents of a renewed Voting Rights Act were sufficient to carry the day. The House hearings were effective in gaining support for the legislation from an unlikely source, Rep. Henry Hyde. The testimony documented the fact that even with legislation on the books for 17 years there were still numerous barriers to voting, and the only way potential minority voters would have access to the ballot was with a strengthened and renewed Voting Rights Act. The picture painted by proponents of the act in 1982 was just as compelling as that presented in 1965; it was just not as visible to the public. The public was of the opinion that the legislation was on the books and that all covered jurisdictions were in full compliance with the act. This was the case because they were made aware only of the electoral successes created as a result of the act. It took the debate over renewal to refocus the public's attention on the issue of voting rights. Congress and the public were swayed more by the argument of fairness than by the argument of too much government intrusion or the illegitimacy of government actions.

Proponents were greatly helped by the fact that the resisters did not have a clearly defined set of goals. In the early ad hoc meetings during the fall of 1980, the proponents were able to thrash out and define what it was they wanted out of the 1982 legislation. There was a consensus that they might not get everything they wanted. Nevertheless, they knew what it was that they wanted if they got their way. The resisters had not clearly defined what they wanted, and when the House bill was formulated they were put on the defensive by having to respond to the agenda that had already been set by the proponents. In addition, the proponents were able to marshall very strong support in both the House and the Senate. The House Judiciary Committee's hearings' overwhelming support did not leave the resisters with much of an opportunity to challenge what appeared to be a fait accompli. Also, the resisters were on the defensive because they had to preface all of their remarks with "I'm not against voting rights, but . . . " which made their position more tenuous. When the debate shifted to the Senate they were again at a loss. They did not attempt to introduce their own legislation; instead, they attempted to amend and debate the proponents' bill.

The debate over the renewal was primarily a legislative debate, unlike the debate over the enactment of the Voting Rights Act in 1965, which was a national referendum. In 1965 protest and public opinion were two of the compelling factors in the enactment of the Voting Rights Act. This was not the case in 1982; letters and telegrams were more important in 1982 than was public opinion. Reverend Joseph Lowery of the Southern Christian Leadership Conference did lead a march to Washington in an attempt to rekindle the enthusiasm that was prevalent in 1965, but its effect was minimal in getting the Voting Rights Act passed. The mobilization of support on the part of various national leadership organizations to put pressure on members of Congress in their home districts was much more instrumental in getting the legislation passed. The reference public in 1982 were the members of Congress who responded to pressure from constituents either by direct mail, letters to the editor, or phone calls to the home offices. This type of pressure was most important to members whose districts were not directly affected by the legislation and therefore did not have a direct stake in it. Constituent pressure was significant because it made members aware that there was support for this legislation from a cross-section of the public. Conversely, the opponents of the Voting Rights Act were unable to mobilize a cross-section of opposition. The opposition was for the most part in Congress or in the academy. With no external pressure on members to reject the Voting Rights Act in whole or in part, it was difficult to mobilize significant opposition in Congress.

NOTES

1. Abigail M. Thernstrom, "The Odd Evolution of the Voting Rights Act," Public Interest 55 (1979): 59-60.

2. See Mack H. Jones, "The Voting Rights Act as an Intervention Strategy for Social Symbolism or Substance" (1983): 5. Presented at The Voting Rights Act: Consequences and Implications conference at Pomona College, Claremont, CA.

3. United States Civil Rights Commission, Political Participation (Washington, D.C.: Government Printing Office, 1968), p. 223.

4. Lorn S. Foster, "The Voting Rights Act: Black Voting and the New Southern Politics," Western Journal of Black Studies 7 (1983): 120-124.

5. United States Civil Rights Commission, The Voting Rights Act: Ten Years After (Washington, D. C. : Government Printing Office, 1975).

6. See Ball, Krane, and Lauth, Compromised Compliance (Westport: Greenwood Press, 1982), p. 68.

7. Interview with L. M. Murphy, lobbyist, American Civil Liberties Union, June 1, 1983.

8. Ibid.

9. Dianne M. Pinderhughes, "Interest Groups and the Passage of the Voting Rights Act in 1982," 6-10. Presented at the National Conference of Black Political Scientists Convention, Houston, Texas, 1983. See also "Interest Groups and the Extension of the Voting Rights Act in 1982," 24-25. Presented at the meeting of the American Political Science Association, Chicago, IL, 1983.

10. Interview with Ralph Neas, Executive Director Leadership Conference on Civil Rights, June 16, 1983.

11. Interview with Representative Don Edwards (D-Cal.), Chair of the Subcommittee on Constitutional and Civil Rights, House Judiciary Committee, June 14, 1983.

12. Interview with Frank Parker, Committee for Civil Rights Under Law, June 14, 1983.

13. Neas, op. cit.

14. Interview with Helen Gonzalez, former Staff Counsel for the Subcommittee on Constitutional and Civil Rights, House Judiciary Committee, June 14, 1983.

15. United States Civil Rights Commission. The Voting Rights Act: Unfulfilled Goals (Washington, D. C. : Government Printing Office, 1981), pp. 91-93.

16. Minor, op. cit.

17. Hugh Heclo, A Government of Strangers (Washington, D. C. : Brookings Institution, 1977), p. 102.

18. Michael L. Goldstein, "Whatever Happened to the Voting Rights Debate" (1982): 7-8. Presented at the meeting for the study of Afro-American Life and History, Baltimore, MD.

19. Armand Derfner, "Affirmative Action in Districting," Policy Studies Journal 9 (1981): 852.

20. Attorney-General William French Smith, Conservative Political Action Conference, Washington, D. C., February 25, 1982.

21. John Shattuck, head of the Washington office of the ACLU, June 16, 1983.

22. Parker.

23. Smith, statement made in Washington before the Third National Young Leadership Conference of the United Jewish Appeal, March 14, 1982.

24. United States House of Representatives, <u>Voting Rights Extension 97-227</u> (Washington, D.C.: Government Printing Office, 1981), p. 62.

25. United States Senate, <u>Congressional Record</u> 128 (1982): pp. 6893-6897.

26. United States Senate, <u>Voting Rights Act Extension 97-417</u> (Washington, D.C.: Government Printing Office, 1982), pp. 126-127.

27. Ibid., pp. 147-148.

28. Ibid., p. 201.

29. Goldstein, pp. 14-15.

6
Legislative Responsiveness And the New Southern Politics
Mark Stern

INTRODUCTION

In June 1982 the Voting Rights Act Extension (HR 3112) was over-whelmingly passed by both houses of the Congress. In the House of Representatives more than 90 percent of all white southern Democrats voted for the bill (63Y-13N). In the Senate, 18 of 22 southern senators voted for the bill, and this included support from all southern Democrats. In Southern Politics, V. O. Key maintained that when less than 10 percent of the members of a voting group dissented on a roll call vote, this represented an "extremely high degree of solidarity."[1] The vote on the 1982 Voting Rights Act Extension thus represents a new meaning for an old term, the "Solid South," as applied to southern Democrats. In 1949 Key demonstrated that "on the race question, and that question alone, does a genuine southern [congressional] solidarity exist."[2] And, of course, it was an antiblack solidarity.

Now, for southern Democrats (although less so for southern Republicans), a problack-rights solidarity is exhibited on this highly symbolic and tangible issue. This occurred despite the Reagan administration's continuing opposition to the bill in the form it came to the floor for final passage and the presence of the extremely controversial Section 2 (the intent versus results section). Passage of this bill was, as Congressional Quarterly Weekly Report put it, "a major victory for a coalition of civil rights groups."[3] This chapter examines hypotheses put forward as to the bases of white southern congressional support for black voting rights.

Only a decade ago Shannon concluded his analysis of southern congressional roll call votes by noting that congressmen from the region had become "a truly isolated sectional minority" with an in-

transigent negative record on black rights.[4] In the wake of the passage
of the 1965 Voting Rights Act, with increased black voting and registration expected in the South, there were scholars who questioned
whether this would fundamentally alter the position of the black in
southern electoral politics.[5] Recent studies of roll call voting find
that from the Ninety-third through the Ninety-fifth Congresses, southern congressmen had begun to support black civil rights, although they
did not support other areas of concern to blacks. Alan Abramowitz
shows that on other issues the southern Democratic congressional
delegation still diverges from the roll call voting patterns of other
Democrats as indicated by their dissent on party unity scores.[6] Utilizing the conservative coalition scores and the Leadership Conference
on Civil Rights scores indicates that on social welfare, foreign policy,
and civil liberties issues southern congressional voting remained non-
liberal, but on black civil rights a liberalization has occurred.[7] Sinclair finds that by the Ninety-third through Ninety-fifth Congresses
civil liberties "had become the least divisive of the domestic issue
areas. . . along regional lines" as the South joined the nation in this
area.[8] Other scholars confirm that southern congressional voting support for black rights issues has become noticeably more positive in
recent years.[9] In large part this has been attributed to increased
black voter participation in the wake of the 1965 Voting Rights Act.

Black's work utilizes roll call votes on final passage of the five
major bills effecting black voting rights from 1957 to 1975 to assess
the validity of three hypothesized patterns of southern white congressional support related to black voter mobilization and the black proportion of district populations.[10] A "Solid South" hypothesis as proposed by Key is first examined.[11] This hypothesis holds that southerners unite when there is any proposed federal legislation that would give
blacks the vote or alter the traditional pattern of southern race relations. Second is the "black belt" hypothesis also proposed by Key[12]
and extensively examined by, among others, Cosman,[13] Mathews and
Prothro,[14] and Black.[15] Although southerners as a whole may oppose
black rights, this hypothesis suggests that it is particularly in states
and districts with high proportions of blacks that resistance is most
likely to occur and persist. Third, Black explores the "curvilinear
hypothesis" as proposed by Keech. Keech's argument is as follows:

> If we assume that federal law has guaranteed the right to
> vote of all southern Negroes, and that the percent of eli-
> gible Negroes registered is relatively uniform over the
> whole region, we might expect a curvilinear relationship
> between the percent of the electorate Negro and the payoffs
> of voting. Up to about 30 percent of the electorate Negro
> the relationship would be positive because the threshold

of white resistance seems to be about 30 percent of the
population Negro. Between 30 and 50 percent of the electorate Negro the relationship might become neutral or
negative, because white resistance will be higher in communities with larger Negro population bases. Beyond 50
percent of the electorate Negro the relationship will become positive again because . . . a Negro voting majority
can overcome a lot of white resistance. [16]

There is ample documentation by Daniel, [17] Feagin and Hahn, [18]
Rogers and Bullock, [19] Murray and Vedlitz, [20] and the U.S. Commission on Civil Rights [21] that after passage of the 1965 Voting Rights Act
millions of southern blacks were added to the voter-registration rolls.
Of course, there was white countermobilization as noted by Hammond [22]
and Bartley and Graham. [23] Salamon and Van Evera demonstrate there
was also white intimidation of blacks who attempted to vote in certain
areas. [24] The effect of the 1965 act is evident in Black's findings. [25]
The Solid South hypothesis holds in 1957 and 1960, and the black belt
hypothesis holds for 1965 and 1970, but by 1975 "the increase and diffusion of black political mobilization" combined with "the changing
calculation of electoral advantages by white politicians" become critical as the curvilinear hypothesis fits the pattern of white southern
congressional support.

Bullock argues that there may be three distinct patterns of southern congressional roll call voting on black rights. [26] First, with little
or no black voter participation and high proportions of blacks present
in the population, the peak of white resistance to black rights is found.
Second, "as blacks have begun to register and vote, researchers have
often found a curvilinear relationship between the size of the black
constituency and legislator voting records." Finally, "once blacks
are fully participating members of the electorate," as perhaps at the
present time where the black and white proportions of the voting age
population registered to vote are roughly comparable, then perhaps
legislative responsiveness would "increase linearly as percent black
rises." Bullock finds, however, that in examining voting on the Leadership Conference on Civil Rights Index (a measure of support for black
rights issues), "increased black political participation has had an impact at the upper extreme [of the black proportion of the population]
although the relationship is far from linear." [27] Using a broad measure
of white southern support for black rights, Bullock's findings are directly counter to Black's in this respect. The present study examines
white southern House voting on passage of the 1982 Voting Rights Act
Extension to assess whether the pattern of roll call support fits the
curvilinear hypothesis supported by Black's findings or Bullock's finding of support in districts with a high proportion of blacks in their pop-

ulation. Hypotheses about generational replacement, partisanship, and subregionalism as each affects white southern representatives' voting on passage of black rights bills are also examined in utilizing the vote on the 1982 Voting Rights Act Extension.

There tends to be a relationship between the replacement of incumbents by challengers and shifts in policy voting. Fiorina finds this occurs when a district changes partisan representation.[28] Clausen believes that newer members of Congress are generally more supportive of civil liberties than are senior members of the institution.[29] Stern finds that within the South, junior representatives as compared to their senior colleagues are more likely to be supportive of black rights across a series of issues.[30] The entry of Republicans into the southern House delegation has meant, as Bullock puts it, that "southern Republicans have taken the most conservative end of the spectrum away from the Democrats."[31] Bass and DeVries provide some earlier evidence on this finding.[32] Asher and Weisberg[33] and Black[34] find that generally Republicans are increasingly moving into an anticivil-rights position in Congress. Black distinguishes between the New South generation of Democrats, first elected to the House after passage of the 1965 act, and the Old South Democratic generation, who were first elected to the House prior to the passage of the 1965 act.[35] He finds the New South Democrats generally abandoned the "posture of unyielding racial conservatism." He also finds that southern House Republicans, regardless of the racial composition of their districts, are the least likely of all southerners to support black voting rights legislation.

Research findings concerning the effects of generational change and partisanship on southern representatives' support for black rights appear to reach two conclusions: first, the more recently elected generation of Democrats tends to be more supportive of black rights than are other delegation members; and second, Republicans have become the least supportive of black rights. A second concern of this chapter is to examine the extent to which these findings hold for the roll call vote on passage of the 1982 voting bill.

Key noted a persistent difference between the Rim South and the Deep South in the virulence of their antiblack stances.[36] The states of Arkansas, Florida, North Carolina, Tennessee, Texas, and Virginia constitute the Rim South; the remaining states of the Confederacy constitute the Deep South. By virtue of the presence of fewer blacks in their populations and a history of a somewhat more moderate approach to race relations, Key hypothesized that the Rim South states would be the most likely southern states to cast aside the politics of race. Bullock's analysis of southern House voting on issues related to black interest concludes: "Rim South representatives continue to be less conservative although the magnitude of the differences is diminishing."[37] (Bullock's analysis, however, treats North Carolina as a Deep

South state.) The persistence of the hypothesized difference between the Rim South and Deep South delegations on the 1982 vote is thus an area of concern in this chapter.

A much neglected area of research has been southern senators' roll call voting on black rights issues. To what extent have there been changes in support of black rights by southern senators? The second section of this chapter explores this question. Little has been done in the way of any systematic analysis of changes in southern senatorial support for black rights. Stern has shown that some parallels exist between changes in southern senators' roll call votes on economic and racial issues and changes along these dimensions in southern gubernatorial rhetoric as analyzed by Black. [38] Due to the limited number of 22 senators from 11 states, caution must be given to the results found in any particular study of this subject. Indeed, it would be foolhardy to directly ascribe black population data from any given state as being related to senatorial voting. One should note, however, that based on the 1980 census data, the black percentage of the population in the Rim South is uniformly lower in each case, with a low of 12 percent in Texas and a high of 22 percent in Virginia, than it is in any of the Deep South states, with 26 percent in Alabama being the low proportion and 35 percent in Mississippi being the high proportion. As of 1980, the mean black proportion of the population in the Rim South states is 16.3 percent, almost half that of the mean black proportion of 29.4 percent in the Deep South states.

Southern Senate roll call voting on voting rights bills from 1957 to 1982 is used to examine whether the hypotheses explored in relation to House roll call voting hold for the Senate in the areas of: generational changes within the southern Senate delegation; partisanship changes within the southern Senate delegation; and subregional variation (Rim South versus Deep South differences).

The following hypothesized relationships are suggested from the House literature: more recently elected southern senators (Black's New South versus Ole South dichotomy) are more likely to be supportive of black voting rights; Democrats are more likely to be supportive of black rights than are Republicans; and Rim South senators are more likely to be supportive of black voting rights than are Deep South senators.

METHODS

The roll call votes of all white southern House and Senate members from the 11 states of the Confederacy are analyzed in this study. The votes on final passage of the voting rights bills of 1982 (HR 3112), 1975 (HR 6219), 1970 (HR 429), 1965 (S 1564), 1960 (HR 8601), and 1957 (HR 6127) are employed for the House and the Senate.

The final votes on these particular bills are used for several reasons. First, they provide comparability and continuity with the analysis done by Black.[39] Second, these bills involve all of the major pieces of voting rights-centered legislation that have been passed since 1957. Third, as both Black and Keech have argued, votes on final passage of the bill as amended are the symbolic votes for or against the principle at issue.[40] In this case one hundred years of southern resistance to federal interference with the southern black franchise is the principle at hand. Placing one's self on the record by roll call or pairing of a vote is considered equivalent for purposes of this analysis.

The black percentage of the population in each district in 1980 is employed as one independent variable for the House vote. This figure is drawn from the 1980 Census report as cited for each district in Barone and Ujifusa.[41] Stern has shown that in the only states where there are available official black voter-registration data (Florida, Louisiana, North Carolina, and South Carolina), there exists a strong correlation (r = .82) between the black percentage of the population and the black percentage of the total voters registered.[42] For both the southern House and Senate analyses, the date of first election to Congress is employed to assess the impact of congressional generation. Key's classification of Rim South versus Deep South is employed to assess whether a subregional effect still persists.

DATA ANALYSIS: THE HOUSE

Figure 6.1 and Table 6.1 present evidence to test the various black population effect hypotheses and directly extend the data presentation of Black. Figure 6.1 shows the percentage support for the voting rights bills from 1957 through 1982 for varying percentages of the black proportion of the population in each district as compiled by Black prior to 1982 and by the author for 1982. Table 6.1 shows the percentage of the white southern delegation favoring the voting rights bills in each of the earlier Congresses as compiled by Black and in 1982 as compiled by the author. In 1965 31.8 percent of white southerners in the House supported the Voting Rights Act. In 1970 only 28.3 percent supported the bill. In 1975 the figure jumped to 62.5 percent support and in 1982 it became 81.7 percent. All the members of Congress from districts with 40 percent or more blacks in their population voted for the bill.

Black finds that a shift over time occurs as to which hypothesis is accurate in reflecting the effect of the black population on white representatives' voting. As noted previously, in 1957 and 1960 he finds the Solid South hypothesis is accurate. In 1965 and 1970 the black belt hypothesis fits the pattern. In 1975 he finds the curvilinear hypothesis

FIGURE 6.1: White Southern Representatives and Support for
Federal Voting Rights by Racial Composition of Districts

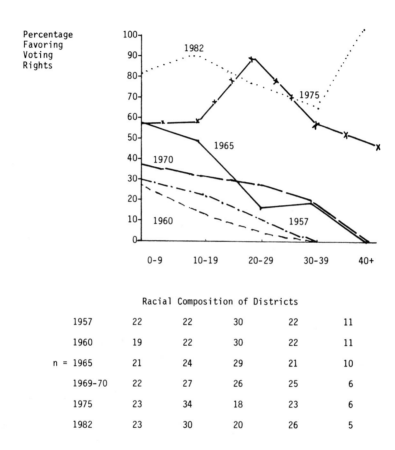

	Racial Composition of Districts				
1957	22	22	30	22	11
1960	19	22	30	22	11
n = 1965	21	24	29	21	10
1969-70	22	27	26	25	6
1975	23	34	18	23	6
1982	23	30	20	26	5

Sources: 1982 compiled by the author. Previous data compiled
by Black (1978).

TABLE 6.1: Decline of the Solid South: Percentage of White
Southern Representatives Supporting Federal Voting Rights
on Final Passage, 1957-1982

	Democrats	Republicans	Total
1957	14.3 (98)	13.3 (7)	13.3 (105)
1960	7.2 (97)	28.6 (7)	8.7 (104)
1965	32.9 (88)	23.5 (11)	31.4 (104)
1970	33.8 (80)	11.5 (26)	28.3 (106)
1975	72.7 (77)	33.3 (27)	62.5 (104)
1982	91.3 (69)	62.9 (35)	81.7 (104)

Sources: 1982 compiled by the author. Previous data compiled
by Black (1978).

to be most fruitful. In 1982 the point on the curve of Figure 6.1 fits
the pattern of the districts with the largest proportions of black populations as among the most supportive of black voting rights.

This is but one limited data point, but it does appear to fit well
with Stern's and Bullock's results from broader data sets.[43] The latter
found that districts with the smallest and largest proportions of blacks
are most likely to have representatives who vote in support of black
rights. Key's statement that "Departures from the supposed uniformity
of southern politics occur most notably in those states and districts
with the fewest Negroes"[44] must now be amended as follows: and in
those districts with the highest proportions of Negroes. In these districts it requires but relatively few whites to form coalitions with
blacks, if the latter turn out at the polls at rates comparable to their
proportion in the population. The key electoral assumption in a democracy is that politicians do pay attention to electoral possibilities. In
this case, with very high proportions of black voters in a district,
there would appear to be a distinct possibility of effective black re-
taliation at the polls if representatives were to ignore this constituency
on such a highly symbolic issue. This can aptly be called the "democratic coalition" hypothesis. It holds that when a minority population
makes up a large proportion of a district, on highly visible and symbolic issues of impact for this population, the representative will vote
in a manner consistent with the minority's preferences.

In 1965 31.8 percent of the white southern House delegation supported black voting rights. In 1970 only 28.3 percent gave such support, but by 1975 the support figure jumps to 62.5 percent and it jumps
again to 81.7 percent in 1982. Yet, as Table 6.1 shows, it is primarily

Democrats who have moved into a supportive position on this issue. Only six southern Democrats voted against the 1982 bill as compared to 13 negative Republican votes. In addition, as Table 6.2 indicates, regardless of the proportion of the black population in the districts, Democrats were more likely to support the 1982 bill than were Republicans. This result is similar to Black's finding,[45] and it provides some additional evidence on the primacy of partisanship on this issue. In earlier studies, as I have noted previously, it was the older generation who opposed civil rights legislation.

TABLE 6.2: White Southern House Support for 1982 Voting Rights Bill on Final Passage, by Party and Proportion of Black District Population

| | Proportion Black in District Population | | | | |
	0-9	10-19	20-29	30-39	40+
Democrats (n)	91.7 (12)	100.0 (23)	85.7 (14)	82.4 (16)	100 (4)
Republicans (n)	72.7 (11)	57.1 (7)	50.0 (6)	60.0 (10)	100 (1)

The role generational change played apparently has been altered in comparing the 1975 and 1982 votes. None of the six Democrats voting against the 1982 bill was elected to Congress prior to 1965. Only one of the five Republicans elected prior to 1965 was among the 13 negative votes cast by southern GOP representatives. Thus, by 1982, recently elected Democrats and Republicans cast the negative votes on black rights issues. Such votes were not cast by the senior Democrats as in 1975.

One interesting finding that still appears to hold for the Democrats is that subregionalism plays a role in differentiating the anti-black-rights votes in 1982. Five of the six negative Democratic votes were cast by members from Deep South states. On the other hand, only two of the 10 Deep South Republicans cast negative votes on this bill, whereas 11 of the 25 Rim South Republicans cast negative votes. The Virginia House delegation almost unanimously cast their votes in opposition to the 1982 bill: eight of the nine Republicans and the one Democrat voted in the negative.

In summary, analysis of the hypotheses using the votes of white southern House members on the 1982 Voting Rights Act Extension indicates the following: districts with the highest and lowest proportion of blacks are most likely to be supportive of black voting rights; Democrats compared to Republicans, regardless of the proportion of blacks in their districts, are more likely to be supportive of the issue; generational change does not appear to increase supportive voting; and subregional effects still appear to be present for Democrats in a very limited fashion, but not for Republicans.

DATA ANALYSIS: THE SENATE

The overall southern Senate record on black voting rights acts parallels that of the southern House record. Figure 6.2 graphically shows the overall pattern. In 1957 22.7 percent of southern senators supported the voting rights bill. This figure declined to 18.2 percent in both 1960 and 1965, but rose continuously since then from 27.3 percent in 1970 to 47.6 percent in 1975 and 81.8 percent support in 1982. The Rim South senators were continuously more supportive than the Deep South senators, with no Deep South support evident until 1975. In both the House and the Senate the 1982 vote marks the first time that the Deep South delegation casts a majority of its support for a voting rights bill. As Key hypothesized, it is the senators from the three southern states with the lowest proportion of blacks in their populations (Texas, Florida, and Tennessee) who were the first to depart from the southern tradition. Senators from these states cast positive votes in 1957, 1960, and 1965. In 1970 the two states with the next smallest proportion of blacks (Arkansas and Virginia) each had a senator joining in support of the voting rights bill. In 1975 the last rim state (North Carolina) had a senator join with the senators from the other rim states to vote for black voting rights. They were also joined by at least one senator from Georgia, Louisiana, and South Carolina. In 1982 only South Carolina had both its senators vote in opposition to the voting rights bill, and they were joined by one senator from Alabama and Virginia.

Three Republicans and the one Independent from Virginia were the only southerners to vote against the 1982 Voting Rights Act extension. Table 6.3 shows the partisan division on the voting rights bills from 1957 through 1982. Again, the need for caution in generalizing from this number is in order, but we can note two results from these data. First, from 1970 on the Democratic percentage for black voting rights consistently increased. Second, although the Republicans have been less consistent in their support for black voting rights, a solid majority of their members did vote for the 1982 bill.

The 1975 vote appears to represent a watershed in the Senate, as it does in the House, for southern black voting rights support. Deep South members of Congress in significant numbers, for the first time,

FIGURE 6.2: Overall Southern Senate Support for Federal Voting Rights and Support Subregion (Rim South or Peripheral South), 1957-1982

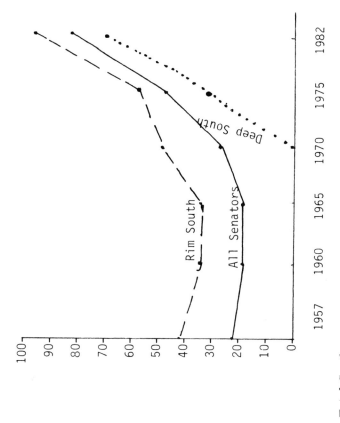

N = 22 for Total South, except 1975 when N = 21 as Eastland (D-Mi.) did not go on record with a position for that vote. N = 22 for Rim South. N = 10 for Deep South.

TABLE 6.3: Southern Senate Support for Voting Rights Bills
on Final Passage by Party, 1957-1982

	Democrats (n)	Republicans (n)
1957	22.7% (22)	—
1960	18.2% (22)	—
1965	14.3% (21)	0.0% (1)
1970	23.5% (17)[1]	50.0% (4)
1975	46.7% (15)[1,2]	40.0% (5)
1982	100.0% (11)[1]	70.0% (10)

[1]Does not include Byrd (Ind.-Va.), who cast a negative vote.
[2]Does not include Eastland (D-Mi.), who did not go on record
for this vote.

cast affirmative votes on this issue. Black found that New South Democratic representatives (those first elected to the House after 1965)
were much more supportive on this issue than were their more senior
Old South Democratic colleagues, and southern Republicans were the
least supportive of this issue. Among southern senators a similar pattern of support for the 1975 bill is evidenced. Three of the five Old
South Democrats and three of the five Republicans voted against the
bill, but all 11 New South Democrats voted for the bill. In 1982 only
three Republicans and an Independent voted against the voting rights
bill. The two Old South Democrats stood with the other Democrats in
casting a positive vote.

In summary, analysis of southern Senate votes on bills related to
black voting rights indicates initial and steady support for this issue
by Rim South senators from states with lower proportions of blacks
in their populations. The 1975 vote appears to mark a dividing point
in southern Senate support for black voting rights, as Deep South senators with high proportions of blacks in their state populations joined
their fellow southerners in support of this legislation. Whereas the
black belt hypothesis does describe southern Senate voting patterns
prior to 1975, by 1982 southern support for this issue is so diffuse
that subregional comparisons lack much discriminative ability. A
generational effect appeared to be operative for both the House and
Senate in the 1975 vote but, again, for the 1982 vote this is no longer
present. Partisan differences appear to be persistent in House and
Senate voting. The Republican southern representative to the national
legislature is less likely than a Democratic colleague to be supportive
of black voting rights.

CONCLUSIONS

Two features of the southern political landscape emerge starkly from this study: Republican representatives in Congress provide the base of antiblack-rights votes, and there is now a general diffusion of support for black voting rights across the region. The so-called southern strategy, nurtured and maintained by Republican White House occupants since Nixon, was repeated again in the 1982 legislative maneuvering by the White House staff. Clearly, only a minority of Republicans followed this cue in a manner that led to their voting against the 1982 bill, and Republican Senator Dole was a major actor in the process of getting a strong bill out of the Senate. Finally, after all was said and done by the executive staff, the 1982 bill was signed by the president. But the tone of the southern strategy was there and apparent not only on this issue but in other arenas as well. The Civil Rights Commission appointments battle in 1983 again evoked the symbols of the Republican southern strategy.

Black argues that it is because successful southern biracial campaigns have centered on Democratic candidates that the representatives of this party have altered their positions on black voting rights.[46] With few potential supporters among black voters, given their attachment to the Democratic party, southern Republicans find they have little of an electoral price to pay as they become the conservatives on this issue. One may also argue that southern Republicanism arose in part as a reaction to the increasing federal interventionist stance for black rights taken by Democrats in Congress. The southern strategy is part and parcel of the growth of southern Republican representation in Congress. Few and far between are the southern Republicans with whom blacks are offered the possibility of a coalition that involves a candidate who will take policy positions consistent with black needs. One can suggest that this holds because it would mean a violation of the southern strategy on the part of the southern Republican candidate.

Southern Democratic solidarity in the House and Senate in support of the 1982 bill is impressive. A new era of southern politics has arrived. The old hypotheses related to the Solid South and Old South Democrats no longer hold. Deep South versus Rim South differences have also lost much of their descriptive accuracy in this area. Key's (1949, p. 11) statement that "the fundamental explanation of southern politics is that the black belt whites succeeded in imposing their will . . . and thereby presented a solid regional front in national politics on the race issue" is a description that is now only for the history books.[47] Blacks now vote in large numbers even in the states that are in the heart of Dixie. Black vote dilution is still an issue that must be dealt with, but the shift in southern congressional voting on black rights issues is a manifestation of the black suffrage extension in recent years.

One last critical question begs to be answered: To what extent has the support for black voting rights extended over into support of other areas of concern to blacks? Studies of shifts in tangible benefits to blacks accruing as a result of shifts in black electoral participation have yet to be undertaken on a broad scale. This should be part of the research agenda for studies of the new southern politics.

NOTES

1. V. O. Key, Jr., Southern Politics (New York: Vintage Books, 1949), p. 667.

2. Ibid., p. 359.

3. Congressional Quarterly, Congressional Quarterly Weekly Report 26 (1982): 1504.

4. W. Wayne Shannon, "Revolt in Washington," in The Changing Politics of the South, ed. William C. Havard (Baton Rouge, La.: Louisiana State University Press, 1972), p. 662.

5. See, for example, Hanes Walton, Jr., Black Politics: A Theoretical and Structural Analysis (Philadelphia: Lippincott, 1972); William R. Keech, The Impact of Negro Voting (Chicago: Rand McNally, 1968), p. 109; Donald, R. Mathews and James W. Prothro, Negroes and the New Southern Politics (New York: Harcourt, Brace and World, 1963), p. 481.

6. Alan I. Abramowitz, "Is the Revolt Fading: A Note on Party Loyalty Among Southern Democratic Congressmen," Journal of Politics 42 (May 1980): 572.

7. Charles S. Bullock, III, "Congressional Voting and the Mobilization of the Black Electorate in the South," Journal of Politics 43 (August 1981): 669.

8. Barbara Sinclair, "House Voting Alignments in the 1970s— The Effects of New Issues and New Members," paper presented at the Annual Meeting of the Midwest Political Science Association (Chicago, 1980), p. 20.

9. Merle Black, "Racial Composition of Congressional Districts and Support for Federal Voting Rights in the American South," Social Science Quarterly 59 (December 1978): 665-79; Mark Stern, "Southern Congressional Civil Rights Voting and the New Southern Political Demography," Southeastern Political Review 11 (Spring 1983): 69-90.

10. Black, "Racial Composition," pp. 435-50.

11. Key, Southern Politics, pp. 245-382.

12. Ibid., pp. 3-12.

13. Bernard Cosman, Five States for Goldwater (University, Al.: University of Alabama Press, 1966).

14. Mathews and Prothro, Negroes and the New Southern Politics, passim.

15. Earl Black, Southern Governors and Civil Rights (Cambridge, Mass.: Harvard University Press, 1976), passim.

16. Keech, The Impact, p. 101.

17. Johnie Daniel, "Negro Political Behavior and Community Political and Socio-economic Structural Factors," Social Forces 47 (March 1969): 274-79.

18. Joe R. Feagin and Harlan Hahn, "The Second Reconstruction: Black Political Strength in the South," Social Science Quarterly 34 (May 1972): 484-99.

19. Harrell R. Rodgers, Jr. and Charles S. Bullock, III, Law and Social Change (New York: McGraw-Hill, 1972), pp. 15-54.

20. Richard Murray and Arnold Vedlitz, "Race, Socio-economic Status and Voting Participation in Large Southern Cities," Journal of Politics 39 (November 1977): 1064-72.

21. U.S. Commission on Civil Rights, The Voting Rights Act: Ten Years After (Washington, D.C.: U.S. Government Printing Office, 1975).

22. John L. Hammond, "Race and Electoral Mobilization: White Southerners," Public Opinion Quarterly 41 (Spring 1977): 13-27.

23. Numan V. Bartley and Hugh D. Graham, Southern Politics and the Second Reconstruction (Baltimore: Johns Hopkins University Press, 1975), p. 188.

24. Lester M. Salamon and Stephen Van Evera, "Fear, Apathy and Discrimination: A Test of Three Explanations of Political Participation," American Political Science Review 67 (December 1973): 1288-1306.

25. Black, "Racial Composition."

26. Bullock, "Congressional Voting," pp. 663-64.

27. Ibid., pp. 672-79.

28. Morris P. Fiorina, Representatives, Roll Calls, and Constituencies (Lexington, Mass.: D. C. Heath, 1974), pp. 100-08.

29. Aage R. Clausen, How Congressmen Decide (New York: St. Martin's Press, 1973), p. 14.

30. Mark Stern, "Assessing the Impact of the 1965 Voting Rights Act: A Microanalysis of Four States," in Contemporary Southern Political Attitudes and Behavior, ed. Laurence W. Moreland et al. (New York: Praeger, 1982), pp. 261-62.

31. Bullock, "Congressional Voting," p. 663.

32. Jack Bass and Walter DeVries, The Transformation of Southern Politics (New York: Basic Books, 1976), pp. 377-78.

33. Herbert B. Asher and Herbert F. Weisberg, "Voting Change in Congress: Some Dynamic Perspectives on an Evolutionary Process," American Political Science Review 72 (May 1978): 568-72.

34. Merle Black, "Regional and Partisan Bases of Congressional Support for the Changing Agenda of Civil Rights Legislation," Journal of Politics 41 (May 1979): 665-79.

35. Black, "Racial Composition," pp. 446-47.

36. Key, Southern Politics, p. 669.

37. Bullock, "Congressional Voting," p. 679.

38. Mark Stern, "Southern Senators and Political Change: Roll Call on Racial Segregation and Economic Development," Public Affairs Forum 6 (October 1976): 1-6; Black, Southern Governors, passim.

39. Black, "Racial Composition."

40. Ibid., p. 440; Keech, The Impact, p. 13.

41. Michael J. Barone and Grant Ujifusa, The Almanac of American Politics (Washington, D.C.: Barone, 1982).

42. Stern, "Assessing the Impact."

43. Stern, "Southern Congressional"; Bullock, "Congressional Voting."

44. Key, Southern Politics, p. 668.

45. Black, "Racial Composition."

46. Ibid., p. 448.

47. Key, Southern Politics, p. 11.

PART IV
Administrative Enforcement

7
Implementation of the Voting Rights Act: Enforcement by the Department of Justice

Dale   Krane

Twenty years after the passage of the 1965 Voting Rights Act (VRA), debate about its enforcement flourishes. Whether one reads the reports of federal agencies such as the U.S. Department of Justice (DOJ), the U.S. Commission on Civil Rights (CCR), and the General Accounting Office (GAO) or the reports of private organizations such as the Joint Center for Political Studies, the Lawyers Committee for Civil Rights Under Law (LCCRUL), and the Twentieth Century Fund, contradictory and often highly polarized viewpoints clash with one another. Some reviews of the VRA's implementation applaud the act's pivotal role in opening the doors to full citizenship for blacks in the United States. Other reviews decry the continuing underrepresentation of blacks in public office, especially in those areas of the country where the black population is concentrated.

Resolution of these divergent views has been obscured by several common misperceptions or myths about the enforcement of the Voting Rights Act and particularly Section 5 of the act. These misperceptions often have been engendered by highly visible public officials who were pursuing their own political objectives. A second source of confusion about voting rights enforcement springs from the failure of many evaluation studies to examine the attitudes and actions of the local officials who actually must abide by the 1965 law. Because the U.S. federal arrangement compounds the task of voting rights enforcement, ignorance of the behavior of local officials seriously undermines the quality of any assessment of the act's success.

This essay focuses on the implementation of Section 5 of the 1965 Voting Rights Act from two distinct perspectives. First, four of the most common myths about Section 5 enforcement will be analyzed. Second, the viewpoints of local officials who ultimately must comply with this national policy will be described. No effort to arrive at a definitive judgment about Section 5 enforcement is made in this chapter; rather the purpose of amalgamating these two disparate elements into one essay is, quite simply, an attempt to highlight several problems that plague the enforcement of voting rights policy by the DOJ.

COMMON MISPERCEPTIONS ABOUT SECTION 5 ENFORCEMENT

> MYTH 1: "Johnson's instructions as far as [drafting] that act was concerned, he said, 'I want you to write the goddamnedest toughest voting rights act that you can devise.'"

> Nicholas Katzenbach
> U.S. Attorney General[1]

The extremely radical character of the Section 5 provision has led commentators on U.S. politics to assume that the Civil Rights Division (CRD) of the Justice Department can easily enforce this national policy.[2] After all, the 1965 Voting Rights Act (P.L. 89-110) mandates that "covered jurisdictions" must submit all proposed changes in electoral rules or procedures to the U.S. Attorney General or the U.S. District Court for the District of Columbia and may not put the proposed change(s) into operation until the Attorney General or the U.S. District Court has determined that the proposed change(s) would be nondiscriminatory. In a very real sense, Congress made use of an old-fashioned administrative technique—the bottleneck or gateway—when it devised the Section 5 preclearance provisions. That is, because proposed voting changes must pass review by the federal authorities, Voting Rights Act enforcement should be an ordinary administrative chore akin to application processing typical of granting licenses or permits. A quick glance at the annual Section 5 workflow through the CRD seems to confirm the ease of enforcement: for example, in 1980, 7,340 changes were submitted to and reviewed by the DOJ and only 30 objections were interposed by the Attorney General.[3]

But enforcing Section 5 requirements is not a straightforward process; severe logistical problems must be overcome by the DOJ. Under the original 1965 provisions, the DOJ was given the responsibility to issue a federal imprimatur for all changes in electoral qualifications, practices, or procedures in all of the covered jurisdictions. The geographic area of the original covered states comprises all or parts of seven southeastern states (Alabama, Georgia, Louisiana, Mississippi, South Carolina, Virginia, and 37 counties in North Carolina). To understand the scale of the enforcement task, this region encompasses an area of more than 300,000 square miles, has a population of over 25 million, and includes 549 counties and several thousand cities, towns, villages, and special districts.[4] The 1970 and 1975 amendments to the Voting Rights Act extended voting protection and/or minority language ballot protection to citizens living in Alaska, Arizona, and Texas as well as designated portions of Connecticut, California, Colorado, Florida, Hawaii, Idaho, Kansas, Maine, Massachusetts, Michigan, Minnesota, Montana, Nebraska, Nevada, New Hampshire, New York, North Dakota, Oklahoma, South Dakota, Utah, Washington, Wisconsin, and Wyoming.[5] These recently added "covered jurisdictions" expanded the DOJ's enforcement responsibility by approximately 1 million square miles containing over 25 million persons living in 487 counties and thousands more local units of government.[6]

The job of processing Section 5 submissions from all of these governmental units falls to the attorneys and paralegal staff of the CRD's Voting Section (VS).[7] Although the Office of the Attorney General is as old as the Constitution itself, the CRD was not established until 1975. CRD attorneys were organized by geographic areas during the first four years after the passage of the 1965 Act. With the 1969 reorganization, a separate Voting Section emerged that was divided for operational purposes into a submission unit and a litigative unit (see Figure 7.1). Before the 1975 amendments, CRD attorneys reviewed voting changes with assistance from five paraprofessionals who were paired with the attorneys to serve as "law clerks." With the anticipated growth in submissions resulting from the new minority

FIGURE 7.1: Voting Section Professional and Paraprofessional Staffing as of July 1977

Chief

deputy chief[a]

Submission unit	Litigative staff
1 senior attorney advisor[b]	1 assistant for litigation
1 paraprofessional director	13 attorneys
11 paraprofessionals	2 paraprofessionals

[a]Responsible for administration of the Voting Section and election coverage activity.

[b]Also performs litigative activity.

Source: U.S. Comptroller General, General Accounting Office, Voting Rights Act—Enforcement Needs Strengthening, February 6, 1978, Appendix VI.

language provisions, Congress added six more paraprofessionals to the VS as part of a 1976 reorganization. The Department of Justice, in reaction to the 1978 GAO report criticizing DOJ enforcement of Section 5,[8] reorganized the VS's submission unit into a Section 5 Unit composed of "three teams of Equal Opportunity Specialists, each team being responsible for analyzing Section 5 submissions for a particular group of States."[9] This new alignment is an attempt at better coordination between the old submission unit and the litigative unit since "each group of States in the Section 5 unit is identical to the group of States assigned to the three teams of attorneys in the Voting Section."[10]

The CRD staffers in the Section 5 Unit receive and process each submitted electoral change and decide either to approve the proposed change or to file an objection. If an objection is interposed, then the VS's litigative unit attempts to seek compliance through the federal courts. Given the very small number of personnel assigned to the VS, one can quickly understand that, from the staff's perspective, the logistics of Section 5 enforcement pose a nearly insurmountable task. This small unit of DOJ without the aid of its own field staff must monitor the actions of thousands of public officials, often located in isolated communities, who have authority to make changes in the local electoral process. To make matters even more difficult, Section 5 requirements must be enforced in a fiscally dry environment. The 1965 act did not authorize monies that could be used to lure or induce compliance from unwilling subnational partners. Without the "financial carrots" so common to other federal policies, voting rights policy is unique because compliance cannot be purchased. Of course, the CRD could resort to disincentives such as the criminal penalties provided for in the act, but curiously the penalties have never been used! Because the CRD political leadership fears that a covered jurisdiction might win a court case overturning the penalties, the CRD prefers not to impose them, but to retain them as a bluff. Since 1975, a growing demand for the establishment of civil penalties or damages against state and local officials who violate Section 5 by implementing electoral changes without having obtained preclearance has been pushed by the U.S. Commission on Civil Rights.[11] Although various penalties were discussed during the congressional hearings on the 1982 extension of the act, new sanctions were not added.

Compounding these problems, the VS functions under a time limit uncommon in other federal programs. Because the 1965 legislation insists that submissions be acted upon within a 60-day time limit, the Section 5 Unit must gather, analyze, and verify the necessary evidence and then arrive at a decision with a speed uncharacteristic of other regulatory agencies or adjudicatory proceedings. Failure to review a submission in 60 days results in its preclearance, even if the proposed change is discriminatory. Consequently, unlike other federal bureaucrats, the Voting Section cannot delay!

What emerges from this description of the principal organizational features of the Voting Section is a portrait of an administratively hamstrung regulatory agency. Congress, in response to the bloodshed of the "Freedom Summers," passed the milestone Voting Rights Act, but provided little in the way of new resources for the act's long-term enforcement. This paucity of compliance-inducing instruments (that is, grant money, field personnel, viable penalties), when examined in the light of the logistical dimension of Section 5 enforcement, raises the obvious question of how then does the Voting Section achieve compliance? The answer can be found in addressing other misperceptions about the act's implementation.

> MYTH 2: "Because a large number of voting changes must necessarily undergo the preclearance process, centralized review enhances the likelihood that recurring problems will be resolved in a consistent and expeditious way."
>
> Drew S. Day, III
> Assistant Attorney General
> Civil Rights Division (DOJ)[12]

In its haste to draft voting rights legislation as fast as possible after the events of Selma, Congress contrived two avenues of "preclearance," but did not precisely delineate the differences between the kinds of submissions that ought to go to the D. C. court and those that should be submitted to the U. S. Attorney General. John Roman, in describing the origins of Section 5, observes that preclearance via the Attorney General was added to the act in an almost after-thought fashion.[13] The apparent congressional intent was twofold: the provision of a less expensive and less onerous method of obtaining federal approval of "simple" voting changes "susceptible" to ready appraisal and the prevention of case overload in the federal courts. Because local communities were given the option of two routes with distinctly different degrees of difficulty, the obvious result occurred—once the regulations (28 CFR 51) were published, virtually all of the proposed electoral changes were directed to the Attorney General rather than to the D.C. court. As a consequence, "the administrative route has wholly supplanted the judicial one,"[14] and the Voting Section has become the prime decision maker for Section 5 determinations.

Enforcement of the 1965 Voting Rights Act involves two interrelated but analytically separate problems that the VS staff must solve in order to insure compliance. The first problem concerns the substantive meaning of "discriminatory purpose or effect." The basic question confronted by the staff lawyers of the Voting Section (as well as all other interested parties) is devilishly complex: under what circumstances and given what characteristics should a voting change be objected to as "discriminatory"? Put another way, once the DOJ began to receive preclearance submissions, it faced the conceptual task of devising an <u>operational definition</u> of "discriminatory purpose or effect."

Instead of adopting a specific "normative" rule that would postulate an optimal "nondiscriminatory" situation, the CRD has approached this definitional problem pragmatically; that is, the determination of discrimination has evolved out of a series of standard operating procedures and discretionary judgments. With the end of the voter registration drives, the 1969 <u>Allen</u> v. <u>State Board of Elections</u> (393 U.S. 544) decision (on the types of electoral changes covered by Section 5), the 1969 reorganization of the CRD, and the 1970 extension of the VRA, the number of electoral changes submitted for preclearance rapidly increased from 255 in 1970 to 1,118 in 1971. Since 1965, for example, the VS has received about 5000 submissions each year and this volume averages to a daily workload of approximately 20 proposed changes. Given this volume of submissions coupled with the agency's shortage of personnel and its 60-day time limit, it is not surprising that the VS developed a set of routines to cope with its workload. [15]

After an initial phase that logs the submission and checks for necessary documentation, the second phase—case analysis by a paraprofessional—is pivotal because the paralegal research analysts make the initial (and typically upheld) determinations with respect to whether or not a proposed change is discriminatory. The first important point of discretion in the VS's standard operating procedure comes with the analysis of the submitted documents. Since 28 CFR 51 specifies that covered jurisdictions will transmit a copy of the proposed local ordinance or regulation and other relevant records such as census data, voter registration figures, and maps, there is room for difference of opinion about the quality of the submitted data, as well as the distinct possibility of data manipulation. In most cases, this issue does not pose a serious problem; but, in more extreme cases, the VS staff may be faced with arriving at relatively sophisticated judgments about census and registration figures that can be interpreted as "secondguessing by Washington bureaucrats."[16] The quality of the submitted information is not a trivial matter because Section 5 determinations ultimately rest on the validity of the transmitted documents. Since the covered jurisdictions bear the burden of proof, it is the local election commission or local board or council, not the VS, that gathers the necessary materials. Because the urge to engage in vote dilution has not yet died in many covered jurisdictions, the potential for biased data always exists. This is particularly true when the submission includes population estimates prepared by a city housing officer or a county engineer in the Georgia-Alabama-Mississippi black belt or by a school district official in south Texas. Once these documents reach Washington, D.C., the research analyst has the task of deciding the veracity and validity of the supporting documents. To say the least, even with U.S. census materials and standard maps, analysis at long range can, as it has on some occasions, lead to the underestimation of the local minority population.

The second major point of administrative discretion in Voting Section processing routines is the standard procedure "to telephone minority persons in the locality to see if the voting change is going to bother them."[17] To compensate in part for its lack of a field staff, the Section 5 Unit relies extensively on a file of local contacts composed of minority elected officials, minority pressure group leaders, and other informed and interested individuals to help evaluate the discriminatory impact of a proposed electoral change. The number of local minority contacts made per case varies, as one paraprofessional put it, "on the type of change—the more significant the change, the more contacts required."[18] This pool of informants can provide information not normally included in a covered jurisdiction's submission papers and also allows minority political leaders access to the Section 5 decision process that might otherwise be denied by local white officials. One consequence of this "whistleblowing" arrangement is to place the submission unit personnel in an adjudicatory role between the contending parties.

A third point of discretion in the paralegal's work takes the form of a recommendation from among four options: the submission cannot be reviewed under Section 5 at this time; additional information should be requested from the submitting authority; no objection should be interposed; or an objection should be interposed. While the VS staffer can choose among these options, it is the decision to object or not to object that is crucial to all parties. This choice, though ostensibly based on detailed information, embodies the operationalization problem. In essence, the determination of discrimination has become routinized through the adoption of some elementary decision rules. The Section 5 Unit personnel are trained to spot so-called red flags or suspicious type changes.[19] The catalogue of suspicious changes includes proposals to reduce the number of polling places or move their locations, proposals to purge election rolls and reregister voters proposals that make changes without adequate publicity or without minority participation in the decision (see Figure 7.2). Proposed changes such as these examples alert the paraprofessionals to investigate the motive behind the change and the potential impact of the change. Notice then that the investigation of motivation and impact at long-distance in often isolated jurisdictions in the Southeast and Southwest puts a premium on telephone calls to on-site persons. Yet, even after a number of contacts and examination of the extensive documentation, the operationalization of discrimination remains situational. In the words of one director of the submission unit staff, "one looks at the circumstances

FIGURE 7.2: Obstacles to Black Participation in the Electoral and Political Process

---

A. Diluting the black vote
   1. Switching to at-large elections
   2. Consolidating counties
   3. Reapportionment and redistricting measures
   4. Full-slate voting required

B. Preventing blacks from becoming candidates or obtaining office

   1. Abolishing the office
   2. Extending the term of incumbent white officials
   3. Substituting appointment for election
   4. Increase filing fees
   5. Adding requirements for getting on the ballot
   6. Withholding information or providing false information
   7. Withholding or delay of certification of nominating petition
   8. Improving barriers to the assumption of office

C. Discrimination against black registrants

   1. Exclusion from precinct meetings
   2. Omission of registered blacks from voter lists
   3. Failure to provide sufficient voting facilities
   4. Harassment of black voters by election officials
   5. Refusal to assist or permit assistance to illiterate voters
   6. Giving inadequate or erroneous information to black voters
   7. Disqualification of black ballots on technical grounds
   8. Denial of equal opportunity to vote absentee
   9. Discriminatory location of polling places
   10. Racially segregated voting facilities and voter lists

D. Exclusion of and interference with black poll watchers

E. Vote fraud

F. Discriminatory selection of election officials

G. Intimidation and economic dependence

   1. Intimidation and harassment of politically active blacks
   2. General intimidation affecting the exercise of political rights
   3. Economic dependence as a deterrent to free political activity
      by blacks

Source: U.S. Commission on Civil Rights, Political Participation (Washington, D.C.: 1968).

130

of the change: the area, the people affected, what's going to hurt the people."[20]

Because of the time involved in case analysis by Section 5 personnel (commonly an individual research analyst has anywhere from a dozen to two dozen separate submissions in various stages of progress on his/her desk at any one time), the final activity within the 60-day time limit is the most hectic. Casework by the analysts undergoes procedural and legal reviews before a final determination is made by the Section 5 Unit attorney. Simple cases like a slight revision of office hours for the official responsible for voter registration receive a basic form letter of the decision "not to object." On the other hand, complex and/or controversial cases (for example, a major annexation or redistricting) will be reviewed by the chief of the Voting Section and often by the assistant attorney general for civil rights, especially when a recommendation "to interpose an objection" is made by the Section 5 Unit.

Should the Section 5 Unit decide to seek additional information from the covered jurisdiction, a follow-up procedure is utilized that restarts the 60-day clock. If the local officials respond promptly, the submission process begins again at day one and moves once again through the routine steps. However, if the local officials should stall for more than 30 days, the VS will ask the FBI to visit the jurisdiction.

> We don't ask the FBI to get the information. If local officials try to give it to the FBI, it wouldn't count as a submission. . . . We don't ask the FBI to get the information, but to find out when it is likely to come. Chances are that it comes more quickly than it would otherwise.[21]

Although VS personnel believe that the FBI is fairly effective in stimulating a response, the 1978 and 1983 GAO reports (and my interviews of local attorneys) on voting rights enforcement suggest that local officials do not necessarily tremble and quiver before the federal "muscle."[22] Some jurisdictions, for example, have not responded in over two years after receipt of a request for additional information about a proposed voting change. Much more damaging to minority rights than lack of response is the implementation of proposed voting changes and the conduct of elections without completion of the Section 5 preclearance process.

This decision system, developed by the Voting Section in response to its Congressional mandate (and its logistical problems), consists then of some elementary decision rules that are applied on a case-by-case basis to each new submission. The individual research analysts in the Section 5 Unit learn these cognitive rules from experience rather than from any formal set of guidelines of basic principles.

By searching for red flags among the submission documents, the paralegals can process the VS's workload at a pace sufficient to meet the 60-day time limit. If any one litmus test for discrimination has emerged out of the VS's processing routines, it is the no-retrogression test that was articulated in the 1976 benchmark case of Beer v. U.S. (425 U.S. 130). In the opinion written by Justice Stewart, the Supreme Court held that the purpose of Section 5 "has always been to insure that no voting procedure changes would be made that would lead to a retrogression in the position of racial minorities with respect to their effective exercise of the electoral franchise."[23] This simply means that a proposed change that results in an improvement of the position of minority voters is not likely to be objected to even if a different voting procedure could achieve a better condition. An attorney in the Section 5 Unit concisely restated the no retrogression test: "If a change makes something better, we're not supposed to object even if it is still not very good."[24]

What appears to be most remarkable about Section 5 enforcement has been the VS's ability to foster compliance with a national policy that is still bitterly opposed in some communities. In spite of his agency's lack of compliance-inducing instruments, Gerald Jones, who has been chief of the Voting Section since its inception, claims that over 90 percent of all electoral changes are reported to the Attorney General and that those remaining unreported are the most insignificant and the least dangerous with respect to vote dilution.[25] Also, the VS has precleared almost 97 percent of the submitted changes. When seen against the history of massive resistance to voting rights policy that occurred in the 1960s, the VS's mechanical application of its processing routines seems unlikely to engender the high rate of submissions and preclearances claimed by the VS. Why should local communities under the political control of white public officials submit electoral changes? After all, the CRD cannot withhold federal dollars (for example, like the Department of Education does in school desegregation cases) and it has never imposed criminal sanctions on a recalcitrant jurisdiction. At worst, the litigative unit can file a law suit that can potentially drag on for years (which is fine with many local officials). The answer must be elsewhere than in the VS's standard operating procedures. Examination of the next common misperception about Section 5 enforcement will illustrate how the VS has encouraged such high submission rates and achieved such low objection rates.

> MYTH 3: "Local Officials Have To Go To Washington,
> Get On Their Knees, Kiss The Ring And Tug Their
> Forelock To All These Third-Rate Bureaucrats."
>
> U.S. Senator Thad Cochran (R-MS)
> April 29, 1981[26]

The most persistent misperception about Section 5 enforcement originated with Justice Hugo Black's combined concurring and dissenting opinion to South Carolina v. Katzenbach (383 U.S. 301). While Justice Black agreed with the suspension of literacy tests and other devices to deny voting rights, he objected to Section 5 on the grounds that it violated fundamental principles of U.S. federalism.

> Section 5, by providing that some of the states cannot
> pass state laws or adopt state constitutional amendments
> without first being compelled to beg federal authorities
> to approve their policies, so distorts our constitutional
> structure of government as to render any distinction
> drawn in the Constitution between state and federal power
> meaningless. . . . If all of the provisions of our Consti-
> tution which limit the power of the Federal Government
> and reserve other power to the states are to mean any-
> thing, they mean at least that the States have power to
> pass laws and amend their constitutions without first
> sending their officials hundreds of miles away to beg fed-
> eral authorities to approve them. . . . I cannot help but
> believe that the inevitable effect of any such law which
> forces any one of the states to entreat federal authorities
> in far away places for approval of local laws before they
> can become effective is to create the impression that the
> state or states treated in this way are little more than
> conquered provinces. [27]

Black's "conquered provinces" theme, of course, struck a ready chord in the deep South and has been echoed in constant protest to Section 5 implementation.

Because the Voting Rights Act does constitute a radical departure from what many believe to be the ordinary concepts of federalism, the intergovernmental dimensions of Section 5 enforcement pose a serious dilemma for the CRD.

Frederick M. Wirt, in a study of the impact of the Voting Rights Act on one Mississippi county, describes the quandary in this fashion:

> . . . [federalism] is a system devised for a multifaceted
> people upon which federal law had to impose some unity.
> Federal officials have to develop methods of adjusting
> their centralizing authority to the conflicting demands of
> a decentralized nation. If they pushed too hard, reasoned
> CRD, the South would create greater problems of enforce-
> ment, spiraling downward with diminishing compliance. [28]

Basically, the CRD was caught in the middle: on one side stood state and local officials who despised the federal presence in their jurisdictions and on the other side stood the civil rights workers who demanded action under the new law (as well as under the Constitution) rather than simply a federal "presence" and half-hearted attempts to persuade the "racists" to alter local laws so that blacks could exercise their rightful democratic franchise. A sign on the office wall of Assistant Attorney General for Civil Rights Burke Marshall summed up the national government's dilemma: "Blessed are the peacemakers—for they shall catch hell from both sides."

To escape from this quandary, CRD leadership over the past 17 years has opted for an enforcement posture that does not interfere excessively in the local policy-making processes of covered jurisdictions. Because it is a small, resource-poor enforcement unit, the VS by law depends on the covered jurisdictions to make submissions of proposed electoral changes. In response to this excessive dependence on the willingness of local officials, many of whom were and are hostile to the Voting Rights Act, the staff of the VS has tried to make the preclearance process a relatively simple and painless procedure. Drews Days, assistant attorney general for civil rights during the Carter Administration, explained this to Congress by saying:

> For while I regarded it as my central responsibility under
> the Act to ensure against changes having a discriminatory
> purpose or effect with respect to minority participation in
> the electoral process, I was also determined to carry out
> that mission in a manner that was fair to the submitting
> jurisdictions and properly respectful of the integrity of
> their local electoral processes. [29]

This concern for the integrity of local elections has been translated into an informal advice and consultative relationship between the personnel in the Section 5 Unit and the local attorneys who file preclearance requests. The following comment from the attorney in charge of the pre-1979 submission unit illustrates this preclearance counseling:

> I've worked with them [local attorneys] quite a bit. . . .
> I get involved when the counties have problems and they
> need a response from us; they need to know how to make
> a submission . . . they want to know what we are going
> to look for. They're going to revise their city charter and
> the city attorney will call me up to ask . . . and this is a
> widespread type of request . . . they have a job to do and
> they want to get our clearance . . . we'll do what we can

for them . . . we try to make things go smoothly for
them so they can hold elections.[30]

From these comments by DOJ officials who have had direct responsibility for Section 5 enforcement, one can see that the VS perceives its
principal task to be the guidance of local legal counselors (who represent the local election officials) through the details of the preclearance
process. In fact, it has become standard operating procedure for the
Section 5 Unit attorney to be telephoned by local city or county attorneys in order to obtain advice as to whether a proposed voting change
would pass muster when formally submitted.

To focus only on the processing of the legally required documents
by the paraprofessional research analysts would miss an important and
substantial portion of the interaction between the covered jurisdictions
and the Section 5 Unit. This presubmission counseling of the regulated
communities has meant that almost all submissions receive the preclearance stamp of approval; that is, the sticking points often are resolved before the formal preclearance request is mailed to the Justice
Department.

Even if there is a possibility of an objection interposed by the
Attorney General, the enforcement of Section 5 remains a cooperative
venture between lawyers because of the focus on legal procedures inherent in voting rights policy and because of the restraining force of
the legal profession's behavioral norms. At times, some jurisdictions
have simply refused to enact a voting change because they could not
come to a workable preclearance agreement with CRD attorneys. While
such a situation may produce an objection and may even wind up in federal court, nevertheless, the litigative unit doggedly pursues a course
of informal bargaining. From the perspective of a VS staff attorney,
this fraternal relationship is a key element in the compliance process:

> It's generally not an emotional thing. They have their
> clients and we have our client. Lawyers tend to be fairly
> friendly usually, even if they're on opposite sides. I'm
> handling a case now in _____ County and the lawyers
> on the other side and I get along fine together; we don't
> have a whole lot in common. It's not like I think they are
> immoral people because they are defending a jurisdiction
> that wants to have an at-large election.[31]

The rationale behind the VS's enforcement strategy based on the discussion of proposed voting changes and the counseling of covered
jurisdictions prior to the submission of a preclearance request is
twofold: the reduction of local officials' resistance to Section 5 requirements and the reduction of alienation between local officials and

federal officials. By adopting an almost fraternal relationship between
professionals, the VS staff believe they maximize the level of compliance with the act. As one local attorney in a Mississippi town that
has benefitted from this type of fraternal advice states: "It's easier
to work with them [the Voting Section staff] than with the electric
power company."

> MYTH 4: "Blacks have a toll-free line to the Justice
> Department . . . and some blacks make a career out
> of informing for the Department of Justice."
>
> Mayor of a deep South city

Anyone perusing southern newspapers will find headlines an-
nouncing a civil rights group's public opposition to a proposed change
in the local electoral process. Typically, the accompanying story details the organization's open threat(s) to inform the Justice Department
about the discriminatory effect of the proposed change. During the
review of the preclearance decision steps, it was noted that the research analysts rely heavily on local whistleblowers to help them (in
lieu of a field staff) spot discriminatory changes. As a member of the
Section 5 Unit explained:

> It doesn't seem likely that there are a whole lot of very
> discriminatory changes out there that haven't been sub-
> mitted. There might be some. . . . If there were real
> big problems, I think we would have heard about them.
> . . . If they're really controversial like that, they'll get
> caught quickly by civil rights groups.[32]

But despite all the VS's efforts to aid the covered jurisdictions obtain
a preclearance, the CRD still labors under allegations that it acts as
a lackey of the civil rights organizations. On the other side of the political battle line, the U.S. Commission on Civil Rights has stated
bluntly, "Minority political strength, despite progress under the Voting
Rights Act, is not yet able to prevent structural changes that limit the
effectiveness of that strength."[33] A closer look at the VS's communication links with the covered jurisdictions can help us understand more
fully the persistence of these contradictory views.

Without a doubt, a major source of action devoted to preventing
vote dilution has been private civil rights groups who have become
quite sophisticated about Section 5 requirements and have used 28
CFR 51 to their advantage. In addition to the permanent registry of
local contacts who are telephoned by the research analysts, the VS
publishes a weekly listing of submissions that is available to anyone

upon request. The recipients of the weekly submissions list are not necessarily the same as the VS's primary local contacts. Although the weekly list is intended to elicit local opinion as to the effect of a proposed voting change, the sparse information on the weekly list (date, type of change, and name of jurisdiction) presumes that the individual scanning the list understands the situation from this skeletal description and will either mail or telephone to DOJ an informed opinion about the proposed change.

In 1978, the GAO issued a report on the DOJ's enforcement of the Voting Rights Act. [34] One of the serious enforcement shortcomings identified in the report was the VS's system of communications with local election officials and local minority representatives. The 1978 GAO report, in the section devoted to communication with local officials, noted that local attorneys who must initiate the preclearance process for the covered jurisdictions do not possess copies of the relevant regulations and that they also have difficulty interpreting the regulations once they obtain copies. Since effective enforcement of national policy in a federal system depends in part on the capacity of national officers to transmit the necessary information (for example, the federal regulations) in a clear, consistent, and understandable manner, failure to insure that the appropriate local officials receive and comprehend procedural rules can easily shortcircuit enforcement by creating a legitimate alibi for noncompliance. To assume that local attorneys, hired typically on a case-by-case basis, can inform themselves about the law or know enough to even telephone the VS is not justified. Culpable ignorance of Section 5 procedures may be inexcusable in Atlanta, Georgia, or in Charleston, South Carolina; but in more typical Southeastern towns, like Smut Eye, Alabama, or Chunky, Mississippi, where many minority citizens live, the Federal Register may not be available in the local library, if a library in fact exists!

The Civil Rights Division initiated a number of actions designed to remedy the enforcement flaws identified by the 1978 GAO report. Examples of these actions include a letter sent in 1978 to the municipal league of each state with a covered county explaining Section 5 requirements, the assistant attorney general for the CRD spoke to the 1980 National Conference of State Legislatures, and revised Section 5 guidelines were promulgated in 1981. [35] Unfortunately, two of these three actions were not directly aimed at local officials and the third action did not cope with the isolation and/or resistance of many covered jurisdictions.

Despite the weaknesses inherent in the use of local whistleblowers, the Justice Department continues to rely on the actions of private individuals and groups to ferret our noncompliance with Section 5. In a letter commenting on the draft version of GAO's 1983 investigation of Section 5 enforcement, Assistant Attorney General for Administration (DOJ) Kevin D. Rooney wrote:

There are several means being used by the Department
to obtain disclosure of noncompliance with Section 5. One
of the first decisions by the Supreme Court with respect
to the Voting Rights Act recognized that there is a private
right of action for individuals to enforce Section 5 by
bringing lawsuits to enjoin the use of unprecleared voting
changes. . . . Such actions by private individuals always
have been an important element in assuring compliance
with Section 5, and we encourage the continued filing of
Section 5 enforcement suits by others as well as the Department.

   As another information source, we always have
sought, and have found indispensable, information from
civil rights organizations regarding violations of federal
civil rights laws. This is particularly true with respect
to jurisdictions preparing to use, or using, new voting
practices that are subject to Section 5 but have not been
precleared. Members of the Civil Rights Division routinely
speak with staff members of civil rights organizations
about situations involving possible violations of the Voting
Rights Act in general, and about specific submissions
under Section 5.

   In addition to the above, at every opportunity the
Department has encouraged civil rights organizations to
provide information on violations of federal civil rights
laws, and we believe most organizations have done so
with one notable exception: as the GAO report notes, for
over two years the Southern Regional Council claims to
have had information on numerous changes which have
not been submitted for preclearance, but they have provided information on only 47 of those changes. Since the
Southern Regional Council has not responded to our several requests for information, we welcome any suggestions on how this information might be obtained. [36]

The 1983 GAO document on voting rights enforcement, just as its 1978
predecessor, pointed out problems associated with DOJ's belief that
procedures for monitoring compliance with objections to voting change
submissions did not require revision. As the new GAO study states:

   Even though Justice has taken positive steps to improve
   its enforcement efforts, areas still exist that need Justice's attention. These are summarized below and detailed
   on the following pages.

—Jurisdictions have implemented changes without first
obtaining preclearance from the Justice Department.
—Jurisdictions have implemented changes that Justice
has objected to.
—All data required by Justice regulations was not being
submitted by jurisdictions to support proposed changes.

As a result of the above problems, we believe Justice needs to modify its procedures so as to enhance the
enforcement of the Act's requirements that (1) all covered jurisdictions submit changes for preclearance and
(2) jurisdictions do not implement changes over Justice's
objections. [37]

The 1983 GAO report goes on to itemize several tactics that DOJ could
initiate to improve its enforcement of Section 5.

One piece of information extremely germane to this debate between GAO and DOJ is the perspective of minority group leaders. As
part of its research for the 1978 report, GAO conducted interviews
of 31 minority organization officials in 11 states. [38] The survey found
that 35 percent of the minority leaders lacked knowledge about DOJ
preclearance procedures and over 90 percent said they were not on
the VS's mailing list—over half were unaware of its existence! Approximately 25 percent stated that they knew of unreported changes and
most felt that these unreported changes were significant enough to
cause concern in the local community. After sampling the records of
the preclearance requests, GAO discovered that minority persons
commented on 55 percent of the submissions, but local minority groups
were informed of the VS's review decision in less than 1 percent of
cases sampled.

Part of the sense of removal from the process felt by minority
group leaders can be attributed to the flawed assumption that the weekly
list of submissions is an adequate stimulus for generating informed
local opinion. Even if an individual receives the weekly notice and
discovers that his/her jurisdiction has made a submission, the opinion
may well be too late. First, the local government body most likely
will have worked out the necessary political accommodations among
its own members and will have discussed the proposed change with
an attorney in the Section 5 Unit prior to submission. Obviously, a
certain amount of inertia and sunk costs will have been built up that
will be hard to overturn; that is, the parameters of any proposed
change may well be firmly set before interested parties become informed of the proposed change. Second, reliance on local minority
contacts as whistleblowers also assumes that they can participate in
the local decision processes and/or can gain sufficient knowledge about

the proposed change. With city councils still meeting in executive session or county boards meeting in the county's record storage vault to avoid local reporters, [39] it may be very difficult, if not impossible, for minority leaders to have a voice in the local decision process. This situation has been a constant complaint by the U.S. Commission on Civil Rights.

All of these comments and observations about communication between the covered jurisdictions and the CRD lead to a critical feature of the preclearance process—the Voting Section has developed a two-track system of communication with the covered jurisdictions. The parallel streams of information are not strictly formal channels; rather two routes have evolved from the Section 5 Unit's division of labor and sequence of work. One track consists of the fraternal relationship between local attorneys and the Section 5 attorneys. While this track has grown to carry the bulk of the formal relationship between the covered jurisdictions and the CRD (that is, the submission letter and supporting documents), it is the presubmission counseling and negotiation fostered by the norms of the legal profession that set the tone of communication in this track. A second communication track connects the research analysts in the Section 5 Unit with the local minority contacts for the purpose of spotting red flags. These local minority contacts do provide valuable information about proposed electoral changes that are announced publically. But one should not presume that local election officials and minority leaders are in communication with each other; the obstacles put in the path of minority group representatives by some local election officials mean that this second track often may be late with its assessment of a proposed change and even worse, this second track may be silent about a preclearance submission.

By building two separate and parallel pipelines to the covered jurisdictions, the VS not only has streamlined the flow of submissions, but it also has created a relatively low-cost system for monitoring local electoral activity. These two considerations bear directly on the issue of compliance. Since Section 5 preclearance procedure is not an immensely popular requirement among officials in the covered jurisdictions, the VS's advice and counseling posture toward local attorneys serves as an inducement to submit. By minimizing the paperwork and procedural hassle, the VS eases the pain of preclearance. The 1978 GAO investigation indicates that local attorneys do not find the administrative costs, staffing requirements, or preparation time of Section 5 procedures to be an obstacle to reporting changes. [40] On the other hand, by maintaining the permanent registry of local minority contacts, the VS has access to an extensive number of locally based watchdogs who can ensure that many (but not all) local election officials will submit voting changes for preclearance. Although numerous cases exist

where voting changes have been submitted and then have been precleared without the knowledge of local minority leaders, nevertheless,
a majority of the covered jurisdictions make submissions because
their officials want to obey the law, "even if it isn't a law they have
chosen themselves."[41]

This review of four common misperceptions about DOJ's enforcement of Section 5 preclearance requirements helps account for
the conflicting assessments of the 1965 Voting Rights Act. On the one
hand, the Department of Justice, by enforcing a national mandate in
regard to voting rights, has made considerable progress in the reduction of most blatant techniques of minority vote denial and dilution.
On the other hand, the Department of Justice, through its advice and
counseling posture with covered jurisdictions, sometimes has sacri-
ficed full redress of minority vote dilution to the maintenance of fraternal working relationships with local election officials. In a sense,
the covered jurisdictions have not so much been conquered as they
have been courted to become reluctant partners in a bargain. The willingness of DOJ policy directors to foster negotiations between local
officials, the staff of the Voting Section, and sometimes local minority
representatives helps soften the sting of enforcement, but the implementation of this policy also results in the preclearance of voting
changes that create electoral arrangements that do not fully represent
the proportion of minority citizens in a covered jurisdiction.

SUBNATIONAL OFFICIALS: THE MISSING LINK
IN VOTING RIGHTS POLICY

Since the passage of the Voting Rights Act in 1965, the political
leadership in the Civil Rights Division has believed that "the Justice
Department has neither the personnel nor the resources to become
the primary enforcer of the Voting Rights Act."[42] Trapped in the
crossfire from segregationists and civil rights marchers, Burke
Marshall and Nicholas Katzenbach adopted an enforcement strategy
in 1965-66 that relied on "the smallest possible federal intrusion into
the conduct of state affairs"[43] and tried "to avoid at all costs an oc-
cupation of the South by federal troops, lawyers, registrars, and
marshalls."[44] Instead, successful implementation would depend not
only on measured actions by the national government, but also on responsible subnational officials acting out of respect for the national
law and on the political pressure of locally-situated black citizens.
Assistant Attorney General Drew Days III reiterated this same enforcement posture in 1981 during his testimony before the House Judiciary subcommittee on civil and constitutional rights.

> . . . it might be appropriate that we explain, generally,
> how we view the role of the Civil Rights Division in en-
> forcing the Voting Rights Act. We are an enforcement
> agency—that is, we are charged with the responsibility
> for enforcing the Voting Rights Act through preclearance
> procedures, litigation, and examiner-observer activities—
> but we do not have sole responsibility for vindicating vot-
> ing rights [emphasis added]. Under the Voting Rights Act
> we share that responsibility with private litigants, as
> well as with the very jurisdictions subject to the Act. . . .
> It was never contemplated that an official of the federal
> government would be on hand in each jurisdiction to pre-
> vent violations of this act. While we do have a substantial
> role in monitoring compliance, it is impossible for a unit
> [the Voting Section] which consists of 17 attorneys and 15
> paralegals to be looking over the shoulder of officials in
> some 1,115 jurisdictions.[45]

"Shared responsibility," Days argued, was in accord with original
congressional intent.

Sharing the compliance responsibility with local political forces—
blacks and other disenfranchised minorities and the white election
officials—makes eminent sense for a small, resource-poor enforcement unit like the Voting Section. By having "the target population pass
through a central point rather than having to be sought out by the con-
trollers,"[46] Voting Section personnel and their political managers
can concentrate their scarce resources on the maintenance of a relatively easy-to-use system of preclearance for Section 5 submissions.
Simply put, it is up to local black and white political leaders to work
out their differences to the satisfaction of both parties before the covered jurisdiction files for a Section 5 preclearance. As described in
the previous section, the CRD will make its staff available to give
advice and counsel to local attorneys. The voting change(s) submission, embodying the locally hammered out compromise, then will be
routinely approved by the U.S. Attorney General. The key presumption and the catch-22 in CRD's "shared responsibility" enforcement
strategy is the belief that there will be a viable minority political
community in place in each jurisdiction (over 7,000, not 1,115) covered by the act. Furthermore, the DOJ assumes that this local minority political force, acting as a countervailing power in the city or
county, will be able to dissuade local white leaders from taking actions
to dilute the minority franchise. Unfortunately, if this critical minority political force is absent or unorganized, then the DOJ's "stamp of
approval" posture comes to rest only on the "good faith" belief that
southern election officials possess the volition to uphold the Voting

Rights Act despite the continuing resistance to the law by some elements in the white population.

Given the DOJ's "shared responsibility" philosophy of enforcement, it is curious to discover that the debate over the merits of voting rights policy has not been illuminated by the perspective of those officials in the covered jurisdictions who must actually abide by the 1965 Voting Rights Act. Section 5 regulations state that a preclearance submission must be made "by an appropriate official" of the "submitting authority" (28 CFR Part 51.2). Typically, the "submitting authority"—be it a municipality, school or utility district, or a county—employs a local attorney, often hired on a case-by-case basis, to act as "the appropriate official."[47] Other than the 1978 GAO Report, the crucially relevant views of these city/county attorneys generally have been ignored. As part of a larger study of Section 5 implementation,[48] a mail survey of Georgia and Mississippi city/county attorneys was conducted in 1980 to fill this information gap.[49] The responses to the inquiries provide interesting glimpses into the attitudes and behavior of local level officials who must initiate the preclearance process. While the images drawn from this limited survey capture only certain aspects of the complete enforcement process, the answers of the local attorneys nevertheless reveal much about their own compliance behavior and thus permit some basis for appraising the degree of protection for minority franchise that is possible through "shared responsibility."

For purposes of analysis, the responses of the city/county attorneys have been grouped into categories that reflect the percentage of black citizens in a given jurisdiction. This arrangement was adopted because the effect of Section 5 protection varies with the proportional size of the minority population. That is, at one extreme where only a small number of black citizens live in a community (less than 25 percent), there is little that the DOJ can do, other than prevent vote denial, to enhance a minority population's impact on local electoral decisions. The converse is true at the other end of the population spectrum; where black citizens constitute a sizeable majority (above 60 percent) and are politically organized, the need for DOJ assistance diminishes. But in communities where black citizens are not dominant but constitute a viable political force (25-60 percent), electoral politics has become an intense struggle fought many times along racial lines.

Because Section 5 enforcement hinges on the local attorneys' knowledge of federal policy and procedures, the sources of information about the act directly condition compliance. Table 7.1 provides an overview of the intergovernmental communication process between the covered jurisdictions and Washington, D.C. as perceived by those city/county attorneys who personally have filed preclearance requests (59.2 percent).[50] While almost two-thirds of the attorneys who have filed submissions stated that the DOJ had sent them information about

TABLE 7.1: Sources of Information about Section Procedures[a]

Percent City/County Attorneys in Agreement with Statement	Percent Minority Population in Jurisdiction					
	100-60	59-50	49-40	39-25	24-0	Totals
Personally submitted a preclearance request	58.8 (17)	91.7 (12)	63.6 (22)	61.0 (41)	42.4 (33)	59.2 (125)
For city/county attorneys who have submitted a preclearance request:						
DOJ has sent information about submission procedures	50.0 (10)	45.5 (11)	71.4 (14)	60.0 (25)	85.7 (14)	63.5 (74)
DOJ was jurisdiction's primary source of information about VRA	30.0 (10)	36.4 (10)	35.7 (14)	64.0 (25)	64.2 (14)	50.0 (74)
DOJ assistance was:						
a) adequate	60.0	45.5	50.0	72.0	64.3	60.8
b) inadequate	40.0 (9)	54.5 (11)	50.0 (14)	28.0 (25)	35.7 (14)	39.2 (74)
Knowledge of DOJ standards for evaluating Section 5 submissions:						
a) familiar with standards	11.1	18.2	35.7	24.0	7.7	20.8
b) unsure or unaware of standards	88.9 (9)	81.8 (11)	64.3 (14)	76.0 (25)	92.3 (13)	79.2 (72)

[a]Georgia and Mississippi attorneys.

Note: Numbers in parentheses indicate percentage base.

144

the act, only 50.0 percent of these attorneys with preclearance experience said that the DOJ was their primary source of information about VRA procedures. Open-ended comments about sources of information indicate that approximately 45 percent of the city/county attorneys who have made Section 5 requests did not receive any information from the DOJ prior to the submission and instead relied on their state's attorney general for advice.[51] Of those attorneys who had made Section 5 submissions, about 60.8 percent rated the assistance they received from the DOJ as "adequate" or "more than adequate." The principal complaints with DOJ's assistance include: lack of timely reply; ambiguous answers to questions; and difficulty in identifying the appropriate official within DOJ.[52]

Since the burden of proof under Section 5 procedures is on the submitting authority, officials in the covered jurisdictions ought to know what counts as evidence of nondiscriminatory changes. Kenneth Culp Davis has argued that administrative actions should be subject to predetermined or prospective rules that are known in advance by the affected parties.[53] With almost 80 percent of the city/county attorneys who have filed submissions stating that they were either "unsure" or "unaware" of the CRD's standards for Section 5 determinations, it is apparent that many local attorneys remain misinformed and perplexed about the 1965 Act and Section 5 rules.

Turning to the actual steps taken to obtain a preclearance, Table 7.2 indicates that a majority of the attorneys (60.8 percent) with preclearance experience contacted DOJ prior to filing a submission. As suggested by the comments of the Voting Section staff (see previous section), local attorneys telephone (56.7 percent) and/or write (32.8 percent) Washington to seek "guidelines" and discuss points of difference. Materials accompanying a submission usually include a copy of the local ordinance and other pertinent records such as census data, voter registration figures, and maps. Beyond these typically included items, some Section 5 submissions also contain reports from consultants, court proceedings, resolutions of the city council or county board, and occasionally even statements of support from local minority group leaders. Once a submission has been sent to the U.S. Attorney General, it is not surprising to learn that a majority (58.0 percent) of the city/county attorneys continue to track its progress by contacting the Voting Section while the submission is under review.

Another crucial component of compliance concerns the conduct of elections prior to approval of a preclearance request. Despite the claims of the Voting Section that such elections are not a serious problem,[54] over one-third of the city/county attorneys who have personally made submissions assert that elections have proceeded in their jurisdictions while Section 5 submissions were still under review. This subnational disregard for federal procedures calls into question the

TABLE 7.2: Actions Taken to Comply with Section 5 Preclearance Requirement[a]

Percent City/County Attorneys in Agreement with Statement	Percent Minority Population in Jurisdiction					Totals
	100–60	59–50	49–40	39–25	24–0	
Communicated with DOJ prior to a Section 5 submission	60.0	45.5	78.6	60.9	56.3	60.8
	(10)	(11)	(14)	(25)	(14)	(74)
Communication prior to a Section 5 submission via:						
a) letter	12.5	28.6	42.1	25.0	41.2	32.8
b) telephone	75.0	71.4	52.6	62.5	41.2	56.7
c) personal visit	12.5	0.0	5.3	6.3	5.9	6.0
d) State Attorney General	0.0	0.0	0.0	0.0	5.9	1.5
e) U.S. Congressman	0.0	0.0	0.0	6.3	5.9	3.0
	(8)	(7)	(19)	(16)	(17)	(67)
Materials included in Section 5 submission:[b]						
a) local ordinance	60.0	81.8	92.8	72.0	71.4	75.7
b) census data	10.0	27.3	57.1	48.0	57.1	43.2
c) voter registration data	50.0	36.4	78.6	72.0	71.4	64.8
d) maps	40.0	54.5	78.6	68.0	92.8	68.9
e) report by consultant	20.0	9.1	57.1	8.0	14.3	20.3
f) statement by local citizen group(s)	30.0	18.2	21.4	28.0	28.6	25.7
g) other	30.0	36.4	42.9	20.0	35.7	31.1
	(24)	(29)	(60)	(79)	(52)	(244)
Contacted DOJ while Section 5 submission was still pending	50.0	45.5	64.3	71.4	53.8	58.0
	(10)	(11)	(14)	(21)	(13)	(69)
Election proceeded while Section 5 submission was still pending	44.4	30.0	50.0	36.8	35.7	36.4
	(9)	(10)	(14)	(19)	(14)	(66)

[a]Georgia and Mississippi attorneys.
[b]Multiple responses allowed.

effectiveness of the DOJ's ability to monitor local election officials.
In fact, improvement of DOJ's ability to discover elections that proceeded while a submission was pending is one of the principal recommendations for strengthening Section 5 enforcement made by the 1978
GAO report and again by the 1983 GAO report. Despite the GAO's
sharp criticism on this point, the DOJ has continued to deny that it
is guilty of faulty monitoring.[55]

A collateral problem to monitoring elections that proceed while
a submission is pending arises out of a covered jurisdiction's deliberate inaction on electoral changes. When asked about the manner of
elections in the city or county and the length of time that this form of
election had been used, those local attorneys who had never filed a
preclearance request (40 percent) typically answered with responses
like "50 years" or "forever." This suggests that many jurisdictions
simply have ignored the 1965 Voting Rights Act by not modifying their
election laws or procedures. Put bluntly, in this type of governmental
unit, local white political power holders have decided to defend the
status quo ante in the hope of outlasting the lifespan of the 1965 Voting
Rights Act.[56]

For all of the Voting Section's work to make the submission process convenient, the feeling of federal intrusion into local affairs persists. Close to 70 percent of the local attorneys who have participated
in the submission process claim that the DOJ asked them for additional
information above and beyond that incorporated in the jurisdiction's
original submission documents. The sense of intrusion is heightened
by the CRD's necessary modus operandi of validating submission materials through its institutionalized network of local minority contacts.
To counter-balance its lack of field staff, the Voting Section maintains
a permanent registry of minority officials, minority group leaders,
and other informed citizens to help evaluate the impact of a proposed
voting change. White officials, as indicated in Table 7.3, are quite
aware of this monitoring linkage between the Voting Section and local
black community groups.

From the viewpoint of the local attorneys, the Voting Section's
adherence or nonadherence to the legislatively mandated 60-day time
limit for notification also exacerbates the sense of federal intrusion.
While just half of the attorneys who have submitted preclearance requests (50.7 percent) said they received word of the U.S. Attorney
General's decision by the sixtieth day, the other half claimed notification arrived after the legal deadline, with some letters (4.1 percent)
arriving more than four months after the proposed voting change was
submitted. Much of this irritation stems from confusion on the part
of local attorneys over the tolling of the 60-day period. Georgia v.
United States (411 U.S. 526, 1973) permits the clock to be restarted
whenever the U.S. Attorney General requests additional information
and that information is returned to Washington, D.C.

TABLE 7.3: Perceptions of DOJ Preclearance Policy[a]

Percent City/County Attorneys in Agreement with Statement	Percent Minority Population in Jurisdiction					
	100–60	59–50	49–40	39–25	24–0	Totals
DOJ has requested more information about initial submission of preclearance documents	50.0 (10)	70.0 (10)	85.7 (14)	68.0 (25)	64.3 (14)	68.5 (73)
DOJ has sought information from sources outside your office	77.8 (9)	50.0 (10)	85.7 (14)	100.0 (15)	64.3 (14)	77.4 (62)
DOJ has sent an officer to your jurisdiction to seek more information	0.0 (10)	9.1 (11)	21.4 (14)	16.7 (24)	7.1 (14)	12.3 (73)
DOJ has suggested:						
a) significant revision(s)	10.0	20.0	16.7	23.5	16.7	18.1
b) minor revisions, if any	90.0 (10)	80.0 (10)	83.3 (12)	76.5 (17)	83.3 (12)	81.9 (61)
DOJ has informed your jurisdiction of its decision in:						
a) 60 days or less	60.0	72.7	35.7	52.4	53.8	50.7
b) 61–90 days	30.0	9.1	28.6	28.6	23.1	23.3
c) 91–120 days	10.0	18.2	28.6	14.3	15.4	21.9
d) 121 days or more	0.0 (10)	0.0 (11)	7.1 (14)	4.8 (21)	7.7 (13)	4.1 (73)

[a]Georgia and Mississippi attorneys who personally have submitted a preclearance request.

TABLE 7.4: Interposition of an Objection to a Voting Change[a]

Percent City/County Attorneys in Agreement with Statement	Percent Minority Population in Jurisdiction					Totals
	100-60	59-50	49-40	39-25	24-0	
Has the U.S. Attorney General ever imposed an objection	6.3 (16)	25.0 (12)	30.4 (23)	11.8 (34)	5.9 (34)	14.3 (119)
for jurisdictions under an imposed objection:						
DOJ provided detailed information in support of their objection	0.0 (1)	0.0 (3)	0.0 (7)	50.0 (4)	0.0 (2)	11.7 (17)
The objection has been resolved	0.0 (1)	67.0 (3)	57.0 (7)	75.0 (4)	50.0 (2)	58.8 (17)
Elections proceeded while an objection was still pending	0.0 (1)	33.0 (3)	71.4 (7)	25.0 (4)	50.0 (2)	47.0 (17)

[a]Georgia and Mississippi attorneys.

Even though confusion exists in the federal-local understanding about the timing of the 60-day clock, the usual Section 5 decision, even if it arrives late by local perceptions, is either one of approval or of approval contingent upon one or two minor revisions. DOJ's concern for the integrity of local election processes is substantiated by the high proportion (81 percent) of proposed voting changes approved without significant revision. Both the responses to open-ended questions and in-depth interviews with CRD personnel confirm that the Voting Section's presubmission counseling and guidance of local attorneys is actually a form of intergovernmental negotiation that usually resolves problems prior to the submission of the formal request for preclearance. Wholesale revisions occur rather infrequently (19 percent) and tend to be concentrated among the submissions from racially divided "battleground" jurisdictions (that is, those communities with a minority population in the 25-60 percent range). The lesson for covered jurisdictions is straightforward; when the presubmission communication process breaks down (or is not attempted), the likelihood of significant revisions in a submission increases.

Although the U.S. Attorney General, through February 1981, interposed only 815 objections to some 35,000 voting changes submitted since 1965 (2.3 percent rate), objections to submissions from Georgia (17.4 percent) and Mississippi (11.9 percent) jurisdictions were considerably higher.[57] Election changes that most commonly have engendered objections are method of election (41.3 percent) and annexations (29.9 percent).[58] Besides the substantive disagreement over the discriminatory effect of a proposed voting change, city/county attorneys expressed strong dislike for the DOJ's handling of the objection process. Attorneys representing covered jurisdictions that had experienced an objection uniformly were upset by the DOJ's failure to explain or justify satisfactorily the basis for the interposition of an objection. While the number of cases in Table 7.4 is quite small, the exasperation is evident. Explanatory comments by attorneys (for example, "I do not recall any reasons being cited" or "DOJ said it would adversely affect members of the minority race") make it clear that the local attorneys felt that they were not being adequately informed of the reasons for an objection. Eventually, most objections are resolved, yet about half of the jurisdictions under an objection (47.0 percent), according to their attorneys, proceeded with elections prior to the removal of the objection. It is possible to consider these few cases as part of the imperfections associated with any enforcement responsibility; on the other hand, these outright violations of the 1965 Act confirm the GAO's allegations that CRD fails to follow-up on objections.

COMPROMISED COMPLIANCE

If one combines the review of misperceptions about Section 5 enforcement procedures with the responses to the survey of local attorneys in Georgia and Mississippi, what can be said in summary about the compliance of covered jurisdictions and their "appropriate officials" with respect to Section 5 requirements? As mentioned earlier in this essay, the VS staff believes that their enforcement strategy results in the submission of over 90 percent of all voting changes. Unfortunately, the data from this survey do not permit a direct test of this contention. Nevertheless, the figures in Table 7.5 are suggestive, especially when viewed within the context of southern white hostility to minority political power and the ingenious and tenacious efforts of some local election officials to frustrate the purpose of the Voting Rights Act.

TABLE 7.5: Section 5 Compliance Behavior by City/County Attorneys[a] (in percent)

Attorney has personally made a submission	59.2
Attorney has not made a submission, but knows jurisdiction has made a submission since August 1965	11.2
Attorney has not made a submission nor knows if jurisdiction has made a submission since August 1965	29.6
	100.0
	(125)

[a]Georgia and Mississippi attorneys.

Of the attorneys who responded to the questionnaire, approximately 60 percent stated that they personally had filed one or more proposed electoral changes with the U.S. Attorney General. Jurisdictions represented by these attorneys are probably in compliance with the act. Another group of attorneys (11.2 percent) had not personally filed a preclearance request, but stated that their jurisdiction had made submissions since 1965. This set of jurisdictions also is probably in compliance with Section 5. The remaining attorneys (29.6 percent) did not file preclearance requests nor were they aware of any submissions made by their jurisdictions. Election law changes—especially inasmuch as they are construed so broadly by the Justice Department—typically occur frequently in cities and counties. It seems quite likely that many of the jurisdictions in this latter category—comprising almost one-third of the total—have in fact made such changes and have not reported them to the Attorney General. If this is the case in even half of these jurisdictions, then there is a larger noncompliance rate in these two states than the 10 percent overall rate estimated by the CRD.

In addition to outright noncompliance by failing to tender required submissions, there is a strong likelihood that some of these covered jurisdictions have remained in compliance precisely to frustrate the purpose of the act. In other words, discriminatory voting procedures may have been in place at the time the 1965 act was signed and officials deliberately have chosen not to modify local electoral practices because to do so would mean that the change would have to be precleared.[59] Prior to the 1982 renewal of the VRA, this strategy was secure from DOJ action; but with the revision of Section 2, this deliberate avoidance of electoral change now can be challenged by the Voting Section.

A second conclusion suggested by the data is that some local attorneys have learned to play the Section 5 preclearance game to the full advantage of their jurisdiction. Table 7.2 indicates that 36.4 percent of the local attorneys said that their communities went ahead with elections even though a preclearance request was still pending. While this may partly indicate ignorance of correct procedures under 28 CFR 51, it also seems to reflect a rational strategy by which attorneys presented the Voting Section with a fait accompli and gambled (with very good odds) that the CRD's solicitude for smoothly working local election processes would override any decision to abort the election. Other attorneys, it was discovered during the survey, withheld contemplated voting changes until a week or two before the upcoming election in a "brinkmanship" strategy to take advantage of the VS's posture of accommodation. In still other cases, local attorneys followed a strategy of protracted negotiations over minute details of a preclearance request of interposed objection. Their goals were to delay as long as possible any change in the local political status quo and to obtain through attrition the smallest amount of change acceptable as nondiscriminatory. While this short list of compliance games played by local attorneys is not exhaustive, each strategy falls under the aegis of Section 5 and thus the Voting Section staff must constantly develop counterstrategies.

These avoidance activities exemplify the basic shortcoming inherent in an enforcement philosophy of shared responsibility. To compensate for the minimal resources provided for by Congress to enforce the 1965 Voting Rights Act, the Department of Justice had to devise an enforcement procedure that relied heavily on the good faith of state and local officials to uphold national policy, even one that these local officials themselves strongly disliked. Prevented from constructing a far-reaching and powerful enforcement organization, the Civil Rights Division translated the 1965 Voting Rights Act into a series of regularized procedures—the preclearance process—that eased the costs of compliance for the local officials throughout the area of the covered jurisdictions and also reduced the costs of enforcement for the DOJ. Unfortunately, shared responsibility, while lowering the price of Section 5 enforcement, has not purchased a correspondingly reasonable supply of compliance with the 1965 Voting Rights Act. This trade-off between vigorous enforcement of Section 5 and the maintenance of amicable relationships with local officials traps Voting Section personnel in an administrative quandary that allows local election officials to exploit the Section 5 process to the detriment of the minority franchise.

NOTES

1. Howell Raines, My Soul Is Rested: Movement Days in the Deep South Remembered (New York: Bantam Books, 1978), p. 371.

2. For example, see James C. Harvey, Black Civil Rights During the Johnson Administration (Jackson, MS: University and College Press of Mississippi, 1973), pp. 155-167, and Milton D. Morris, The Politics of Black America (New York: Harper and Row, 1975), pp. 161-163.

3. U.S. Commission on Civil Rights, The Voting Rights Act: Unfulfilled Goals (Washington, D.C.: September, 1981), pp. 183-184.

4. U.S. Bureau of the Census, Statistical Abstract of the United States (Washington, D.C., 1981).

5. U.S. Commission on Civil Rights, The Voting Rights Act: Unfulfilled Goals, pp. 264-267.

6. Statistical Abstract of the United States.

7. Much of the detailed description of the internal operation and organization of the Civil Rights Division and its Section 5 enforcement activities presented in this essay is drawn from Howard Ball, Dale Krane, and Thomas P. Lauth, Compromised Compliance: Implementation of the 1965 Voting Rights Act (Westport, CN: Greenwood Press, 1982). This monograph contains a complete set of sources for the materials and statements made in this essay. Other than the specific quotations and data found in this text, the reader should consult Compromised Compliance for sources relevant to particular items.

8. U.S. Comptroller General, General Accounting Office, Voting Rights Act—Enforcement Needs Strengthening (Washington, D.C.: February 6, 1978).

9. U.S. Comptroller General, General Accounting Office, Justice Can Further Improve Its Monitoring of Changes in State/Local Voting Laws (Washington, D.C.: December 19, 1983), p. 43.

10. Ibid. The CRD also established in 1983 a fourth team of attorneys to be responsible for litigation under the revised version of Section 2 of the 1982 extension of the Voting Rights Act.

11. U.S. Commission on Civil Rights, The Voting Rights Act: Ten Years After (Washington, D.C.: January, 1975), pp. 331-347.

12. Drew Days, III, Testimony on the Extension of the Voting Rights Act, Subcommittee on Civil and Constitutional Rights, House Committee on the Judiciary, Washington, D.C., July, 1981.

13. John J. Roman, "Section 5 of the VRA: The Formation of an Extraordinary Federal Remedy," American University Law Review, 22 (1972): 111-133.

14. David H. Hunter, The Shameful Blight: The Survival of Racial Discrimination in Voting in the South (Washington, D.C.: The Washington Research Project, 1972), p. 167.

15. A detailed description of the Voting Section's administrative routines for processing preclearance submissions can be found in Howard Ball, Dale Krane, and Thomas P. Lauth, Compromised Compliance: Implementation of the Voting Rights Act (Westport, CN: Greenwood Press, 1982), pp. 77-86. Since the 1983 reorganization of the Voting Section, some of the position titles and exact processing steps have been altered, but the essential work has remained the same.

16. Local officials in the covered jurisdictions frequently have expressed this opinion to the author.

17. Interview with David Hunter, Staff Attorney, Voting Section, Civil Rights Division, U.S. Department of Justice, September 1, 1977, Washington, D.C.

18. Interview with Liz Dunagin, Research Analyst, Voting Section Civil Rights Division, U.S. Department of Justice, September 2, 1977, Washington, D.C.

19. Hunter interview.

20. Interview with Janet Blizzard, Voting Section Paralegal Supervisor, Civil Rights Division, U.S. Department of Justice, September 2, 1977, Washington, D.C.

21. Hunter interview.

22. U.S. Comptroller General, GAO, Voting Rights Act; U.S. Comptroller General, GAO, State/Local Voting Laws.

23. 96 S Ct. 1361 (1976).

24. Hunter interview.

25. Interview with Gerald Jones, Chief, Voting Section, Civil Rights Division, U.S. Department of Justice, September 2, 1977, Washington, D.C.

26. Jackson Clarion Ledger (Jackson, MS), p. 1B.

27. South Carolina v. Katzenbach, 383 U.S. 301 (1966), p. 359.

28. Frederick M. Wirt, Politics of Southern Equality (Chicago, IL: Aldine, 1970), p. 82.

29. Drew Days, Testimony, 1981.

30. Hunter interview.

31. Ibid.

32. Ibid.

33. U.S. Commission on Civil Rights, The Voting Rights Act: Ten Years After, p. 326.

34. U. S. Comptroller General, General Accounting Office, Voting Rights Act—Enforcement Needs Strengthening (Washington, D.C.: February 6, 1978).

35. U.S. Comptroller General, GAO, State/Local Voting Laws, pp. 33-34.

36. Ibid., pp. 42-44.

37. Ibid., p. 13.

38. Also included in the survey were "67 private citizens with expressed interest in minority voting rights in covered jurisdictions in 11 States." See page 45 of the 1978 GAO report for a complete discussion of the methodology utilized to produce the survey.

39. During a 1982 visit of CRD attorneys to one Mississippi county, the members of the Board of Supervisors, the consultant assisting the Board with redistricting of the county, and the DOJ personnel carried out some negotiations inside the county's living room sized vault in order to avoid being overheard.

40. This information can be found in an internal GAO memorandum, entitled "Impact of Voting Rights Act as Seen by Minority Interest Groups and Selected Individuals," made available to the author by the GAO's General Government Division.

41. Hunter interview.

42. Jackson Clarion-Ledger, June 16, 1978, p. 11.

43. David J. Garrow, Protest at Selma: Martin Luther King, Jr. and the Voting Rights Act of 1965 (New Haven, CN: Yale University Press, 1978), pp. 21-22.

44. Howell Raines, My Soul Is Rested, p. 372.

45. Jackson Clarion-Ledger, June 16, 1978, p. 11.

46. Andrew Dunsire, "Implementation Theory," in Implementation, Evaluation and Change (U.K.: The Open University, 1980), pp. 5-54.

47. The "appropriate official" at the state level is, of course, the state's attorney general. These legal officers are not the focus of this essay.

48. Lauth, Compromised Compliance.

49. To obtain the views of local attorneys on Section 5 requirements, the author mailed questionnaires to county attorneys in Georgia (159) and Mississippi (82) and to city attorneys in Mississippi (236). While the responses do not constitute a random sample (125 jurisdictions out of a population total of 477, or a 26 percent response), the

responses come from a complete range of jurisdictions by population size, racial mix, and degree of urbanization. Despite its limitations, this survey is the only available in-depth examination (of which I am aware) of those individuals who must actually comply with the 1965 Voting Rights Act. A copy of the questionnaire may be obtained from the author.

50. The percentages shown in Tables 7.1-7.4 should be read across the rows. Each percentage value and its appropriate base is provided. On Table 7.1, for example, the second row (that is, "DOJ has sent information about submission procedures") should be read as follows: each figure in parentheses indicates the number of attorneys who said they had made a preclearance submission for a jurisdiction within a given range of minority population, and the percentage figure represents the percent of city/county attorneys who have made a preclearance submission for a jurisdiction within a given range of minority population who are in agreement with the questionnaire statement. For example, 5 of the 10 attorneys (50.0 percent) who have made submissions and who represent jurisdictions with a minority population in the 100-60 percent range agree that the DOJ had sent their office information about Section 5 procedures. Note that the total number of responses by city/county attorneys who personally made a submission will vary from question to question (that is, be less than the total of 74) because not all of these attorneys answered every item on the questionnaire.

51. Several of the close-ended questions asked for further explanation of a particular answer. For example, the question about "primary source of information" read as follows:

Was the Department of Justice your jurisdiction's primary source of information about the 1965 Voting Rights Act?

Yes ( )   No ( )

If no, please explain _____

_____

Some of the attorneys' attitudes and behavior offered in this essay are derived from these open-ended follow-up questions.

52. These complaints were garnered from both open- and close-ended questions.

53. Kenneth Culp Davis, Discretionary Justice: A Preliminary Inquiry (Baton Rouge, LA: Louisiana State University Press, 1969).

54. Letter from Kevin D. Rooney, Assistant Attorney General for Administration, U.S. Department of Justice, submitted to the Honorable Abraham Ribicoff, Chairman, Committee on Governmental Affairs, U.S. Senate, Washington, D.C., June 7, 1978.

55. Rooney letter to Ribicoff.

56. The 1982 amendment of Section 2 now prohibits voting practices that result in discrimination on account of race, color, or mem-

bership in a language minority group. This change overturns the U.S. Supreme Court decision in City of Mobile v. Bolden (466 US 55 1980) that allowed challenges to voting practices only on the basis of discriminatory intent. The revised Section 2 provides the CRD with a legal weapon to challenge jurisdictions that have stayed with the status quo since November 1964.

57. U.S. Commission on Civil Rights, The Voting Rights Act: Unfulfilled Goals, p. 184.

58. Ibid.

59. Howard Ball, Testimony on the Extension of the Voting Rights Act, Subcommittee on Civil and Constitutional Rights, House Committee on the Judiciary, June 25, 1981, Washington, D.C.

8
The Federalization of
Voter Assistance:
Section 208

David H. Hunter

INTRODUCTION

During the 1981 and 1982 debate on renewal of the Voting Rights Act, attention was focused primarily on extension of the special provisions of the act, the bailout formula, and the wording of Section 2.[1,2,3,4] What may ultimately prove to be of greater practical importance for the voter and the politician, more resource consuming for the federal courts, and more problematical as a matter of policy and federalism is the new Section 208.

Section 208 of the Voting Rights Act of 1965, as amended by Section 5 of the Voting Rights Act Amendments of 1982, establishes, as of January 1, 1984, the right of a voter in need of assistance (because of blindness, disability, or illiteracy) to receive such assistance from a person of his own choice.[5] The only limitation on such choice is that the voter will not be permitted to receive assistance from his employer, an agent of his employer, or an officer or agent of his union.

Prior to the 1965 enactment, the literacy test had been used in the South to prevent illiterate as well as literate blacks from registering to vote and voting.[6] Attempts made after the passage of the act to

The views expressed in this chapter are those of the author and not necessarily those of the United States Department of Justice. An earlier version of this article was presented at the Conference on the Consequences and Implications of the Voting Rights Act, Pomona College, Claremont, California, February 4, 1983.

prevent participation of illiterate blacks by denying them needed assistance were quickly struck down by the courts, thus establishing the right of illiterate voters to receive assistance.[7]

There remained, however, the issue of possible bias or intimidation in the assistance process. One civil rights lawyer explained:

> The question of an alternative to assistance from an official is no small issue. The chilling effect on a black illiterate voter of being assisted by a white election official can be significant. The black voter faces the prospect of revealing his vote to an unfamiliar or hostile white person without having any assurance that his vote will be cast as he directs. Faced with this prospect, many illiterate voters have forfeited their votes by staying home or by spoiling their ballots in vain attempts to cast them without assistance.[8]

On the other hand, the opportunity to provide assistance to black voters has been seen by some as an invitation to provide guidance—both to illiterate and to literate black voters—to assure that they vote in the desired way. In addition, the privilege of receiving assistance in marking the ballot has been seen by some voters as an opportunity to receive political guidance and advice while in the voting booth.

Behind the enactment of Section 208 is the policy judgment that voters in need of assistance should be able to receive it from the persons of their choice. Such a policy, which appears to be unexceptionable, is based on the following paradigm: Two persons, Mr. Green and Mr. Gray, are available to assist the voter, Mr. Blue; Blue wants to be assisted by Green; he does not want to be assisted by Gray. In this situation, it seems reasonable to allow Blue to be assisted by Green, the person of his choice. In the real world, however, the situation is usually more complicated. The value of honoring the voter's choice is less clear; the procedure for determining that choice, moreover, is problematical. Mr. Blue may need to choose among: a campaign worker for a political faction that he generally but not uniformly agrees with, a poll worker appointed by officials that he voted against in the last election, a spouse who is barely more literate than he is, a daughter in whom he does not wish to confide his choice of candidates. In this situation, Mr. Blue may prefer a rule that arbitrarily assigns a helper to him than to be forced to select a helper himself.

This chapter discusses the history of Section 208, the context of state law on voter assistance in which Section 208 is placed, assistance procedures in five southern States, the relationship between Section 208 and state law and between Section 208 and other provisions of the Voting Rights Act, and the exceptions contained in Section 208 with respect to employer and union assistance. The conclusion questions whether the enactment of Section 208 was justified.*

---

*The constitutionality of Section 208 is beyond the scope of this chapter. Recent cases concerning the constitutionality of other federal legislation regulating the franchise leave room for doubt with respect to the status of Section 208, especially with respect to its application in nonfederal elections. In South Carolina v. Katzenbach, 383 U.S. 301 (1966), the Supreme Court upheld Section 4(a) of the Voting Rights Act, which banned the use of literacy tests in the South, and Section 5 of the act, the preclearance requirement. In Katzenbach v. Morgan, 384 U.S. 641 (1966), the Court upheld Section 4(e) of the VRA, 42 U.S.C. 1973b(e), which required the states to accept schooling in an American flag (though non-English language) school as evidence of literacy. In City of Rome v. United States, 446 U.S. 156 (1980), the Court upheld the continued application of Section 5 following the 1975 extension of the act.

The constitutional status of several provisions of the Voting Rights Act Amendments of 1970, P.L. 91-285, was before the Supreme Court in Oregon v. Mitchell, 400 U.S. 112 (1970). The Court upheld the five-year nationwide ban on the use of literacy tests added as Section 201 of the amended Voting Rights Act by Section 6 of the 1970 Amendments. The Court also upheld Section 202 of the amended VRA, 42 U.S.C. 1973aa-1, which abolished durational residency requirements for voting for President. Finally, the Court upheld, with respect to voting in federal elections, and only by a five to four vote, the enfranchisement of eighteen-year-olds added as Section 302 of the amended Voting Rights Act by Section 6 of the 1970 Amendments. On the other hand, the Court struck down, also by a five to four vote, the imposition of eighteen-year-old voting in state and local elections.

There have been no reported cases on the constitutionality of the permanent nationwide ban on the use of literacy tests enacted as part of the 1975 Amendments to the Voting Rights Act, Section 201 of the 1965 Act, 42 U.S.C. 1973aa; the requirements, also added to the Voting Rights Act in 1975, that minority languages be used in the electoral process, Sections 4(f)(4) and 203(c) of the VRA, 42 U.S.C. 1973b(f)(4) and 1973aa-1a(c); the Overseas Citizens Voting Rights Act, P.L. 94-203, 89 Stat. 1143 (Jan. 2, 1976), 42 U.S.C. 1973dd-2(b), which enfranchised, for federal elections only, American citizens living abroad who are unable to claim residence in a State; and the Federal Voting Assistance Act of 1955, as amended in 1978, P.L. 95-593, 92 Stat. 2537 (Nov. 4, 1978), 42 U.S.C. 1973cc(b), which guaranteed to military personnel and their dependents the right to register and vote absentee in federal elections.

CONGRESS

When reported out of the House Judiciary Committee, H.R. 3112, which later became the Voting Rights Act Amendments of 1982, did not contain a provision concerning voter assistance.[9] On October 5, 1981, during the floor debate on the proposed bill, Congresswoman Fenwick offered an amendment that evolved into the Section 208 that was ultimately adopted. Her amendment would have added the following section to the act:

> Section 208. Nothing in this Act shall be construed in such a way as to permit voting assistance to be given within the voting booth, unless the voter is blind, or physically incapacitated.[10]

The proposed amendment can be given either a strong or a weak interpretation. Under the strong interpretation, it would be a violation of the act for an illiterate or non-English speaking voter to receive assistance in the voting booth. Under the weak interpretation, states would be permitted to prohibit illiterate voters from receiving assistance in the voting booth. Under either interpretation, the illiterate voter could receive "instruction and assistance" in a public area; only conduct within the voting booth is affected. The debate on the amendment prior to its adoption by voice vote was short. Mrs. Fenwick introduced and explained the amendment; Congressman Hyde, the ranking Republican member of the Judiciary Committee's Subcommittee on Civil and Constitutional Rights, offered his support; Congressman Edwards, the Subcommittee chairman, explained his opposition, and Mrs. Fenwick responded. The highlights of the brief debate were as follows:

> Mrs. FENWICK. My colleagues, I think we all were moved by the words of the Speaker. Yes; we have voted in this Hall today to keep for all our people the right to vote. But we have not quite finished it because the secret ballot, that is the real key.
>
> This is where my amendment would seek to keep the bosses out of the ballot booth. The voter should not be accompanied unless blind or physically incapacitated, unable to vote on their own. All the instruction and assistance can be given in the hall. But in the booth it should be private.
>
> As one of the great teachers has told me, Victor Gottbaum, there is not any vote that is any good if it is not secret. We know what the bosses can do when they have the right to go into the booth with the voter, and I

hope very much that this amendment will be accepted.
I do not want to put my colleagues to the strain of a
vote. . . .

Mr. EDWARDS of California. . . . [W]e have a
responsibility here, and no provision of the Voting
Rights Act requires that jurisdictions allow persons
assisting persons to enter the voting booth with them.
How assistance is provided is determined by state laws
and is not properly a federal responsibility.

It should also be noted that the subcommittee which
heard over 100 witnesses did not receive any testimony
on this issue which the amendment addresses. . . .

Mrs. FENWICK. I would say to the gentleman if we
had to depend, and I am sure my honored colleague knows
if we had to depend on States for every kind of justice we
would not have the kind of justice that we want in this country. There are times when the Federal Government must
intervene.

Now may I also say that I believe the Justice Department has said that the States cannot allow people to go into
the voting booth. This merely reiterates one of the essential rights. . . .

Because the language proposed by Mrs. Fenwick was not included
in what was ultimately adopted by Congress, one need not dwell long
on the questions it raises. It is clearly based on the distrust of those
who give assistance to voters. It is assumed that the helper will influence how the voter's ballot is marked. The amendment does not tell
us, however, how the illiterate voter, having received "instruction
and assistance" in "the hall," is supposed to cope in the privacy of the
booth. If the voter does not know that "REAGAN" stands for Reagan
and "CARTER" stands for Carter, the help he receives in the hall will
not enable him to be an effective voter in the booth. One might also
ask for the source of Mr. Edwards' statement that the Voting Rights
Act does not require jurisdictions to allow the helper to enter the booth
or of Mrs. Fenwick's statement that the Department of Justice has said
that the states cannot allow helpers to enter the booth.

The hearings conducted by the Subcommittee on the Constitution
of the Senate Judiciary Committee between January and March 1982
did not focus attention on the Fenwick Amendment, and the bill reported out by the subcommittee on March 24, 1982, was silent on the
subject of voter assistance. [11] In the full Judiciary Committee, which
met on Voting Rights Act amendments between March and May 1982,
a group of senators introduced and the committee adopted a substitute
bill containing a Section 208 affirmatively providing for voter assist-

ance. Like the section finally adopted, it provided for assistance by a person of the voter's choice, making an exception only for the voter's employer or an agent of that employer. The committee subsequently adopted an amendment that placed on unions a restriction comparable to that on employers. [12] Section 208's final refinement, the delay in its effective date until January 1, 1984, was added by a floor amendment offered on behalf of a majority of the Judiciary Committee. [13] The House accepted the Senate version of H.R. 3112. [14] The Senate Report recognizes the problem that the Fenwick amendment was intended to address, that voters can be improperly influenced by their helpers, by determining that the best way for this problem to be handled is for voters to choose their own helpers. [15]

THE STATES

In enacting Section 208, Congress was not entering virgin territory. There had always been qualified voters who could not reach the voting booth or mark their ballots without assistance, and the states had found it necessary to provide rules for voter assistance decades ago. This section provides an overview of the state systems in effect in 1982 and a more detailed consideration of the systems of a few states.*

The complexity of voter assistance is obscured by the simple language of Section 208 and by the discussion contained in the Senate Report. Assistance can occur at the registration stage or at the voting stage. Voters may need assistance to vote absentee, to enter the polling place or to vote outside the polling place, or to mark the ballot or pull the levers inside the polling place. The state must determine what disabilities give a person the right to receive assistance and the standards and procedures for determining when these disabilities exist. The state must determine who may act as a helper, how the helper is

---

*This account is based primarily on an examination of state election codes; consideration of judicial decisions, regulations, and actual practice would result in corrections and add considerable refinement. In addition, no attempt has been made to discover recent legislation that was not included in supplements or pocket parts to state codes as of late 1982. The procedures described are generally for illiterate voters at general elections. Where no provision for assistance to illiterates is contained in the election code, that for disabled voters is considered. Statutory references for state assistance procedures are found in the appendix at the end of the chapter.

selected, how the assistance is given, and what records are made of the assistance. Different rules or procedures may be followed for different types of elections, types of voting systems, categories of persons needing assistance, and categories of helpers. Finally, the state must determine the legal consequences of violations of the standards and procedures that it has established.

The assistance systems established by the states show great diversity; no two states have the same system. The system mandated by Section 208—free voter choice but with employer or union assistance prohibited—is not to be found among the 50 states or the District of Columbia. Only five of the states—Alaska, California, Idaho, Mississippi, and South Dakota—allow completely free voter choice without the Section 208 restriction. In two others, Delaware and Massachusetts, the only restriction is that the helper be a registered voter. Three of these states, however, Delaware, Idaho, and South Dakota, do not make explicit statutory provision for assistance to illiterates. (While all states and the District of Columbia provide by statute for voter assistance, 12 state election codes do not include illiterates among those entitled to receive assistance.)[16] Mississippi allows free choice by court order, not as a result of legislative judgment. Alaska, California, and Delaware allow the voter to be assisted by two persons. The most popular method of assistance, which is the rule in 17 states and the District of Columbia, is for poll workers alone to be authorized to give it.[17] In 34 states, if a poll worker is to act as helper, two poll workers must participate.[18] In 28 of these, in general elections, the two must be of opposite parties.[19] Two of these 28 states provide additional safeguards. In Texas, poll watchers can watch the assistance; in Utah, the same pair of poll workers cannot assist successive assisted voters. In addition to the 34 states in which two poll workers must participate, in the District of Columbia and New Hampshire the voter may choose to have a second poll worker present, and in South Carolina a bystander must be present in addition to the poll worker.

How the poll worker who serves as a helper is selected also varies. State law may specify that poll workers with certain titles will assist, that a designation should be made at the beginning of the day, that the poll worker in charge will designate the helper for each voter, that the helper will be chosen randomly, or that the voter can select the poll worker by whom he wishes to be helped. Seven states allow free voter choice except with respect to poll workers.[20] Four of these, however, do not provide by statute for assistance to illiterates.[21] In addition, in an eighth state, Hawaii, a voter in need of help can choose any registered voter. Eight states place limits on the number of voters a person other than a poll worker or relative may assist. In Colorado, Louisiana, Missouri, and North Carolina, one person may assist only one other; in Florida, two; in Minnesota, three; in

Texas, five, and in Georgia, ten. In Georgia, Minnesota, and North Carolina, the helper must be a registered voter of the same precinct as the person helped. (In North Carolina, in addition, such assistance is allowed only if a relative of the voter is not available.) In Colorado, the helper must be a registered voter, though not necessarily of the same precinct. In ten states, relatives of the voter in need of assistance have special status as helpers compared to other persons.[22] Which relatives are permitted to assist varies from state to state. Arkansas and South Carolina have the most restrictive rule; only spouses are allowed to assist. In South Carolina, moreover, the spouse must be a registered voter.[23] Five states explicitly bar certain categories of persons from serving as helpers. In Alabama, candidates and poll watchers may not help. In Georgia, poll workers and poll watchers may not help. In Michigan, persons under 21 cannot assist blind voters. In Nevada, poll workers may help no one other than their spouses. In North Carolina, a poll worker may not help unless no one else is available.

In 21 states, the assistance procedure specified by the election code varies depending on the reason assistance is needed.[24] Blind voters are allowed the most freedom in choosing their helpers; illiterates are allowed the least. In six states, physically disabled or blind voters are allowed more freedom than illiterate voters.[25] In 13 states, blind voters are allowed more freedom than otherwise physically disabled or illiterate voters.[26] In Nebraska, blind or paraplegic voters receive favored treatment compared to otherwise physically disabled or illiterate voters. Indiana has a three-tier system, with blind voters on top, other physically disabled voters in the middle, and illiterate voters on the bottom.[27] Three states allow assistance to voters not covered by Section 208. In Arizona, any voter can receive assistance; in Kansas, anyone 65 years of age or older can receive assistance; in Maine, a voter "whose religious faith prevents him from marking his ballot" may receive assistance.[28] Two other states possibly have larger classes of voters entitled to assistance than are recognized by Section 208. In Vermont, mental as well as physical disabilities enable the voter to receive assistance. In Michigan, anyone who needs assistance may receive it. Some states, for example Illinois and Kansas, narrowly define the class of disabled voters to exclude the intoxicated.

Some states specify precisely how the assistance is to be given; others leave this to the discretion of the helper and the voter. Usually the helper is prohibited from seeking to influence the voter and is required to keep secret how the ballot was marked. In Michigan the helper may not use "any written or printed list or slip furnished him by the voter or any other person"; in Texas neither assisted nor unassisted voters may rely on sample ballots.[29]

The Senate Report explains that free voter choice is the assistance method used in "many States."[30] This suggests that free voter choice is a more popular method than it actually is and ignores the complexity and diversity of the approaches of the various states. Restrictions on the right of voters in need of assistance to select their own helpers, moreover, have been upheld in the courts.[31] Compliance with Section 208 will require major changes in assistance practices in most states.

THE SOUTH

Given the history of the disfranchisement of blacks in the South, it is certainly plausible that in some states assistance procedures were designed or have been maintained in order to discourage blacks from voting or to prevent them from voting effectively. In this section the assistance procedures in five southern states, Mississippi, Georgia, Alabama, Louisiana, and Texas, are examined.

In 1892, the Mississippi legislature adopted voter assistance provisions.[32] Blind or disabled voters could receive assistance from anyone of their choice.[33] Illiterate voters could receive assistance only from the election manager assigned the duty of giving assistance; that the ballot was marked with assistance would be marked on the back.[34] In 1965, anticipating the enfranchisement of blacks, the legislature repealed the provision for assistance to illiterate voters.[35] Assistance to illiterates was nevertheless required to be provided by federal court order.[36]

In 1977, the Mississippi Supreme Court held that the distinction made between blind or disabled voters and illiterate voters violated the Equal Protection Clause of the Fourteenth Amendment and required Mississippi election officials to allow illiterates also to receive assistance from a person of their choice and to discontinue the practice of marking the back of ballots completed with assistance.[37] The court upheld the requirement that the voter declare his need of assistance to a manager.[38]

In 1979, the Mississippi legislature again attempted to restrict assistance.[39] Under the new law, the helper would have had to be a registered voter and to be registered in the same precinct as the voter; one helper could have assisted only five others, and a poll manager would have had to be present while the assistance was given. This law was objected to by the Attorney General pursuant to Section 5 of the Voting Rights Act.[40] As a result, Mississippi continues under the standards and procedures set out by the Mississippi Supreme Court in 1977.

The state of Georgia has elaborate procedures with respect to voter assistance. The voter in need of assistance because of a disability should indicate this when he registers to vote.[41] The poll list provided by the registration board will then indicate that the voter has a physical disability that makes assistance necessary.[42] The poll workers must be satisfied that the voter still suffers from the same disability.[43] Alternatively, assistance is allowed if the poll workers determine that the voter suffers from a disability acquired after the time of registration.[44] Both the disabled voter and the voter "unable to read the English language" must take an oath, "giving the reason why" they require assistance.[45] They are then permitted to select as their helper any registered voter of their voting precinct except a poll worker or poll watcher or to select any close relative.[46] The name of the helper is entered on the oath.[47] In addition, no person may assist more than ten voters.[48] It is a misdemeanor for a poll officer to assist a voter or to allow another to assist a voter illegally, for a voter to receive assistance illegally, or for a person to give assistance without authorization, attempt to influence a voter he is assisting, or mark a ballot other than as instructed by the voter he is assisting.[49, 50, 51] Similar but not identical instructions apply to who may give assistance to absentee voters. The absentee voter may be assisted by a registered voter of the same county, a relative, or a notary public, if the voter is outside his own county.[52, 53]

In 1966, Georgia sought to reduce the number of voters that one person could assist from ten to one.[54] This was struck down by the courts as violative of the Voting Rights Act.[55] Both in 1968 and in 1981, Georgia sought again to reduce the number of voters one person could assist, each time reducing the maximum from ten voters to five.[56] Because the new rule would too severely restrict the opportunity of black illiterate voters to receive assistance from a person they could trust, the Attorney General objected pursuant to Section 5 of the Voting Rights Act each time.[57]

Alabama has variations in its rules for assistance depending on whether the election is a primary or a general or a municipal election and whether voting machines or paper ballots are used. In general elections, with paper ballots in use, the voter seeking assistance "shall state to any of the inspectors that by reason of his inability to write the English language or by reason of blindness or the loss of the use of his hand or hands he is unable to prepare his ballot"; he may then receive assistance from any person he may select.[58] The person selected, however, unless he is a poll worker, should be outside the polling place, 30 feet away, waiting to be summoned by the inspector. If the chosen person cannot be found, the voter may select someone else, though not a candidate.

Voters using a voting machine may select the helper of their choice. However, if they desire to be assisted by a poll worker, they must select two of them.[59] The requirement that the helper be called

in from the outside and the prohibition on assistance by a candidate
are omitted. Unlike the case when paper ballots are used, a form
must be completed when a machine voter receives assistance, and
the voter must provide the required information under oath. When
elections are conducted by municipalities, the rules for county-run
elections apply except that, when voting machines are used, neither
candidates nor poll watchers may assist but federal observers are
permitted to act as helpers.[60] Primary election voters can receive
assistance from the person of their choice, other than poll watchers.[61]

In Louisiana, the voter who needs assistance, either because of
a physical disability or because of illiteracy, must file a statement to
this effect with the registrar.[62] The voter's right to assistance is
thereafter indicated on the poll list and the voter does not have to provide any additional evidence of his need for assistance or to complete
an oath.[63] Candidates and commissioners-in-charge (poll managers)
are not allowed to assist voters. A voter needing assistance because
he is blind or suffers from a physical handicap may receive assistance
from anyone of his choice and there is no limitation on how many blind
or disabled voters one person can assist. A voter who needs assistance
because he cannot read has a more limited choice. He "may receive
assistance from (i) his spouse or a blood relative, or (ii) a commissioner of his choice other than the commissioner-in-charge and a second commissioner chosen at random by the commissioner-in-charge,
or (iii) any other person of his selection." A helper in the third category, however, can only assist one voter.[64]

As of 1970, Texas allowed blind and physically disabled voters
to be assisted but not illiterate voters. In that year, the distinction
between the two classes of voters in need of help was struck down and
now the same rules apply to both.[65] Voters needing assistance can
select any registered voter of their precinct as a helper or may receive help from two poll workers.[66] One person, other than an official,
may assist only five others, parents, grandparents, spouses, children,
and siblings excepted.[67] In a general election, the two poll workers
must, if possible, be of different parties.[68] When assistance is given
by poll workers, poll watchers are allowed to be present.[69] The ballot
of the voter helped by someone who has gone over the limit is nevertheless valid.[70] Helpers must give assistance according to prescribed
procedures and, if they are not poll workers, must take a prescribed
oath that they will give assistance properly.[71] Failure to follow the
proper assistance procedures invalidates a ballot.[72]

This account of experience in five southern states indicates that
the courts will act to assure that black illiterate voters are able to
receive assistance, and that the Attorney General will use Section 5
of the Voting Rights Act to prevent states from implementing changes
that might make it more difficult for illiterate black voters to receive

assistance. Whether the assistance procedures provided by the southern states and whether practice in the South at the precinct level actually prevent black voters needing assistance from participating effectively in the electoral process are clearly important factors in an assessment of the need for federal legislation on voter assistance. If such denials do exist, it is equally important to consider whether existing remedies under the Voting Rights Act can be used to prevent them. The Senate Report does not provide information on either topic. *

PROBLEMS OF IMPLEMENTATION

The Senate Report specifies that "state provisions would be preempted only to the extent that they unduly burden the right recognized in this section, with that determination being a practical one dependent upon the facts."[73] State laws regulating the assistance process thus would be invalid only if, or to the extent that, they are inconsistent with Section 208. Such regulatory laws include those setting standards for illiteracy or disability, those establishing procedures for determining illiteracy or disability, those establishing procedures for determining who the voter has selected as helper, those establishing rules for the interaction between voter and helper in the voting booth, and those specifying the electoral consequences and the penalties for departures from the required standards and procedures for assistance. The question of consistency with Section 208 would be a federal question.

The Committee would also permit states to make distinctions among the different groups eligible to receive assistance:

By including the blind, disabled and persons unable to read or write under this provision, the Committee does not require that each group of individuals be treated identically for purposes of voter assistance procedures. States, for example, might have reason to authorize different kinds of assistance for the blind as opposed to the illiterate. [74]

Thus, for example, a state presumably could require an illiterate voter to take an oath attesting to his illiteracy even though it did not require an oath from a blind voter.

---

*The Civil Rights Commission's recent report on voting rights provides no examples of discrimination against blacks in the South in the assistance process. (U.S. Commission on Civil Rights, The Voting Rights Act: Unfulfilled Goals 31-34 (1981).)

Where all voters qualifying to receive assistance must be treated alike under Section 208 is in the selection of the helper. All must be allowed to choose their own helpers. (A problem could arise if the voter refuses to select a helper, preferring to accept whomever the poll manager assigns. Could the voter be told that he cannot receive assistance unless he selects the helper himself?) A state will no longer be able to restrict helpers to poll workers, to relatives of the voter, to registered voters, to residents of the voter's precinct, or to persons over a certain age or to limit the number of persons that one person may assist. It would be contrary to the intent of Section 208, although perhaps not contrary to its language, for a state to require that assistance be witnessed by a poll worker.

The extent to which a state will be able to restrict assistance by poll workers is less clear. One could argue that the voter should be able to select a poll worker just as he can select anyone else. Under this interpretation, state requirements that assistance be given by two poll workers, that the two poll workers be of different parties, and that the poll worker or poll workers to assist be selected by someone other than the voter would be set aside. On the other hand, presumably Section 208 does not impose upon a person selected to help the duty to help. If I am waiting in line to vote and the person in front of me asks me to help him, presumably I can say no. (If a state, however, passed a law requiring, for example, persons waiting to vote to give assistance when requested by a voter, there is no obvious reason why such a law would be invalid. Assisting voters could be analogized to serving on juries.) Is a poll worker in a different position? If an individual poll worker can turn down a request for assistance, cannot a state instruct its poll workers not to assist voters, or to assist voters only if the voters are willing to accept certain conditions, for example, the conditions now specified by state law? A state could argue that since the voter now has the right to select anyone as a helper—friend, relative, campaign worker, etc., there is no longer a need for officials to give assistance, and the efficient conduct of the election and the integrity and appearance of integrity of the electoral process dictate that officials not participate in voter assistance.

If a state can forbid poll workers from helping voters, who else can it forbid? Poll watchers generally have official status under state law; they have rights and duties that normal voters do not have. Can a state require a poll watcher to agree not to assist voters? The relevant provision of the Voting Rights Act to limit such action of the state would appear to be not Section 208 but Section 201, which guarantees to illiterates the right to participate in the electoral process.[75]

In most states, a voter receiving help from someone other than a poll worker can only have one person with him in the voting booth. Does Section 208 authorize a voter to select two (or more) helpers?

Conversely, some states allow the voter to select two helpers.[76] Is Section 208's specification of "a person" intended to prevent multiple helpers?

Although Section 208 appears to be directed at assistance in the marking of the ballot, its application may be broader. The terms "vote" and "voting" are defined in the act to include not only the marking of the ballot but also "all action necessary to make a vote effective . . . including, but not limited to, registration . . . or other action required by law prerequisite to voting. . . . "[77] The Senate Report appears to indicate that this broad definition of voting is intended to apply: "Thus, for example, a procedure could not deny the assistance at <u>some stages of the voting process</u> during which assistance was needed. . . . "[78] It is normal practice when a person unable to write applies to register to vote for the registrar to fill out the form for him. Under Section 208, must the applicant for registration be permitted to have a friend rather than the registrar fill out the form? On the other hand, while Section 201 (and other sections) of the Voting Rights Act refers to "citizens," Section 208 refers to "voters." This suggests that the protected class includes only those who are already registered. Finding the answers to these questions, which are ones of federal law, will be the responsibility of the courts.

If a state refuses to change its law with respect to assistance to allow free choice, or if a poll worker refuses to allow an illiterate voter to be assisted by the person of his choice, what remedy is available? The Attorney General is authorized to bring legal actions to enforce most provisions of the Voting Rights Act. For example, if a state applies a literacy test in violation of Section 201 or fails to provide oral minority language assistance in violation of Section 203(c), the Attorney General is authorized by Section 204 to go to court.[79,80] When Congress added Section 208 to Title II of the Voting Rights Act, however, it neglected to amend Section 204 to authorize the Attorney General to bring enforcement actions. Of course, if the denial of free choice had the effect of preventing an illiterate voter from voting or if a state allowed whites but not blacks to choose the helper of their choice, the Attorney General could take action, but Section 208 was not needed to deal with these problems.[81] While it is possible that Congress decided to restrict enforcement of Section 208 to private litigation, it is more likely, given the absence of discussion in the legislative history, that the lack of authorization for the Attorney General is an oversight, which could easily be remedied by a technical amendment to the act. *

----

*It is possible that the courts will decide that the Attorney General has the authority to enforce Section 208 under Sections 11(a) and

A number of questions will arise with respect to the interpretation of Section 208 and to the relationship between Section 208 and other provisions of the Voting Rights Act. Who is included in the class of voters unable "to read or write" defined by Section 208? Three different groups may qualify: those persons unable to read and write who are enfranchised by Section 201, that is, English speaking illiterates, those language minority citizens enfranchised by Section 4(f)(4) and Section 203(c), and non-English speaking persons not enfranchised by Section 4(f)(4) or Section 203(c). [82,83] The first group is the obvious primary target group. The Senate Report appears to imply that the second group is also included, but there is nothing in the language of Section 208 that would indicate that one group of persons unable to read and write English is included while another is not. [84] Also, the language used in Section 208 is the same as that used in Section 201, which has not been broadly interpreted to enfranchise all non-English speaking citizens.

Section 208, unlike Sections 201, 4(f)(4), and 203(c), is not designed to enfranchise anyone, but to guarantee a certain voting procedure to those already enfranchised. Thus, it would appear most reasonable to assume that it protects those unable to read or write who are enfranchised by Sections 201, 4(f)(4), or 203(c) and any other non-English speaking persons in need of assistance who are eligible to vote under state law or who have been enfranchised by judicial decision.

If a jurisdiction subject to the preclearance requirement of Section 5 makes a change in its assistance procedures to conform to Section 208, must it seek federal preclearance? The Supreme Court has held that even minor changes are covered by Section 5. [85] The Attorney General's Section 5 Guidelines specify that even changes that "ostensibly expand voting rights" are reached by Section 5, and the Attorney General's minority language guidelines take the position that changes made to comply with the minority language requirements of the Voting Rights Act are likewise covered. [86,87] Thus one would expect actions taken to comply with Section 208 to be covered. There may be an exception to this general conclusion if a state takes no legislative action but local election officials, to comply with Section 208, simply cease to enforce the preexisting state restrictions on the choice of the voter. This would be comparable to the cessation of the use of literacy tests after August 6, 1965, which was not considered covered by Section 5.

If a new practice by a jurisdiction subject to the preclearance

---

12(d) of the act, 42 U.S.C. 1973i(a) and 1973j(d), which are general enforcement provisions.

requirement of Section 5 violates Section 208, is that violation, by itself, the basis for a Section 5 objection? Because Section 208 is not designed exclusively to combat discrimination against racial or language minorities, and because there is no basis for assuming that any method of assistance other than free voter choice will be racially discriminatory, an automatic connection between the two sections should not be assumed. When the analogous question arose with respect to Section 4(f)(4), which requires the use of minority languages in the electoral process, the court held that such an automatic connection did not exist. [88]

Are federal observers, present at a polling place pursuant to Section 8 of the Voting Rights Act, authorized to give assistance? [89] Although observers are present "for the purpose of observing whether persons who are entitled to vote are being permitted to vote," their giving assistance to occasional voters who ask them for help is not necessarily inconsistent with this purpose. For observers to participate in an election as helpers would, however, be a greater federal intrusion in the conduct of elections than is their presence as monitors; it would be appropriate for the Office of Personnel Management and the Department of Justice to continue to instruct observers not to serve as helpers.

Section 8 has been interpreted not only to allow observers to be present at a polling place but also, at least where assistance is provided by poll workers, to authorize them to enter the voting booth when a voter is receiving assistance and listen to the conversation between voter and helper and watch the marking of the ballot, if the voter is willing to permit the observation. [90] While such observation may be necessary for a determination whether the person entitled to vote is being permitted to vote—since the right to vote includes the right to have one's ballot marked the way one wants it to be marked— it is an obvious additional compromise of ballot secrecy. When voters receive assistance from someone imposed upon them, the balance between the two values may come out for observation. When voters have free choice in selecting helpers, however, the balance may tilt toward ballot secrecy. Thus if state law only allows the voter and one other person to be in the voting booth and if Section 208 is not interpreted to override this numerical limitation, then one might ask whether the observation of assistance by federal observers is still valid under Section 8.

EMPLOYERS AND UNIONS

There is a tension in Section 208 between two conflicting principles. The first principle is that the voter in need of help should have free choice in choosing his helper. The second principle is that, to safeguard the voter from exploitation and the integrity of the electoral process from compromise, the voter should not be permitted to receive help from certain categories of persons. Having chosen to limit the principle of free choice, it is not clear why Congress chose the limitation it did or who is included in the class of persons ineligible to give assistance.* The premise behind the congressional limitation appears to be that an unequal economic relationship between helper and voter is a danger. If that is the basis, then assistance by landlords and creditors should be banned also.

It is not clear, moreover, why the concern to protect the voter from exploitation should be restricted to concern with economic relationships. Candidates, poll watchers for candidates, and campaign workers have a clear interest to have the assisted voter mark his ballot in a particular way. The threat that assistance by such persons poses could well be as great as that from employers and unions. On what basis did Congress determine that the limitation on assistance that it selected will better safeguard the voter and the electoral process than the various limitations selected by the states? Defining who is an employer or union representative for the purpose of Section 208, determining at the polls whether the forbidden relationship between voter and would-be helper exists, and establishing the status of the ballot marked with the participation of the forbidden helper will not be easy.

The Senate Report indicates that the employer and union ban does not extend to coworkers and fellow union members.[91] How the line is to be drawn between a forbidden employer agent and a permitted coworker, however, is not clear. A forbidden employer agent could be an immediate supervisor of the voter, anyone in the chain of command between the voter and the president of the company, or anyone with higher status in the company. Assistance could be forbidden only if either the voter or the helper is aware of the relationship, only if both are aware of the relationship, or it could be forbidden even if both are unaware of the relationship. For the ban to be effective, poll workers will have to inquire of each voter seeking assistance and of each helper who their employers are; if the employers are the same, further inquiry will be necessary. A less effective but less intrusive alternative would be to rely on poll watchers to challenge assistance given in vio-

---

*The political rationale for the limitations are transparent: Democrats did not trust employers to give assistance; Republicans did not trust union representatives to give assistance. The principled rationale, however, is not clear.

lation of Section 208. Similar problems exist for the union officer or agent.

If the forbidden assistance is not discovered until after the voter and helper have retired to the voting booth or until after the voter's ballot has been put in the ballot box the question arises of the appropriate remedy. If the ballot has not yet been placed in the ballot box (or if the ballot is numbered and thereby retrievable) one alternative would be to give the voter a second ballot and allow him to choose a new helper; another alternative is to reject the ballot. A criminal prosecution for illegal voting may be another option.

The Senate Report attempts to make an exception to the employer ban for voters "who must select assistance in a small community composed largely of language minorities whose language is primarily unwritten or oral, such as those residing in an Alaskan native village or a New Mexican pueblo or reservation," on the basis that in such communities there may be very few employers or most residents may be employees of the same native corporation. [92] Because the statute is not ambiguous on this question, this attempt to legislate through legislative history is dubious. If the ban on employer assistance creates a problem for such language minority communities, it will also create a problem for other small, rural communities or company towns. A consistent and principled approach, not an ad hoc approach such as that set forth in the report, would be preferable.

CONCLUSION

Once Congress has amended Section 208 to give the Attorney General enforcement authority and once the courts have resolved the more pressing questions of interpretation, the implementation of Section 208 should not be difficult or burdensome. The question will remain, however, whether Section 208 was a good idea in the first place.

The free voter choice approach to assistance contained in Section 208 is certainly a plausible solution to the problem of exploitation of illiterate voters by poll workers. Before accepting this solution, however, one might ask: To what extent does the problem of exploitation by poll workers exist? To what extent do illiterates vote differently from how they would otherwise vote in order to avoid offending the poll worker giving assistance? To what extent are illiterates deterred from voting by fear of exploitation? To what extent are illiterates deterred from accepting assistance by fear of exploitation? To what extent is this fear rational? Congress did not attempt to provide answers to these questions.

Before framing a solution, one would also wish to know whether the exploitation is racial in nature or, for example, political; whether it is restricted to certain parts of the country, for example, the South; whether it affects blind and handicapped persons as well as illiterates.

The solution of Section 208 needs to be compared to the solutions adopted by the states. Why is the requirement that assistance be given by two poll workers, of opposite parties, inadequate? Does the restriction that one person may only assist ten others give the voter no recourse except to accept assistance from a poll worker? Prevention of exploitation by poll workers is not, of course, the only goal that a state might have in regulating the assistance process. Many states seek to prevent voter exploitation by helpers other than poll workers and many seek to prevent voters from delegating their votes to helpers. That the former is a reasonable goal is recognized by Section 208 itself. Section 208, however, guards only against exploitation by employers and unions, while exploitation by campaign workers would appear to be a greater danger.

State policies against voter delegation are reflected not only in restrictions on who can give and receive assistance and in regulations on how assistance is to be given but also in secret ballot requirements and in vote buying prohibitions. Section 208, however, will facilitate voter delegation by allowing the voter to receive assistance from the person to whom he wishes to delegate his vote.

There are a number of reasons why a state would want to prevent delegation. Some are practical: There is no easy way to distinguish voluntary delegation from exploitation; the purchase and sale of votes is more difficult to prevent if voters are allowed to delegate. (A consistent prodelegation position, of course, would accept vote buying.) Others are based on concepts of democracy and individual responsibility. Why the resolution of such issues should not be left to the states is not clear.

NOTES

The author wishes to thank Reba Morris for her excellent and patient typing, Barry Weinberg for his helpful suggestions, and Kerry Mueller for her support and encouragement.

1. P.L. 89-110, 42 U.S.C. 1973 et seq., as amended.
2. The special provisions of the act are Section 5, 42 U.S.C. 1973c, the preclearance requirement for voting changes; Section 6, 42 U.S.C. 1973d, the authorization of the Attorney General to send federal examiners to counties to register voters; Section 8, 42 U.S.C. 1973f, the authorization of the Attorney General to send federal observers to monitor elections; and Sections 4(f)(4) and 203(c), 42 U.S.C. 1973b(f)(4) and 1973aa-1a(c), the minority language requirements. These

provisions apply in jurisdictions covered under Section 4(b), 42 U.S.C.
1973b(b), or under Section 203(b), 42 U.S.C. 1973aa-la(b). See 28
CFR Part 51 Appendix, 28 CFR Part 55 Appendix.

3. Section 4(a), 42 U.S.C. 1973b(a).

4. 42 U.S.C. 1973. Section 2 is the general prohibition against
racial discrimination in voting.

5. P.L. 97-205, 42 U.S.C.A. 1973aa-6 (Sept. 1982 Supp.).

6. Section 4(a), 42 U.S.C. 1973b(a), of the act banned the use
of literacy tests in the deep South. Voter assistance has been a national
issue since Congress, in 1970, banned literacy tests nationwide for a
five-year period, and, in 1975, made that ban permanent and required
the enfranchisement of most non-English speaking citizens. P.L. 91-
285 section 6; P.L. 94-73, 42 U.S.C. 1973aa; P.L. 94-73, 42 U.S.C.
1973b(f)(4), 1973aa-la(c). The minority language enfranchisement had
previously been partially accomplished through litigation and by state
legislation. See D. Hunter, The 1975 Voting Rights Act and Language
Minorities, 25 Catholic U.L. Rev. 250, 257-58 (1976).

7. See United States v. State of Mississippi, 256 F. Supp. 344
(S.D. Miss. 1966); United States v. County Executive Committee of
the Democratic Party of Clarendon County, South Carolina, C.A. No.
66-459 (D.S.C. June 1966); United States v. State of Louisiana, 265
F. Supp. 703 (E.D. La. 1966), aff'd per curiam, 386 U.S. 270 (1967);
Morris v. Fortson, 261 F. Supp. 538 (N.D. Ga. 1966). See generally
U.S. Commission on Civil Rights, Political Participation 70-74 (1968);
A. Derfner, Racial Discrimination and the Right to Vote, 26 Vander-
bilt L. Rev. 523, 563-66 (1973).

8. Derfner, supra, at 564-65, n. 171. See Morris v. Fortson,
supra; Hamer v. Ely, 410 F.2d 152 (5th Cir. 1969); James v. Humphreys County Board of Election Commissioners, 384 F. Supp. 114
(N.D. Miss. 1974). In 1975, the U.S. Commission on Civil Rights
recommended the adoption of free voter choice legislation. U.S. Commission on Civil Rights, The Voting Rights Act: Ten Years After 352
(1975). In 1981, however, the Commission only recommended Congressional hearings on the idea. (U.S. Commission on Civil Rights,
The Voting Rights Act: Unfulfilled Goals 92 (1981).)

9. July 31, 1981. See House Committee on the Judiciary, Report on Voting Rights Act Extension, H.R. Rept. No. 97-227, 97th
Cong., 1st Sess. (1981).

10. 127 Cong. Rec. H 7001 (daily ed. Oct. 5, 1981).

11. Subcommittee on the Constitution of the Senate Judiciary
Committee, Report on S. 1992 (Voting Rights Act), 97th Cong., 2d
Sess. (1982).

12. Senate Judiciary Committee, Report on S. 1992 (Voting
Rights Act Extension), S. Rept. 97-417, 97th Cong., 2d Sess. (1982)
(hereafter "Senate Report" or "S. Rept.").

13. 128 Cong. Rec. S 6939 (daily ed. June 17, 1982).

14. 128 Cong. Rec. H 3839-46 (daily ed. June 23, 1982). The bill was signed into law by the President on June 29, 1982.

15. S. Rept. at 62.

16. Connecticut, Delaware, Idaho, Maryland, Nevada, New Jersey, Ohio, Oklahoma, Oregon, South Dakota, Washington, and Wyoming. See Garza v. Smith, 320 F. Supp. 131 (W.D. Tex. 1970), vacated on other grounds, 401 U.S. 1006 (1971), remanded, 450 F.2d 790 (5th Cir. 1971), injunction granted, C.A. No. SA 70-CA-169 (Dec. 6, 1971).

17. District of Columbia, Illinois, Indiana, Iowa, Maine, Michigan, Nebraska, New Hampshire, New Jersey, New Mexico, Oklahoma, Rhode Island, Utah, Virginia, Vermont, West Virginia, Wisconsin, and Wyoming.

18. Alabama, Arizona, Arkansas, Florida, Hawaii, Illinois, Indiana, Iowa, Kansas, Kentucky, Louisiana, Maine, Maryland, Michigan, Minnesota, Missouri, Montana, Nebraska, New Jersey, New Mexico, New York, North Dakota, Ohio, Oklahoma, Oregon, Rhode Island, Texas, Tennessee, Utah, Vermont, Washington, West Virginia, Wisconsin, and Wyoming.

19. The six that do not follow the opposite party rule are Alabama, Indiana, Kentucky, Louisiana, Michigan, and Vermont.

20. Arizona, Kansas, Kentucky, Maryland, Nevada, Oregon, and Washington. In all but Nevada, if a poll worker assists, two poll workers must be present. In Nevada, poll workers are not allowed to give assistance, except to their spouses.

21. Maryland, Nevada, Oregon, and Washington.

22. Arkansas, Colorado, Georgia, Louisiana, Missouri, New York, North Carolina, South Carolina, Texas, and Tennessee. In New Mexico, relatives are given favored status in primary but not general elections.

23. 1975-76 Op. Atty. Gen. No. 42901, p. 119.

24. See James v. Humphreys County, supra.

25. Illinois, Iowa, Louisiana, Maine, New Mexico, and New York.

26. Florida, Michigan, New Hampshire, New Jersey, North Carolina, Ohio, Oklahoma, Rhode Island, Tennessee, Utah, Virginia, Vermont, and Wisconsin.

27. Under a system most recently amended in 1982, P.L. 12 (1982), the illiterate voter in Indiana is assisted by two judges. The disabled but not blind voter is assisted by his parent, spouse, child, sibling, grandparent, or grandchild, or, if none of these is available, by two judges. The blind voter can choose any person. The illiterate voter must complete a written affidavit; for the blind or disabled voter, an oral declaration is sufficient. Ind. Sts. Ann. 3-2-3-1, 3-2-3-2

(1982). Under the prior legislation, both illiterates and the physically disabled but not blind voters were assisted by election judges. Where paper ballots were used, an oral declaration was sufficient. Where voting machines were used, a written affidavit was required. Ind. Sts. Ann. 3-1-23-27, 3-1-24-8.

28. Maine Rev. Sts. Ann. 21:862 (1964).

29. Mich. Sts. Ann. 6.1754 (1971); Tex. Elec. Laws Art. 8.12. But see Gilmore v. Greene County Democratic Execution Committee, 435 F. 2d 487 (5th Cir. 1970).

30. S. Rept. at 63-64.

31. Smith v. Dunn, 381 F. Supp. 822 (M.D. Tenn. 1974); Smith v. State of Arkansas, 385 F. Supp. 703 (E.D. Ark. 1974).

32. Miss. Code of 1892: 3666, 3667.

33. Miss. Code of 1972 Ann. 23-5-157 (1972).

34. Miss. Code of 1942 Ann. 3273 (Supp. 1956).

35. Miss. Gen. Laws Ch. 19 (Extraordinary Sess. 1965).

36. United States v. State of Mississippi, supra. See also Hamer v. Ely, supra; James v. Humphreys County Board of Election Commissioners, supra.

37. O'Neal v. Simpson, 350 So. 2d 998, 1003 (1977). The court first held that section 3273 was still the law in Mississippi because the attempted repeal had not been precleared pursuant to Section 5 of the Voting Rights Act, 42 U.S.C. 1973c. Id. at 1001.

38. Id. at 1009.

39. H.B. 854 (Reg. Sess. 1979).

40. Letter of July 6, 1979. Initially, by letter of June 19, 1979, the Attorney General approved the new law; within the statutory 60-day period, he changed his mind and objected.

41. Ga. Elec. Code 34-1312(a); 34-609.

42. Id. at 34-1312(a); 34-622.

43. Id. 34-1312(a).

44. Id. Information with respect to a disability acquired since registration is provided to the registrar, who enters it, if the disability appears to be permanent, on the registration records. Id. 34-1312(c).

45. Id. 34-1312(a). 34-609 and 34-622 appear to provide for the recording of a voter's illiteracy at the time of registration and for the registrar's indicating this fact on the poll list. 34-1312(a), however, does not mention the prior recording of a need for assistance because of illiteracy.

46. Id. 34-1312(b). The class of relatives permitted to assist even if they are not registered voters or are not residents of the same precinct is defined to include the voter's "mother, father, sister, brother, spouse, or child."

47. Id. 34-1312(a).

48. Id. 34-1312(b).
49. Id. 34-1920(d), 34-1927.
50. Id. 34-1925(a), (c), and (d).
51. Id. 34-1926(a), (d), and (e).
52. The class of relatives eligible to assist is larger for absentees than it is for election day voters. It includes the voter's "mother-in-law, father-in-law, brother-in-law, or sister-in-law." Id. 34-1406(b).
53. Id.
54. Ga. Acts, 1966, p. 185.
55. Morris v. Fortson, supra.
56. Ga. Acts, 1968, p. 881, Acts Nos. 793 and 794 (Ga. Acts, 1981).
57. Objections of June 19, 1968, and Sept. 18, 1981.
58. Ala. Elec. Code 17-8-29, 17-7-18.
59. Id. 17-9-25(a).
60. Ala. Mun. Elec. Code 11-46-111, 11-46-122. The role of federal observers is discussed below.
61. Id. 17-16-26, 17-16-27.
62. For prior history, see United States v. State of Louisiana, supra.
63. La. R.S. 18-564, as amended by Act 229 of 1979.
64. Id. An illiterate voting by absentee ballot can receive assistance from a nonrelative only if no spouse or relative is available. Id. 18-1310(B).
65. Garza v. Smith, supra.
66. Tex. Elec. Laws Art. 8.13 Subdivs. 1 & 2.
67. Id. Art. 15.30a(a).
68. Id. Art. 8.13 Subdiv. 1.
69. Id. Subdiv. 1.
70. Id. Art. 15.30a(d).
71. Id. Art. 8.13 Subdiv. 2.
72. Id. Art. 8.13 Subdiv. 3.
73. S. Rept. at 63.
74. Id.
75. 42 U.S.C. 1973aa.
76. Alaska, California, and Delaware.
77. Section 14(c)(1), 42 U.S.C. 1973l(c)(1).
78. S. Rept. at 63 (emphasis added).
79. 42 U.S.C. 1973aa-la(c).
80. 42 U.S.C. 1973aa-2.
81. The former practice would violate section 201, the latter section 2, 42 U.S.C. 1973, and 42 U.S.C. 1971(a).
82. 42 U.S.C. 1973b(f)(4).
83. Persons who are Native American, Asian American, Alaskan

Natives, or of Spanish heritage and who live in certain countries. See 28 C.F.R. 55.1(c), 55.5, and 55.6 (1981).

84. S. Rept. at 64.

85. Allen v. State Board of Elections, 393 U.S. 544, 566 (1969); Dougherty County, Georgia, Board of Election v. White, 439 U.S. 32 (1978).

86. 28 C.F.R. 51.11 (1981).

87. 28 C.F.R. 55.22 (1981).

88. Apache County High School District No. 90 v. United States, C.A. No. 77-1515 (D.D.C. 1980), slip op. at 15.

89. 42 U.S.C. 1973f.

90. United States v. State of Louisiana, 265 F. Supp. at 715; United States v. Executive Committee of Democratic Party of Greene County, Alabama, supra. See also Morris v. Fortson, supra; Hamer v. Ely, supra; James v. Humphreys County, supra.

91. S. Rept. at 64.

92. Id.

APPENDIX: STATE ELECTION LAW PROVISIONS
WITH RESPECT TO VOTER ASSISTANCE

Alabama	Ala. Elec. Code 17-8-29, 17-9-25, 17-16-26, 17-16-27.
Alaska	Alaska Sts. Ann. 15.15.240.
Arizona	Az. Rev. Sts. 16-580.G.
Arkansas	Ark. Sts. 3-713, 3-1219.
California	West's Calif. Elec. Code Ann. 14234, 14235, 14236.
Colorado	Col. Rev. Sts. 1-7-108.
Connecticut	Conn. Gen. Sts. Ann. 9-264, 9-297.
Delaware	Del. Code Ann. 15-4943.
District of Columbia	D.C. Code Ann. 1-1313(f).
Florida	West's Fla. Sts. Ann. 101.051.
Georgia	Ga. Elec. Code 34-1312.
Hawaii	Hawaii Rev. Sts. 2-11-139.
Idaho	Gen. Laws of Id. Ann. 34-1108, 34-2427.
Illinois	Smith-Hurd Ill. Ann. Sts. 46-17-14.
Indiana	Burns Ind. Sts. Ann. 3-2-3-1, 3-2-3-2.
Iowa	Iowa Code Ann. 49.89, 49.90, 49.91.
Kansas	Kan. Sts. Ann. 25-2909, 25-2911.
Kentucky	Ky. Rev. Sts. Title X 117.255.
Louisiana	La. Rev. Sts. 18-564.
Maine	Me. Rev. Sts. Ann. 21-862.
Maryland	Md. Ann. Code 33-16-12.

Massachusetts	Ann. Laws of Mass. 54-79.
Michigan	Mich. Sts. Ann. 204C.15 subdiv. 1.
Mississippi	Miss. Code of 1942 Ann. 3273.
Missouri	Vernon's Ann. Mo. Sts. Title IX 115.445.
Montana	Mon. Code Ann. 13-13-119.
Nebraska	Rev. Sts. of Neb. 32-460.
Nevada	Nev. Rev. Sts. 293.296.
New Hampshire	N.H. Rev. Sts. Ann. 59:65.
New Jersey	N.J. Sts. Ann. 19:50-3.
New Mexico	N.M. Sts. Ann. 1-12-12, 1-12-13, 1-12-15.
New York	N.Y. Elec. Code 8-306.
North Carolina	Gen. Sts. of N.C. 163.152, 163.152.1.
North Dakota	N. Dak. Century Code Ann. 16.1-13-27.
Ohio	Page's Ohio Rev. Code Ann. 3505.24.
Oklahoma	Okla. Sts. Ann. 26-7-123, 26-7-123.1, 25-7-123.2, 26-7-124.
Oregon	Ore. Rev. Sts. 254.445.
Pennsylvania	Purdon's Pa. Sts. Ann. 25-3058.
Rhode Island	Gen. Laws of R.I. Ann. 17-19-26, 17-19-30.
South Carolina	Code of Laws of S.C. Ann. 7-13-770, 7-13-780.
South Dakota	S.D.C.L. 12-18-25.
Tennessee	Tenn. Code Ann. 2-7-116.
Texas	Tex. Elec. Laws 8.13, 15.30a.
Utah	Utah Code Ann. 20-7-24.
Vermont	Vt. Sts. Ann. 17-2569.
Virginia	Code of Va. Ann. 24.1-132.
Washington	Rev. Code of Wash. Ann. 29.51.200.
West Virginia	W. Va. Code Ann. 3-4-21, 3-4A-22.
Wisconsin	West's Wisc. Sts. Ann. 6.82.
Wyoming	Wyo. Sts. Ann. 22-13-113.

PART V
Electoral Response

9
Aftermath of the Voting Rights Act: Racial Voting Patterns in Atlanta-Area Elections

Charles S. Bullock, III

Many observers consider the 1965 Voting Rights Act to be the most successful of the civil rights laws. Following its enactment, millions of additional southern blacks registered to vote. These new participants have been instrumental in the election of thousands of black officials and have determined the outcomes of numerous elections from President down to local officials. Black political influence doubtless accounts for the moderation in the social welfare and civil rights stands taken by white public officials. [1]

As the implementation of the Voting Rights Act has removed many blatant obstacles to black political participation, attention has shifted to more subtle tactics for curbing black political influence. [2] Special attention has been given to various types of districting plans. A common question has been: Are blacks less likely to be elected under at-large, district, or combinations of these two arrangements for choosing officials? With a few exceptions, [3] researchers find blacks less likely to win municipal office under an at-large system. [4] Black candidates apparently fare less well in at-large elections because they attract too few white voters. Consequently black officeholding has occurred disproportionately where blacks are in the majority. [5] Despite the critical interaction between the type of electoral system and the voting behavior of blacks and whites, little is known about the latter aside from the observation that blacks are likely to bloc vote for black candidates. [6]

Much of the limited research on racial voting patterns has been carried out in conjunction with litigation over whether districting arrangements dilute the influence of black votes. The few published results come primarily from the rural South. [7] These analyses have not provided an extensive review of a single community's elections

over time. A partial exception was the five city study by Murray and
Vedlitz.[8] They report differences in racial support for candidates who
carried predominantly black precincts in 109 elections in Atlanta,
Dallas, Houston, Memphis, and New Orleans. However since blacks
ran in only 17 of the elections, understanding of racial voting when
there are black and white opponents remains incomplete.

A unique, comprehensive, longitudinal analysis of racial voting
patterns in one urban community, Atlanta, is reported here. One objective is to determine how cohesive whites and blacks are in supporting members of their own race. A second objective is to see if racial
voting patterns are consistent across time and across positions or
offices. If there is evidence that the degree of racial bloc voting varies,
then a third objective will be to develop multivariate models with which
to explain the variations that are observed. Fourth, multivariate analyses will be conducted in an effort to explain variations in the share
of the popular vote received by black candidates and to account for
black electoral success.

BACKGROUND

The impact of race on politics has been more extensively studied
in Atlanta than in most other southern cities. Atlanta's reputation as
a progressive city was nurtured by mayors Hartsfield and Allen, who
urged compliance with civil rights laws while many southern officials
joined the unreconstructed or abdicated leadership in this sensitive
area. In seeking to peacefully desegregate schools and public facilities,
Atlanta's mayors responded to the biracial coalition that elected them.
Orderly desegregation encouraged business growth favored by their
white supporters while meeting some of the civil rights expectations
of their black backers.

Black voters have been important in Atlanta since playing a de-
cisive role in a 1946 special congressional election. From 1949 through
1965 blacks joined liberal whites in electing the mayors and in 1969
blacks were essential to Sam Massell's triumph over the city's business leaders who had recruited the two previous chief executives.[9]
As early as 1953, a black was elected to the board of education and
12 years later the first black was elected to the city council. By 1973
blacks held half of the 18 council seats and five of nine seats on the
school board. In that year Maynard Jackson became the first black
mayor of a major southern city, following by a year the election of
Andrew Young as one of the first blacks sent to Congress from the
South in this century.

RACIAL CROSSOVER VOTING

It is widely assumed that voters prefer candidates with whom they share skin color.[10] This is hardly surprising. Intolerant voters will not support anyone but a member of their own race. In addition, some voters will be unable to differentiate candidates on other dimensions. Voters may use race as a cue if they find competitors' policy positions equally attractive. Inability to distinguish candidates' policy stands may result from inattention by the voter, lack of specificity by the candidates, or a genuine similarity in candidate stands. Candidates, knowing that many voters are inattentive to politics, appeal for support by publicizing personal characteristics that reveal little about their competence or their issue stands. Campaign literature reports candidates' religious preferences, military experience, alma maters, and club memberships. This information is publicized in the hope that voters who know little about issues or candidates' stands will assume that the aspirant with whom they share a characteristic will also share their policy preferences. Attentive voters when confronted with attractive, well-publicized choices may opt for the one with whom they share a racial tie if this is the only feature on which they perceive a difference.

Race of the candidate may be a more powerful influence than religion or club memberships. In part this is because race is a more salient feature than most other characteristics and it is certainly more closely associated with a number of policy options. Voters are usually correct in assuming that a black candidate is more liberal than an opposing white. Finally, candidate's race is readily discernable since it can usually be determined by a glance at a campaign poster, brochure, or television advertisement. Neither posters nor television advertising is likely to indicate that a candidate is a Methodist or graduated from the state university. While this information appears in brochures and handouts, voters must read the campaign literature to learn these facts—a greater although certainly not insurmountable obstacle. Supporting a candidate with whom one shares a racial tie need not be a product of racism but instead may result from reliance on a simple, readily available cue, much as a candidate's last name prompts some ethnic voters to foresake their party identification in order to support a fellow ethnic.[11]

DATA

Fifty-two Atlanta-area elections held during 1970-82 were analyzed. Elections that involved a sizable share of the Atlanta population were included. A sizable share is defined to mean citywide elections, at-large elections for Fulton County (which includes most of corporate Atlanta), and elections in the Fifth Congressional District (which includes most of Fulton County and the city). Only primaries, runoffs, and general elections having black and white contestants were analyzed.

All elections in which there were black and white opponents were included even though in some instances the candidates of one race ran poorly. That some candidates attracted little support from their own race suggests that the electorate weighs considerations other than the candidates' race when deciding how to vote. Excluding contests in which there was not fierce competition between black and white candidates might predetermine a conclusion that the elections are characterized by racial bloc voting.

The elections analyzed include five mayoral contests and three contests to choose the president of the city council. There are 11 congressional elections, 12 city council contests, six city board of education elections, seven county commission contests, and eight elections to choose various judicial officials. The offices involved give this study more of a local flavor than in the Murray and Vedlitz research in which most of the contests were for governor, President, senator, or mayor, with only five council elections included. Blacks won or led in 27 of the Atlanta contests analyzed in this chapter.

ECOLOGICAL REGRESSION

Ecological regression was used to estimate the extent of racial crossover voting.[12] Ecological regression was selected in preference to overlapping percentages since the former permits use of data from all precincts. Overlapping percentages that produce an estimate of the minimum amount of racial bloc voting can be used only in precincts in which at least 90 percent of the registrants are of one race.[13] Moreover, overlapping percentages must be computed precinct by precinct, a laborious process.[14]

Precinct-level figures for registered voters and the proportion of the vote for black and white candidates were collected. Ordinary least squares (OLS) regression was performed using the proportion of the electorate that was black as the independent variable and the proportion of the electorate voting for the black candidate(s) as the dependent variable. The intercept is an estimate of the proportion of the white registrants who voted for the black candidate since at the intercept the proportion black in the electorate is zero. A second regression was estimated using the proportion of the electorate voting for the white candidate(s) as the dependent variable. The intercept for this equation is an estimate of the percentage of the white registrants who voted for a white. The proportion of the whites participating in the election who voted for a black is calculated by the following: percent voting for a black/(percent voting for a black + percent voting for a white). Figures for the voting preferences of black voters are calculated using two regressions in which the independent variable is the proportion white in the precincts (since at the intercept all of the voters are black) and the dependent variables are the same as in the equations in which the independent variable was percent black in the electorate. In the regressions equations precincts were weighted by turnout because of the range in the number of participants. Some precincts had fewer than ten voters while others had more than 1000.

Ideally, the independent variables would be computed using the racial identity of the voters who actually turned out. Fulton County does not collect turnout figures by race, necessitating the use of registration figures. When there was more than one candidate of a race, the votes for all candidates of that race are combined and a single figure is used for the dependent variable.

To illustrate the kinds of figures that come from the OLS regressions, in 1981 when John Lewis, a former Carter official and leader of the Voter Education Project and SNCC, was elected to the city council, he received the votes of 35.6 percent of the city's registered blacks while his white opponent won 5.7 percent of the black vote. The remaining 58.7 percent of the registered blacks did not cast a ballot in this contest, so Lewis won 86.2 percent of the votes of blacks who participated. He also was the preference of 20 percent of the whites while 23.2 percent of the whites opted for the white candidate who received 53.7 percent of the white votes cast. Stated another way, 46.3 percent of the whites crossed over and voted for a black and 13.8 percent of the black voters crossed over and supported the white.

INDEPENDENT VARIABLES

In most Atlanta-area elections, voters support a candidate of their own race. In all but four contests, most whites supported a white while in an equal number of elections most blacks voted for a black. At the other extreme, there were eight elections in which essentially all black voters supported a black. The greatest cohesion in the white electorate occurred in the 1973 primary and runoff to choose the president of the city council and the 1976 primary to elect the clerk of the superior court. In each of these elections at least 97 percent of the whites voted for a white. In only four elections did 90 percent or more blacks support a black at the same time that 90 percent of the whites supported a white. There were 14 elections in which at least 80 percent of the black voters opposed at least 80 percent of the whites. Thus high levels of racial polarization were not the rule and there was sub-

stantial variation in the voting patterns across contests. It is therefore appropriate to search for variables that will explain variations
in racial crossover voting. Nine sets of variables will be considered
as possible predictors of racial crossover voting.

Office

Racial crossover voting may be less prevalent for the more important offices since these positions should more often attract stronger
candidates and voters will perceive more to be at stake in these elections. When confronted with attractive candidates of each race, a number of voters will use race as a cue. A bit of evidence that higher positions attract stronger candidates is provided by Michigan's Survey
Research Center that reports that stronger sets of candidates seek
the U.S. Senate than the House.[15] Applying these findings to the Atlanta context leads to the expectation that stronger candidates run for
mayor, president of the council, and Congress than for lesser positions. Research on elections for the period 1949-73 found blacks to
be especially prone to bloc vote in mayoral contests, even in the absence of a black candidate.[16]

As predicted, average black crossovers were least in the congressional and top municipal contests where, as Table 9.1 reports,
only one black in eight voted for a white. The incidence of black crossover voting for the other offices has been substantially higher and, on
the average, 31 percent of the black voters support a white in county
commission elections. Among whites, bloc voting is most pronounced
in elections to fill the top city posts with 80 percent of the whites voting

TABLE 9.1: Racial Crossover Voting by Office (in percent)

Elections[a]	Whites Voting for Blacks	Blacks Voting for Whites	N
Mayor/Council President	20.1	12.9	8
Congress	23.8	12.9	11
City Council	24.4	23.6	12
County Commission	25.4	31.0	7
Board of Education	27.0	18.7	6
Overall Mean	23.6	19.4	52

[a]In addition to the five categories in the table, there are eight
other elections for a variety of judicial branch positions.

white. The mean white crossover figures in the other elections is about one in four, indicating that there is less variation across offices for whites than blacks.

Time

The attitudes of southern whites toward blacks have undergone major change. Whites now express greater willingness to live near blacks, to work with blacks, to have their children attend schools with blacks, and to vote for blacks.[17] These attitudinal changes prompt a prediction that white Atlantans' support for black candidates has increased.

An alternative line of reasoning predicts that despite a general rise in tolerance, white Atlantans may have become less disposed to vote for blacks.[18] Between 1970 and 1980, the proportion black in the city rose from 51 to 67 and the percent black in the Fifth Congressional District rose by seven points to 51 percent. Among the city's registered voters, the percent black increased from 49 to 56 between 1973 and 1981. As blacks became more numerous and the number of black elected officials rose, their political success could have triggered a white backlash.[19] Some whites may be willing to have a few black officeholders but object to a predominantly black local government.[20] If there has been a white backlash, then white crossovers will have declined with time.

When the black population was smaller, it had to present a united front in order to triumph against the more numerous whites.[21] Now that whites are outnumbered, blacks may be more willing to vote for qualified whites so that black crossovers increase with time.

To determine whether racial bloc voting has changed over time, the 12-year period was trichotomized into 1970-73, 1974-78, and 1979-82. Although white crossover voting is always greater than black crossover voting, Table 9.2 shows a similarity in the patterns for the two races. The incidence of crossovers rose by four points for each race from the first to the second periods. It continued to rise during the

TABLE 9.2: Crossover Voting Across Time (in percent)

	1970-73	1974-78	1979-82
Mean White Crossovers	20.4	24.2	25.4
Mean Black Crossovers	15.3	19.8	22.2
N of Elections	14	20	18

third period, although at a reduced rate, particularly among whites. Crossovers were more common among whites in each period, although the gap narrowed. Greater crossover voting by both races may be due to the recruitment of better qualified candidates, more effective campaigning, or a decline in prejudice.

Incumbency

In U.S. House elections incumbency is a major predictor of outcomes. Incumbents are generally unbeatable, with their electoral security having been particularly great since the mid-1960s. [22] While incumbent U.S. senators have not enjoyed the invulnerability characteristic of the House, they nonetheless are usually victorious. [23] The advantages of incumbency, such as name recognition and access to contributors, may scare off potentially strong challengers.[24] Incumbency advantages also apply in local elections. Three recent studies report that incumbents in city council contests win between 73 and 84 percent of the elections that they contest. [25] Therefore it is expected that Atlanta-area incumbents, regardless of race, will fare better than nonincumbents. Not only should incumbents usually win, they should attract a larger crossover vote.

These propositions are supported as shown by some examples. When running against incumbent Fletcher Thompson (R) in the 1970 congressional election, Andrew Young won less than 20 percent of the white vote. Two years later when Young ran for an open congressional seat, he polled almost a quarter of the white vote. In 1974, incumbent Young won more than half of the white vote. Similarly Wyche Fowler received less than 5 percent of the black vote in the 1977 special election runoff to fill Young's seat. In the 1978 primary, Fowler got almost two-thirds of the black vote when challenged by a black state representative.

Table 9.3 shows that the Young and Fowler examples illustrate

TABLE 9.3: Mean Crossover Voting and Vote for Black Candidates by Incumbency (in percent)

	No Incumbent	White Incumbent	Black Incumbent	Incumbent of Each Race
White Crossover	18.5	18.6	47.6	19.5
Black Crossover	11.4	39.1	7.0	18.5
N	25	16	9	2

a general pattern. Incumbents average a much larger crossover vote than do challengers or competitors in contests where incumbency is equal. White incumbents do no better at holding white voters than do whites running in open contests, while white challengers lose almost half the white vote. Black incumbents do especially well, losing only 7 percent of the black vote. Black voters always vote for white candidates in smaller proportions than whites vote for black candidates under comparable conditions.

Newspaper Endorsements

Newspapers believe that they can affect election outcomes and in most Atlanta elections they made recommendations. The hypothesis to be tested is that candidates who received newspaper endorsements attracted more crossover votes than did candidates who were not endorsed. To test the effectiveness of Atlanta's press, the endorsements of the city's two major dailies were coded. Since the Journal and the Constitution disagreed on their endorsements about 40 percent of the time, the two papers were treated separately. For each paper, two dummy codes were used to indicate whether a white was endorsed and

TABLE 9.4: Mean Crossover Voting and Vote for Black Candidates by Newspaper Endorsements (in percent)

	Newspapers' Endorsement Pattern					
	Black/ Black	Black/No Endorse- ment	Black/ White	No Endorse- ment	White/No Endorse- ment	White/ White
White Cross- overs	42.58	26.67	19.16	13.50	26.50	14.53
Black Cross- overs	2.83	6.33	15.92	14.12	17.75	40.60
N	12	3	12	6	4	15

Note: The column heads show the editorial stands taken by the two newspapers. "Black/Black" indicates that both papers supported a black candidate. "Black/No Endorsement" means that one paper endorsed a black candidate for the position while the other paper took no stand.

whether a black was endorsed. The absence of an endorsement was the third category, that is zero for both variables.

The results in Table 9.4 show that crossover voting varies with endorsements. When both papers endorse a white, two in five blacks vote for the white while if both papers endorse a black, fewer than one in 30 blacks vote for a white. One in seven whites vote against white candidates who have received dual endorsements but more than 40 percent support blacks who get two endorsements. When the papers disagree in their recommendations, the crossover rates fall between the extremes noted above. Crossovers are infrequent when neither paper makes an endorsement.

Type of Election

Different factors may be at work in primaries, general elections, and runoffs held when no one obtained a majority. General elections provide a partisan cue that is missing from the others. The presence of a Republican nominee should reinforce white Republicans' inclinations to vote against a black Democrat. Similarly a black Democratic nominee provides an added incentive for black Democrats to vote Democratic. Some whites will be cross pressured when choosing between a black Democrat and a white Republican.[26] Therefore levels of white crossovers in general elections should be higher when there is a black nominee than in other elections. Black crossovers should be fewer in general elections than elsewhere since party and race will be reinforcing.

Fewer blacks may crossover in runoffs than primaries because of the experiences of some black candidates in the South. At times a black has led a field of several whites in the first primary only to lose in the runoff. This has happened only once in Atlanta since 1970, but the phenomenon has occurred enough elsewhere that Atlanta black leaders may go to great pains to mobilize the black community in runoffs. Moreover Atlanta black voters have historically been more cohesive in runoffs than primaries even in the absence of black candidates.[27] Whites there may mobilize to counter activity on behalf of the black candidate or the excitement of the prolonged runoff, which stimulates higher turnout than in the primary, may cause heightened racial bloc voting. This would result if the black versus white arrangement of the runoff stimulated the intolerant of both races to vote. It could also be the product of an influx of relatively inattentive voters who sat out the primary and now rely heavily on race as a cue.

The mean level of white crossovers in general elections, 30.7 percent, is 6 points higher than in primary elections, thus supporting the hypothesis that the party label draws some additional white Democrats to a black nominee. Also as expected, Table 9.5 reports that crossovers among blacks are much lower in general elections than in primaries. When racial and partisan cues are reinforcing, there is little incentive not to support the black candidate. Black polarization in general elections is promoted since the white is a member of the party of Goldwater, Nixon, and Reagan, none of whom is identified with black policy objectives.

TABLE 9.5: Mean Crossover Voting and Vote for Black Candidates by Type of Election (in percent)

| | Type of Election | | |
	General	Runoff	Primary
White Crossovers	30.71	17.73	24.83
Black Crossovers	9.86	13.87	24.40
N	7	15	30

Also as predicted, crossover voting is lower in runoffs than in primaries for both races. Indeed whites are least likely to support a black in a runoff. In the absence of a partisan cue or the added stimulus of a runoff, crossover rates for the two races are almost identical.

Number of Candidates

The total number of candidates and the number of black candidates may influence voting patterns. When there are numerous candidates, voters face higher information costs. As the number of alternatives increases, more voters may turn to race as a voting cue. However, neither the number of candidates nor the number of black candidates has a statistically significant relationship with the incidence of black or white crossovers. The largest correlate occurs for white crossover voting that is somewhat less ($r = -.26$) when there are numerous candidates. An analysis of the means fails to show a consistent pattern.

Black Registration

In discussing the "time" variable it was suggested that the share of the registered electorate might impact on crossover voting in both races. Bivariate analyses indicate little relationship, with the correlation between black registration and black crossover being .12 and a correlation for registration and white crossover of .03.

Although the proportion black among registered voters is only a weak correlate of crossovers, it may be important for understanding the other topic addressed in this chapter, the political success of blacks. There are three possible models for the success of blacks. In racially polarized communities, blacks will win office only when black registration and turnout produce a majority. The share of the vote won by blacks will be determined by these two variables. In communities characterized by white racist voting with some blacks voting for whites, but whites shunning black candidates (the situation Loewen observed in some parts of Mississippi),[28] the political strength of black candidates will depend on black registration, turnout, and crossovers. In communities like Atlanta where the extent of crossovers fluctuates in both races, black politicians' strength should be the product of four factors: the three just mentioned plus white crossovers. Data to test these three models will follow.

Black Turnout[29]

Since blacks almost always vote more heavily for black than white candidates, it is expected that when turnout among blacks is high, black candidates should do better. When black turnout was correlated with the proportion of the vote received by black candidates, the correlation was .39. This variable will also be used to predict black success.

The presence of a black candidate typically heightens black turnout as Harold Washington's 1983 mayoral candidacy in Chicago demonstrated. To the extent that black turnout is associated with black candidacy, it should also result in lower levels of black crossovers. The correlation between turnout and black crossovers, as expected, is a sizable -.33. The relationship with white crossovers is quite modest, r = .11.

MULTIVARIATE ANALYSIS

Using ordinary least squares, multivariate models will be developed first for crossover voting and then for two aspects of black candidate strength: share of the vote and winning the election. In developing models for crossovers, all variables for which there was a theoretical basis were initially included and then those that failed to achieve significance at the .10 level were deleted.

TABLE 9.6: The Effects of Independent Variables on Crossover Voting

Black Crossovers

	Regression Coefficient	Standard Error	Beta
Intercept	8.026		
WINC	20.459[a]	3.687	.477
MAYPRES	17.350[a]	5.786	.307
CONG	9.673[b]	4.471	.194
RO	-6.270	3.330	-.139
YRS	4.850[b]	2.116	.185
JENDWH	9.257[a]	3.339	.226
CENDWH	12.781[b]	4.836	.298
CENDBL	-9.148[b]	4.301	-.224
BTURN	-0.380[a]	.138	-.279

$R^2 = .789$
Adjusted $R^2 = .743$

White Crossovers

	Regression Coefficient	Standard Error	Beta
Intercept	20.097		
WINC	-7.759[b]	3.557	-.217
BINC	13.886[a]	4.226	.334
MAYPRES	-8.060	4.780	-.171
NUMCAND	-3.082[b]	1.301	-.300
GE	-14.731[a]	5.420	-.296
JENDBL	12.344[a]	4.444	.322
CENDBL	7.704[b]	3.602	.227
RO	-10.773[b]	4.625	-.287

$R^2 = .646$
Adjusted $R^2 = .584$

[a] $p \leq .01$.
[b] $p \leq .05$.

Crossover Voting

Nine variables are included in the model for black crossovers presented in Table 9.6. Taken in combination, these account for approximately three-fourths of the variance. Particularly useful predictors are incumbency, newspaper endorsements, and turnout. (The key to the abbreviations used in Tables 9.6 and 9.8 are presented in Table 9.7.) Black voters support white incumbents 20 percentage points more often than they do nonincumbent whites. Endorsements of whites by the Atlanta papers are related to a substantial black crossover vote while black crossovers are 9 percentage points fewer when the Constitution backs a black candidate. As turnout increases, black crossovers become less frequent with a 10 percentage point increase in turnout associated with a 3.8 point decline in black votes for white candidates. Black crossovers have increased with time and crossovers are 6 percentage points less frequent in runoffs.

The relationships for the other variables in the multivariate analysis in Table 9.6 are not as expected from the bivariate relationships. Once other variables are held constant, the incidence of crossovers is positively associated with elections for the top offices. When incumbency, press endorsements, and other factors are considered,

TABLE 9.7: Variables Used in the Multivariate Analyses

BCROS	Black crossover vote in percent
BINC	Black incumbent
BLLEAD	Whether a black was the leading candidate
BLREGIS	Black registration as a percent of total registrants
BLVOTE	Percentage vote for black candidates
BTURN	Turnout among registered blacks, in percent
CBL	Atlanta Constitution endorsed a black
CONG	Fifth District congressional contests
CWH	Atlanta Constitution endorsed a white
GE	General election
JBL	Atlanta Journal endorsed a black
JWH	Atlanta Journal endorsed a white
MAYPRES	Elections of mayor or council president
NUMBCAN	Number of black candidates seeking the office
NUMCAND	Number of candidates seeking the office
RO	Runoff election
WCROS	White crossover vote in percent
WINC	White incumbent
YRS	Year of election, trichotomized

Table 9.6 shows that blacks are more likely to vote for whites in contests for member of congress, mayor, and council president.

The positive sign for these top offices is produced by the combination of office variables and endorsement variables in a single equation. When both papers endorse a black, average black crossovers in a top city election is 2 percent. When endorsements are split, mean black crossovers are more than 9 percent and when a white wins both endorsements, more than a third of the blacks vote for a white. Applying the same controls to congressional elections, the mean black crossover is less than 1 percent when both papers endorsed a black, about the same when the endorsements were split, but 35 percent when a white received both endorsements.

The model for white crossovers presented in the right hand side of Table 9.6 has eight variables and can explain about 60 percent of the variance. As with black crossovers, incumbency and newspaper endorsements are important. A black incumbent polls 14 percentage points more of the white vote than does a black nonincumbent. Thus the drawing power of an incumbent of the opposite race is only two-thirds as great on white as on black voters. Another racial difference is that the presence of a white incumbent significantly deters white crossovers while black incumbents did not reduce the rate of black crossovers. Press endorsement of black candidates led whites to vote for blacks, but the endorsement of a white did not significantly reduce white crossovers. White bloc voting was more pronounced in runoffs and general elections than in primaries. The finding for runoffs was foreshadowed in the bivariate analysis, but the finding for general elections was unanticipated. Whites are more cohesive in elections for the top municipal offices—as was expected from Table 9.1—and when there are large numbers of candidates. The effect of top city contests is less for whites than for black voters while runoffs have a larger effect on white than black voters in producing solidarity. Table 9.2 showed that crossover voting has risen for both races, but the multivariate analysis indicates that time makes a significant independent contribution only among black voters.

Support for Black Candidates

Three models for predicting the vote for black candidates were presented earlier. If people voted only for members of their own race, black political success would be determined by black turnout and black registration. If some blacks but no whites voted for candidates of the other race, the electoral performance of black candidates could be predicted by turnout, registration, and crossovers among black voters. The model that should best predict black political strength in Atlanta

TABLE 9.8: Three Models of Black Political Success

	BLVOTE		BLLEAD	
	b	beta	b	beta
1. Racial polarization				
Intercept	25.95		.195	
BLREGIS	.156	.074	-.003	-.048
	(.279)		(.009)	
BTURN	.411[a]	.381	.013[a]	.389
	(.142)		(.004)	
	$R^2 = .16$		$R^2 = .15$	
	Adjusted $R^2 = .12$		Adjusted $R^2 = .11$	
2. White racist				
Intercept	36.24		.382	
BLREGIS	.412[b]	.195	.002	.024
	(.183)		(.008)	
BTURN	.123	.114	.008	.232
	(.098)		(.004)	
BCROS	-.603[a]	-.760	-.001[a]	-.446
	(.072)		(.003)	
	$R^2 = .66$		$R^2 = .32$	
	Adjusted $R^2 = .63$		Adjusted $R^2 = .28$	
3. Crossover				
Intercept	23.44		.108	
BLREGIS	.300[b]	.142	-.0009	-.013
	(.095)		(.0073)	
BTURN	.158[b]	.146	.008[b]	.254
	(.051)		(.004)	
BCROS	-.394[a]	-.496	-.006[b]	-.262
	(.042)		(.003)	
WCROS	.537[a]	.563	.011[a]	.391
	(.047)		(.004)	
	$R^2 = .91$		$R^2 = .44$	
	Adjusted $R^2 = .90$		Adjusted $R^2 = .40$	

[a]$p \leq .01$.
[b]$p \leq .05$.
Note: Standard errors in parentheses.

where crossovers occur in both races includes black and white crossovers along with black registration and turnout as independent variables. Black political success will be measured in two ways—the share
of the vote polled by black candidates and whether a black won or was
the leading candidate.

Table 9.8 reports results for the three models. The two variable racial polarization model proved to be inappropriate for Atlanta
since it could explain very little of the variance. When black crossovers was added as a predictor, the adjusted R^2 rose substantially to
.63. However, in the four variable model, which includes both crossover terms, 90 percent of the variance can be accounted for and all
four variables are significant at the .01 level. As anticipated, black
candidates run stronger when blacks constitute a larger percent of the
registrants, black turnout is high, relatively large numbers of whites
vote for the black candidate, and few blacks support a white candidate.
The most important predictor is the behavior of white voters. To be
successful, black candidates' platforms and appeals must attract a
share of the white vote while holding the bulk of the black vote.

As the right half of Table 9.8 shows, the proportion of the variance that can be explained in models for whether black candidates poll
more votes than whites improves as we go from the two to the four
variable model, indicating the superiority of the crossover model.[30]
However the R^2 values are substantially smaller than in the models
for share of the vote won by blacks. Another difference is that black
registration is never statistically significant in models for whether
blacks win. However, once again the behavior of white voters is the
most important variable.

The results in Table 9.8 illustrate the conflict faced by black
candidates. When there is a substantial white vote, black politicians
must choose between making biracial appeals in order to attract white
votes that are often essential for election or castigating the inequities
that they see and promising correctives but losing because of a white
voter boycott. Too blatant an appeal for white votes may antagonize
blacks who feel that the candidate is insensitive to their needs. A
strategy that attracts whites may bring victory even if it alienates
some blacks, however, since the coefficient for white crossovers is
larger than that for black crossovers. The full model for the share
of the vote going to a black indicates that a 5.4 percentage point increase in white crossovers is associated with a 3.9 point loss of black
support. Even in Atlanta with its sizable black majority, candidates
who are unacceptable to whites have difficulty getting elected.

SUMMARY AND CONCLUSIONS

This analysis of 12 years of black-white electoral competition in the Atlanta area reveals great variety in the degree of racial bloc voting. Clearly the electorate considers factors other than race when voting. If Atlanta were racially polarized, then the extent of crossover voting would be uniformly small and registration and turnout rates among blacks would determine the success of black candidates. Neither proposition is sustained by the data.

One might suggest that when racial crossovers have been numerous, it is due to ignorance of the race of the competitors. This is unlikely since whites have voted in large numbers for some well-known blacks as in the 1981 council president contest and in several of Andrew Young's congressional elections. Similarly, large numbers of blacks voted for Wyche Fowler when he was elected council president and when he sought re-election to Congress.

Crossover voting has allowed candidates to win when their race was in the minority. Young was elected to Congress when blacks constituted less than 40 percent of the registered voters. Three other blacks have won countywide offices even though the majority of the voters in Fulton County are white. White candidates have won citywide positions despite the presence of a black majority among registrants since 1977.

Additional evidence that race is not the only consideration comes from the absence of candidates of both races for some positions. Among the more visible offices for which one race has not had a candidate are the absence of white challengers to Andrew Young in 1974 and 1976 and to Carl Ware in the 1977 election to choose the council president. If the race of the candidate could insure a sizable vote from the electorate sharing the racial tie, then in a polity in which the electorate is as evenly divided between blacks and whites as in Atlanta, candidates of both races would have a reasonable chance to win and we would expect that blacks and whites would offer for all positions. That some incumbents of each race are perceived to be unbeatable is evidence that Atlanta politicians perceive that their skin color alone is insufficient to mount a serious campaign, much less to win public office.

The failure of race to adequately account for voting patterns as it did in several rural communities Loewen[31] analyzed creates an environment in which incumbency and newspaper endorsements play major roles. Incumbency advantages candidates of both races, allowing them to make inroads among voters of the opposite race. Incumbency may help by facilitating fund raising and name recognition. Incumbents may also run better because they win over skeptics through performance. Some blacks who thought that Wyche Fowler could not represent their interests in Congress may have been converted. Some white voters who opposed Andrew Young or Maynard Jackson when they first ran may have been won over by the performances of these two men once in office. Less informed voters appear to turn to the newspaper for recommendations.

The frequency with which voters will back a candidate of the opposite race has risen in both races and time makes a significant independent contribution to the explanation of black crossover voting. This contradicts Murray and Vedlitz who concluded "that racial polarization increases as blacks become a larger proportion of the urban electorate and move to exercise a more independent role in local politics."[32] Possible explanations for the differences in the findings presented here and those of Murray and Vedlitz are the length of time that Atlanta blacks have played critical roles in elections, this chapter considers only local elections, and the exclusion from this chapter of elections contested exclusively by whites (which was the situation in 86 percent of the Murray and Vedlitz elections).

Recently, in the typical election, one white in four votes for a black and more than one black in five votes for a white. Less white than black cohesion is another pattern unlike what Loewen observed in the rural South.[33] Indeed average white crossovers in Atlanta in recent years have exceeded the 20 percent figure reported in mayoral contests in the Northeast.[34] The slightly greater cohesion among blacks may be due to the long history of discrimination and exclusion from officeholding to which their race was subjected. Habit or better organization may be factors since when choosing between two whites, blacks display more cohesion than do whites.[35]

Despite crossover voting in both races and the history of blacks and affluent whites supporting moderate to liberal candidates, some observers contend that the era of biracial politics in Atlanta has ended. The most compelling evidence underlying this assertion is the 1981 mayoral elections. The primary and the runoff were extremely polarized with 92 percent of the whites supporting Sidney Marcus in the runoff while Andrew Young garnered 91 percent of the black vote. This level of racial voting was exceeded only in the 1977 primary and runoff elections to fill the Fifth District Congressional seat.

It appears that 1981 did not usher in a new era of racial cleavage. The polarization of the mayoral contest did not even spread to the other positions at stake in 1981. On the day of the first primary while 89 percent of the whites were voting for a white for mayor, fewer than 14 percent voted for the white candidate for the council presidency. The three whites running for at-large council seats that day received between 53 and 86 percent of the white vote. Blacks who faced white candidates on primary day obtained as little as 44 percent and as much as 97 percent of the black vote. Although the range was less on the date of the runoff, polarization was far more pronounced in the mayor's contest than in the council and school board elections decided at the same time.

The atypically high racial bloc voting that occurred in the 1981 mayoral elections may well be due to the comparability of the leading black and white candidates. Andrew Young had been a very popular congressman. His service in that capacity and as President Carter's ambassador to the United Nations had given him high name recognition. His leading opponent was Sidney Marcus, a respected state legislator with strong liberal credentials augmented by a reputation for promoting the city's commercial interests. Presented with a choice between competent, experienced contenders who had records of service to blacks and whites and who promised to strengthen the city's financial situation by attracting new industry (Young claimed that contacts developed at the United Nations would allow him to entice foreign firms to invest in Atlanta), many voters fell back on race as a cue.

This research has implications for future officeholding in Atlanta. Since the share of the vote received by black candidates, and thus the elections of blacks, is partly a product of black registration and turnout, the number of black elected officials in the Atlanta area should continue to rise as the black population increases. If Jesse Jackson's efforts to register additional southern black voters succeeds, the replacement of white by black officeholders in Atlanta may be accelerated. However the replacement of white officeholders by blacks will be slowed to the extent that there are white incumbents and that the press endorses whites. Black candidates will be most successful in seeking open positions and when they get press backing.

Blacks have frequently been successful when seeking public office in Atlanta. This success has usually required support from a segment of the white electorate. Likewise, whites who have won office have secured some backing in the black community. Winners in both races have typically been men and women who could build biracial coalitions.

NOTES

I appreciate the suggestions for improving this chapter made by John Alford and the assistance in data collection provided by Susan Duffin.

1. Earl Black, Southern Governors and Civil Rights. (Cambridge, Mass.: Harvard University Press, 1976); Charles S. Bullock, III, "Congressional Voting and the Mobilization of a Black Electorate in the South," Journal of Politics, 43 (1981): 662-682; Charles S. Bullock and Keith S. Henry, "The Impact of Increased Black Political Participation: Legislative Voting in the South," Civil Rights Research Review, 9 (1981): 7-23.

2. U.S. House of Representatives, Extension of the Voting Rights Acts, Hearings before the Subcommittee on Civil and Constitutional Rights of the Committee on Judiciary Parts 1-3 (Washington, D.C.: U.S. Government Printing Office, 1982).

3. Susan A. MacManus, "City Council Election Procedures and Minority Representation: Are They Related?", Social Science Quarterly, 59 (March 1978): 153-161; Leonard A. Cole, "Electing Blacks to Municipal Office," Urban Affairs Quarterly, 10 (1974): 17-39.

4. Chandler Davidson and George Korbel, "At-Large Elections and Minority Group Representation: A Re-Examination of Historical and Contemporary Evidence," Journal of Politics, 43 (November 1981): 982-1005; Richard D. Engstrom and Michael D. McDonald, "The Election of Blacks to City Councils: Clarifying the Impact of Electoral Arrangements on the Seats/Population Relationship," American Political Science Review, 75 (June 1981): 344-354.

5. Charles S. Bullock, III, "The Election of Blacks in the South: Preconditions and Consequences," American Journal of Political Science, 19 (August 1975): 727-739.

6. Harlan Hahn and Timothy Almy, "Ethnic Politics and Racial Issues: Voting in Los Angeles," Western Political Quarterly, 24 (1971): 719-730; Thomas F. Pettigrew, "When a Black Candidate Runs for Mayor: Race and Voting Behavior," in Harlan Hahn, ed., People and Politics in Urban Society. (Beverly Hills, Cal.: Sage, 1972): 95-118.

7. James M. Loewen, "Continuing Obstacles to Black Electoral Success in Mississippi," Civil Rights Research Review, 9 (Fall-Winter, 1981): 24-39; Testimony before the Subcommittee on Civil and Constitutional Rights of the Committee on the Judiciary, on the Extension of the Voting Rights Act, 97th Congress, 1st Sess., House of Representatives (Washington, D.C.: U.S. Government Printing Office, 1981): 255-278.

8. Richard Murray and Arnold Vedlitz, "Racial Voting Patterns in the South: An Analysis of Major Elections from 1960 to 1977 in Five Cities," Annals, 439 (1978): 29-39.

9. Berdie Ricks Hardon, "A Statistical Analysis of the Black-White Voting Coalition in Atlanta, 1949-1970," unpublished Masters thesis, Georgia State University, 1972; p. X; Alton Hornsby, Jr., "The Negro in Atlanta Politics, 1961-1973," Atlanta Historical Society Bulletin (1977): 7-33; Mack H. Jones, "Black Political Empowerment in Atlanta: Myth and Reality," Annals, 439 (1978): 99; Jack Walker, "Negro Voting in Atlanta: 1953-1961," Phylon, 24 (1963): 379-387.

10. Murray and Vedlitz, "Racial Voting Patterns in the South," pp. 29-39.

11. Robert A. Lorinskas, Brett W. Hawkins, and Stephen Edwards, "The Persistence of Ethnic Voting in Rural and Urban Areas:

Results from the Controlled Election Method," Social Science Quarterly, 49 (December 1969): 891-899.

12. Leo Goodman, "Some Alternatives to Ecological Correlation," American Journal of Sociology, 64 (1959): 610-625; E. Terrence Jones, "Ecological Inference and Electoral Analysis," Journal of Interdisciplinary History, 2 (1972): 249-269; W. Phillips Shively, "'Ecological Inference': The Use of Aggregate Data to Study Individuals," American Political Science Review, 63 (December 1969): 1183-1196.

13. James W. Loewen, Social Science in the Courtroom. (Lexington, Mass.: Lexington Books, 1982), p. 186.

14. Estimates of racial crossover voting that seem to be based on some form of overlapping percentages analysis have appeared for some elections. These are available from the press, reports of the Voter Education Project, and press releases of the late Clarence Bacote of Atlanta University. Ecological regression seems to provide conservative estimates of crossover voting in Atlanta. When estimates from the regression equations were compared with 26 reports of crossovers based on analyses of heavily one-race precincts, the regression estimates were lower 17 times, higher 5 times, and approximately equal 4 times.

15. Thomas E. Mann and Raymond E. Wolfinger, "Candidates and Parties in Congressional Elections," American Political Science Review, 74 (September 1980): 617-632; Alan T. Abramowitz, "A Comparison of Voting for U.S. Senator and Representative in 1978," American Political Science Review, 74 (September 1980): 633-640; Barbara Hinckley, Congressional Elections (Washington, D.C.: Congressional Quarterly, 1981).

16. Hardon, "A Statistical Analysis of the Black-White Voting Coalition in Atlanta," pp. 28-31; William P. Collins, "Race and Political Cleavage: Ten Positions in a Local Election," Journal of Black Studies, 11 (1980): 121-136.

17. Everett Carll Ladd, "The State of Race Relations—1981," Public Opinion, 4 (1981): 32-40.

18. Hardon, "A Statistical Analysis of the Black-White Voting Coalition in Atlanta," pp. 87-88, proposes this idea.

19. Jones, "Black Political Empowerment in Atlanta," pp. 90-117.

20. Hornsby, "The Negro in Atlanta Politics, 1961-1973," p. 26 explains that some white business leaders supported Maynard Jackson over a white councilman in the 1969 election for vice-mayor because of a feeling that blacks were entitled to additional influence.

21. Hardon, "A Statistical Analysis of the Black-White Voting Coalition in Atlanta," p. 82.

22. Robert S. Erikson, "Malapportionment, Gerrymandering, and Party Fortunes in Congressional Elections," American Political

Science Review, 66 (December 1972): 1234-1245. David R. Mayhew, "Congressional Elections: The Case of the Vanishing Marginals," Polity, 6 (1974): 295-317. Hinckley, Congressional Elections; John R. Alford and John Hibbing, "Increased Incumbency Advantage in the House," Journal of Politics, 43 (November 1981): 1042-1061.

23. Charles S. Bullock, III and Michael J. Scicchitano, "Partisan Defections and Senate Reelections," American Journal of Political Science, 19 (1982): 482.

24. Gary C. Jacobson and Samuel Kernell, Strategy and Choice in Congressional Elections (New Haven: Yale University Press, 1981).

25. John Kirlin, "Electoral Conflict and Democracy in American Cities" Journal of Politics, 37 (February 1975): 266; Kenneth Prewitt, "Political Ambitions, Volunteerism, and Electoral Accountability," The American Political Science Review, 64 (March 1970): 9. Charles Gilbert and Christopher Clague, "Electoral Competition and Electoral Systems in Large Cities," Journal of Politics, 24 (1962): 323-49.

26. In only one contest has a black Republican run against a white Democrat. In the 1982 general election for the Fifth Congressional District, the black Republican won 5.5 percent of the vote against Wyche Fowler.

27. Hardon, "A Statistical Analysis of the Black-White Voting Coalition in Atlanta," pp. 30-31.

28. Leowen, "Continuing Obstacles to Black Electoral Success in Mississippi," pp. 24-39.

29. Since black and white turnout correlate at $r = .93$, only the former will be used in multivariate models.

30. Table 9.8 reports the results of OLS regression equations. Since the dependent variable, that is, whether a black polled the most votes, is dichotomous, logit is a more appropriate technique than OLS regression. A separate logit analysis was performed and it confirmed the results of the regressions. The two variable model correctly classifies 71 percent of the cases while the four variable model accurately classifies 90 percent of the cases. Since the OLS and logit results are so similar, OLS results are presented here because they are more widely understood.

31. Loewen, "Continuing Obstacles to Black Electoral Success in Mississippi," pp. 24-39; Testimony before the Subcommittee on Civil and Constitutional Rights of the Committee on the Judiciary, pp. 255-278.

32. Murray and Vedlitz, "Racial Voting Patterns in the South," p. 33.

33. Loewen, "Continuing Obstacles to Black Electoral Success in Mississippi," pp. 24-39; Testimony before the Subcommittee on Civil and Constitutional Rights and the Committee on the Judiciary, pp. 255-278.

34. Howell Raines, "Major Lesson at Polls," New York Times (November 10, 1983), p. 15.

35. Jack Walker, "Negro Voting in Atlanta," pp. 379-387; Hardon, "A Statistical Analysis of the Black-White Voting Coalition in Atlanta," pp. 30-31.

About the Editor and Authors

CHARLES S. BULLOCK, III is The Richard Russell Professor of Political Science at the University of Georgia. He is on the editorial boards of the <u>American Journal of Political Science</u> and the <u>Annals of Public Administration</u> as well as <u>Social Science Quarterly</u>. He received an A. B. degree summa cum laude from William Jewell College, an M. A. and Ph. D. from Washington University, and attended the Lamar School of Law at Emery University.

KATHERINE INGLIS BUTLER is an associate professor of law at the University of South Carolina. She spent three years as a trial attorney in the voting section of the Civil Rights Division of the Department of Justice in Washington, D. C. She is currently writing "Reapportionment, the Courts, and Section 5 of the Voting Rights Act: Still More Thorns. " She received her B. S. in chemistry and zoology and her M. Ed. in counseling from Mississippi State University and holds a J. D. degree from the University of Tennessee.

DON EDWARDS represents the 10th Congressional District of California, which is composed of parts of Santa Clara and Alameda Counties. Since 1971, he has been the chairman of the House Judiciary Committee's Subcommittee on Civil and Constitutional Rights, which has jurisdiction over most constitutional amendments, civil rights, constitutional rights, and the Federal Bureau of Investigation. He was the 1982 recipient of the Leadership Conference on Civil Rights "Hubert H. Humphrey Civil Rights Award" and serves as chairman of the California Democratic Delegation. He was educated at Stanford University and attended Stanford Law School.

RICHARD ENGSTROM is a professor of political science at the University of New Orleans. He was a Fulbright Professor at National Taiwan University and National Chengchi University and a visiting scholar at the Institute of American Culture in Taipei, Taiwan. He is currently working on a book entitled <u>Representational Districting: 'One Person, One Vote' Revisited</u>. He is a 1968 graduate of Hope College and received his M. A. and Ph. D. degrees from the University of Kentucky.

LORN S. FOSTER is an associate professor in the department of government and black studies at Pomona College. Currently on leave, Mr. Foster is a senior fellow at the Joint Center for Political Studies in Washington, D.C. Mr. Foster's research has been in the areas of education, political socialization, and voting rights. He is a 1969 graduate of California State University, Los Angeles, with a B.A. degree in political science. He received his A.M. and Ph.D. degrees in political science from the University of Illinois.

DAVID H. HUNTER is a member of the District of Columbia Bar, admitted to practice before the Supreme Court of the United States. He is currently associated with the U.S. Department of Justice where he drafted the guidelines for the minority language and preclearance provisions of Section 5 of the Voting Rights Act. He graduated magna cum laude with a B.A. degree from Princeton University in 1964 and from Harvard Law School with an LL.B. degree in 1967.

MACK JONES is chairman of the political science department at Atlanta University. He has served as editor of the Journal of Political Repression and as advisory editor of the Social Science Quarterly. In addition, he is a member of the board of directors of the Georgia chapter of the American Civil Liberties Union. He has a B.A. degree in political science from Texas Southern University where he graduated magna cum laude in 1962, and M.A. and Ph.D. degrees from the University of Illinois in political science.

DALE KRANE is an associate professor of political science at Mississippi State University. He is a Danforth Foundation Associate for Instructional Excellence and has written extensively on the subject of voting rights. He has had articles published in the American Journal of Political Science and the American Political Quarterly. He holds B.A. and M.A. degrees in government from the University of Indiana, and a Ph.D. from the University of Minnesota in political science.

MARK STERN is a professor of political science at the University of Central Florida in Orlando, where he was honored as University Teacher of the Year. He has published a number of papers on voting rights including his most recent, "Southern Congressional Civil Rights Voting and the New Southern Political Demography." He has a B.A. degree from Brooklyn College, C.U.N.Y., and a Ph.D. from the University of Rochester.